WHAT IS SACRED THEOLOGY?

What Is Sacred Theology?

Joseph Clifford Fenton

Edited and with an Introduction by Cajetan Cuddy, O.P.

THOMIST  TRADITION
SERIES

CLUNY
Providence, Rhode Island

*"Among all human pursuits, the pursuit of wisdom
is more perfect, more noble, more useful,
and more full of joy."*

~Saint Thomas Aquinas,
Summa contra Gentiles

* * *

THOMIST TRADITION

Book Series

While his birth and death and everything in between remain confined to the thirteenth century, the intellectual legacy of St. Thomas Aquinas perdures to the present day. The Catholic Church continues to recognize the sapiential fecundity of this Doctor whom she invokes as "Common" and "Universal." God gave to the world through the wisdom of his Thomas a gift that does not expire.

There was only one Thomas. However, there have been many Thomists—philosophers and theologians who have assimilated the principles of his instruction and found the freedom that only the truth can provide.

The THOMIST TRADITION book series from Cluny Media arises from a dual conviction: (1) the thought of St. Thomas Aquinas contains an incomparable fullness of wisdom, and (2) the writings of the Thomists who followed him play a necessary role in mediating his wisdom to subsequent generations. Admittedly, those figures who constitute the Thomist tradition were by no means equals in regard to talent, influence, and renown. Moreover, their individual and collective contributions to the Thomist tradition elude facile comprehension or easy summary. Nonetheless, this series attempts to make available the key texts of figures—both classic and contemporary, major and minor—who rightly claim membership in the living tradition which bears the intellectual imprint of their master, Thomas.

The THOMIST TRADITION series makes these books available not merely as static works of antiquated value or anachronistic interest. Rather, the series is the fruit of our conviction that each Thomist has participated in a legacy perennially alive and perpetually relevant. Under this inspiration, each carefully selected volume in the series includes a new introduction that explains the book's original historical and speculative context. These introductions also outline their volume's enduring relevance to contemporary questions and disputes. Finally, the texts themselves have undergone extensive editorial review and certain footnotes have been added in order to highlight, explain, and clarify themes and passages of particular significance.

It is our sincere hope that this endeavor from Cluny Media will contribute to the renewed interest in the Thomist tradition among contemporary philosophers and theologians. For 800 years, Thomas and the Thomists have demonstrated unparalleled service in the defense and exposition of the saving truth Christ confided to his bride, the Catholic Church. The THOMIST TRADITION book series is designed both to honor that service and to provide the Thomists of today and tomorrow with resources for their own service to the Truth who sets us free.

Cajetan Cuddy, O.P.
General Editor

THOMIST T✦T TRADITION

Cluny Media edition, 2018

This is a republication of *The Concept of Sacred Theology*,
originally published in 1941 by The Bruce Publishing Company.

For more information regarding this title
or any other Cluny Media publication,
please write to info@clunymedia.com, or to
Cluny Media, P.O. Box 1664, Providence, RI 02901

VISIT US ONLINE AT WWW.CLUNYMEDIA.COM

Nihil obstat: H. B. Ries, *censor librorum*

Imprimatur: Moyses E. Kiley, *Archiepiscopus Milwaukiensis*
May 31, 1941

Imprimatur: ✠ Thomas M. O'Leary, D.D., *Episcopus* ✠ *Campifontis*
July 8, 1941

ISBN: 978-1944418618

Cover design by Clarke & Clarke
Cover image: *Saint Paul Writing His Epistles* (detail),
attributed to Valentin de Boulogne,
c. 1618–1620, oil on canvas
Courtesy of Wikimedia Commons

Contents

* * *

Introduction to the 2018 Edition

Joseph Clifford Fenton's
Concept of Sacred Theology

Monsignor Joseph Clifford Fenton (1906–1969) originally published this book in 1941 under the title of *The
Concept of Sacred Theology*.[1] The text had its origin in the doctoral
dissertation he completed ten years prior at the Pontifical University of St. Thomas Aquinas (the "Angelicum") under the direction
of Reginald Garrigou-Lagrange, O.P., whom Fenton would later
characterize as "one of the foremost minds of our generation."[2] Following his graduate studies in Rome, Fr. Fenton returned to the
United States and eventually served as a professor of fundamental
and dogmatic theology at The Catholic University of America.[3]

Fenton's years on this earth were few in number, yet his priestly life and literary output exercised a significant influence in the
Catholic Church during the mid-twentieth century.[4] Fenton was
editor-in-chief of the *American Ecclesiastical Review*, co-founder
of the Catholic Theological Society of America, and author of six
books and scores of essays.[5] Notably, he was a formidable and public critic of Jesuit theologian John Courtney Murray's account of
religious pluralism in the modern state.[6] Finally, Saint John XXIII
appointed Fenton as one of the conciliar *periti* at the Second Vatican
Council. The priest also worked closely with Cardinal Alfredo

Ottaviani on the Council's Preparatory Theological Commission as well as its Doctrinal Commission on Faith and Morals.[7]

Fenton was largely forgotten by his immediate successors in the latter-part of the previous century. When he did receive mention it was usually in reference to his influence at the Second Vatican Council or to his criticism of Jesuit Fathers John Courtney Murray and Leonard Feeney. Recently, however, his life and work have begun again to attract the attention of historians and theologians.[8] Certainly his role at the Council continues to elicit interest.[9] Fenton's personal diaries remain a valuable resource for those

1. Joseph Clifford Fenton, *The Concept of Sacred Theology* (Milwaukee, WI: The Bruce Publishing Company, 1941).

2. Joseph C. Fenton, "Modern Thomists," *The Commonweal*, Vol. 20, No. 11 (1934): pp. 279–80 (p. 279).

3. For a brief description of theological education at The Catholic University of America during this period, see Joseph M. White, "Theological Studies at the Catholic University of America: Organization and Leadership before Vatican Council II," *U.S. Catholic Historian*, Vol. 7, No. 4 (1988): pp. 453–66.

4. For a recent and concise summary of Fenton's life, see Christian D. Washburn, "Life and Work of Joseph Clifford Fenton," in Joseph Clifford Fenton, *The Church of Christ: A Collection of Essays By Monsignor Joseph C. Fenton*, ed. Christian D. Washburn (Tacoma, WA: Cluny Media, 2016), pp. vii–xviii.

5. For a bibliographical listing of Fenton's major writings, see the "Bibliography of Msgr. Fenton's Works" in Fenton, *The Church of Christ*, pp. 303–22.

6. See Donald E. Pelotte, S.S.S., *John Courtney Murray: Theologian in Conflict* (New York: Paulist Press, 1976); Philip Gleason, *Contending With Modernity: Catholic Higher Education in the Twentieth Century* (Oxford: Oxford University Press, 1995); William L. Portier, *Divided Friends: Portraits of the Roman Catholic Modernist Crisis in the United States* (Washington, DC: The Catholic University of America Press, 2013); and Barry Hudock, *Struggle, Condemnation, Vindication: John Courtney Murray's Journey Toward Vatican II* (Collegeville, MN: Liturgical Press, 2015).

7. John W. O'Malley, *What Happened At Vatican II* (Cambridge, MA: The Belknap Press of Harvard University Press, 2008), p. 113.

8. Cf. Patrick Carey, "Fenton Returns," *First Things*, No. 282 (April 2018): pp. 54–58.

9. For example, see Karim Schelkens, *Catholic Theology of Revelation on the Eve of Vatican II: A Redaction History of the Schema* De fontibus revelationis *(1960–1962)* (Leiden: Brill, 2010); Roberto de Mattei, *The Second Vatican Council: An Unwritten Story*, trans. Patrick T. Brannan, S.J., Michael J. Miller, and Kenneth D. Whitehead; ed. Michael J. Miller (Fitzwilliam, NH: Loreto, 2013).

interested in the intellectual currents surrounding Vatican II.[10]
However, his dissertation first appeared some thirty years before
the opening of the Council. *What Is Sacred Theology?*, therefore,
represents the fruit of his formative studies as a priest. We might
even say that it summarizes an essential aspect of his identity which
preceded and abided throughout the controversies to which his
name is most commonly associated.[11] Msgr. Joseph Clifford Fenton
was a theologian. And his concept of sacred theology informed his
conception of ecclesial ministry and inspired his literary industry.
His understanding of theology stands as a key principle for those
who wish to understand his work and evaluate his legacy.

THEOLOGICAL INQUIRY: TWO APPROACHES

Fenton introduces his text with a clear summary of its purpose: "This book is meant to aid those who are professionally and
culturally interested in the science of sacred theology better to appreciate the nature and the characteristics of this discipline."[12] Such
an interest, however, does not lose readers in a theoretical world of
floating abstractions. "Sacred theology is essentially a teleological
discipline."[13] It bears real-life and life-changing implications for all
who seek saving truth. "Within the science of sacred theology are
those lessons which will tell man how he can attain an everlasting
and ineffable happiness in the next world and possess the justice,
peace, and security so tragically lacking in this world."[14] The lessons

---

10. The American Catholic History Research Center and University Archives of
The Catholic University of America has digitally scanned and posted the diaries
Fenton kept from 1948–1966, available at http://archives.lib.cua.edu/findin-
gaid/fenton.cfm.

11. For Fenton's exposition of the priestly vocation he received, see his *The Diocesan
Priest in the Church of Christ* (Providence: Cluny Media, 2018) and *The Calling
of a Diocesan Priest* (Westminster, MD: The Newman Bookshop, 1944).

12. Joseph Clifford Fenton, *What Is Sacred Theology?*, ed. Cajetan Cuddy, O.P.
(Providence: Cluny Media, 2018), p. xix.

13. Ibid., p. 4.

14. Ibid., p. xix.

in this discipline touch directly on things of this life and of the life to come. The stakes are high when it comes to sacred theology. Fenton wishes to demonstrate that "theological truth expresses the very meaning which can be proved to *belong* to the body of revealed doctrine rather than merely a teaching *connected with* the divine message."[15] He clarifies that "this discipline [sacred theology] is something more than a science which draws conclusions *out of* that body of teaching which we accept as true on the authority of God who has revealed it." Sacred theology does not exploit divine revelation with human logic or dialectic. It does not corrupt or compromise God's holy teaching. "Sacred theology is actually that science which works toward the clear and unequivocal expression of the divine message." Indeed, "this faithful and exact setting forth of God's teaching is the *essential* function of sacred theology."[16] Neither rationalism nor fideism have a place in the rational creature's reception of the *sacra doctrina*.[17] Reason and faith both—carefully distinguished and properly united—draw the rational soul close to God. In relation to the supernatural truth and goodness of God, reason without faith and faith without reason both betray the human soul. Both of these "withouts" create distance between God and the human person. Reason without faith remains enfeebled by its own natural limitations. It can never attain the most intimate of divine verities. Faith without reason obstructs the transformation divine truth can effect in all aspects of the human soul—which is itself rational in nature. The human creature needs the dual illumination of the light of reason and the light of faith in order to see God in spirit and in truth. Sacred theology represents the proper integration of these two lights. "The scientific form of sacred theology is not an end to itself. It is not calculated to distract men's minds from the teaching of the Gospel. Because of that very technical apparatus, and not in

---

15. Ibid., p. xx. Emphasis in original.

16. Ibid., pp. 3–4. Emphasis in original.

17. See Romanus Cessario, O.P., "*Duplex Ordo Cognitionis*," in *Reason and the Reasons of Faith*, ed. Paul J. Griffiths and Reinhard Hütter (New York: T&T Clark, 2005), pp. 327–38.

spite of it, men are able to grasp and teach the actual meaning of the message which God has given to the world."[18]

Fenton adumbrates the benefits that accrue to those theologians who appreciate the essential nature and function of sacred theology. "*If* American students of our day can be brought to realize clearly that the body of theological literature sets forth the very meaning inherent in the teaching which comes to man from the lips of our crucified Savior, *then* they will be able effectively to use this tremendous resource which God has given them for the happiness and the perfection of their fellow men."[19] Salubrious effects follow upon sacred science conceived in this manner. Theology does not subsist independent from the gospel. Some students of theology recognize the intimate relationship between theology and the teaching of Jesus. Others do not. Those who do, however, participate in Christ's saving mission: the supernatural happiness and perfection of humanity. Theology, according to this true conception, receives its identity from God revealing himself to rational creatures. "God is actually the formal object of attribution for the science [of theology] in the very real sense that every statement put forward in the science contributes toward a more perfect grasp of that concept of God which He has offered to the world in the content of divine revelation."[20] This first account presents a sacred discipline which removes the distance between God and the rational soul. Here we observe a science that facilitates divine intimacy.

Of course, not everyone conceives of theology in this manner—neither in Fenton's time nor in our own. Fenton describes an alternative account of sacred science and the personal implications that follow therefrom. "On the other hand, *if* they [students of theology] conclude, erroneously, that the body of theological teaching is merely a doctrine connected with divine revelation, *then* there is always the danger that they will seek to set aside this treasure for

---

18. Fenton, *What Is Sacred Theology?*, p. 6.
19. Ibid., p. 20. Emphasis added.
20. Ibid., p. 34.

spurious studies which claim to bring men directly to the words
and the meaning of our Lord."[21] Theologians who conceive their
science only in loose connection to divine revelation eventually witness the ever-greater separation of their discipline from the
Lord. This is an infelicitous prospect. A bond of mere association
with divine truth does not guarantee or preserve theology's proper
dignity. Theology's sublimity is directly proportional to its depth of
formal participation in God's holy teaching. This science does not
simply cohabitate with this saving doctrine. Rather, theirs is a nup-
tial relationship. Without such an inviolate bond, the science risks
deforming into something less sublime in nature and less salvific in
end. Any degree of separation from Jesus and his message does not
aid the theologian in particular or the human person in general.

As a discipline merely "connected" with divine revelation, this
account of theological inquiry does not exclude association with
other sources extrinsic to divine revelation. Initially, these other
associations may arrive only by way of consonant extension or ex-
istential application. It is claimed that these *additions* continue to
express elements of the *material* message of divine revelation, but
do so simply from diverse, contemporary perspectives and persua-
sions. However, addition can eventually cede to *supplementation*. At
this stage, additions essentially alien to divine revelation begin to
fill putative gaps within its proper and inherent meaning. Usually
such supplementation enters theological inquiry because the theologian wants to further (more effectively or more compellingly)
divine revelation's salvific end. In other words, the end of theology
remains the happiness and perfection of the human person. But
the theologian believes that it is necessary to graft new elements on
to Christ's teaching in order to help his teaching achieve its purpose. Finally, at this stage, the discipline experiences a self-reflec-
tive recognition of its essential autonomy. Supplementation then
gives way to *substitution*. Principles extrinsic to the gospel message
begin to supplant those of Christ's teaching. Moreover, *formally*,

---

21. Ibid., p. xx. Emphasis added.

this liberated theological inquiry now begins to pursue other alternative ends. These substitutions do not comport with God as the proper and shaping object of the discipline. A new theology now emerges—a theology independent from the principles of divine revelation and dependent upon the *priorities* of the individual theologian. A plethora of customized theologies now replaces what was formerly a unified and sapiential science. The perspectives of theologians now supersede the object of theology. And with the eclipse of theology's true formal object, theological science itself loses its bearing. Its supernatural teleology begins to fade. God no longer stands as the principle end of theological inquiry. Theology is no longer sacred. It is no longer, essentially, about God.

Admittedly, this progression from addition to supplementation to substitution does not always occur from beginning to end. And yet the fundamental point remains: If theology is conceived as merely connected with divine revelation, then a theology separated from God is possible. This erroneous conception bears dire consequences for the science itself and for those who require divine truth. Fenton does not mince words: "The setting aside of the theological resource today would constitute an irreparable harm to those men who stand in such great need of it."[22] The gravity and timelessness of this warning should not escape our attention. We always require God's holy teaching. Therefore, we need theological science in its authentic form—reflecting and expressing the inherent meaning of the Savior.[23] We need a theology that is truly sacred. And "there is no process in sacred theology, however abstruse it may be, which is not centered upon the task of bringing to the student, and through him to the Christian world, the ineffable beauty and simplicity of the message of Jesus Christ, the truth about God."[24]

---

22. Ibid., p. xx–xxi. Emphasis added.

23. Cf. Eugene M. Burke, C.S.P., "The Scientific Teaching of Theology in the Seminary," in *Proceedings of the Fourth Annual Convention* of The Catholic Theological Society of America (1949): pp. 129–73. Burke cites Fenton in his own examination of theology's scientific character.

24. Fenton, *What Is Sacred Theology?*, p. 61.

An Integrated Theology

It is not difficult to recognize that academic theology in the contemporary period has gradually forgotten its sacred identity and purpose. Fenton's book helps remind students why, for Catholics, theology remains an essentially sacred science. Its sacredness is not something accidental or extrinsic to an academic discipline—something akin, perhaps, to an elusive and ideal qualification. Rather, for theologians who work in and with the Church in the service of the *depositum fidei*, a non-sacred theology is not true theology.

Moreover, Fenton's book has a fascinating macrostructure. Students can benefit from many texts which consider the history of Catholic theology from a variety of perspectives and aspects. And many contemporary examinations of Catholic theology give priority to the historical controversy and development that precede the current moment of analysis. Fenton, however, does not follow this methodology. He certainly does not underappreciate the value of historical research. In fact, Fenton laments the lack of comprehensive summaries of theological history. Nevertheless, he chooses a fundamentally different approach. Fenton's method is one of proper scientific division and method ordered to fruitful integration. He does not ignore historical developments in the practice of sacred theology, but considers them as dependent upon the prior and essential establishment of theology as a sacred science and a holy wisdom. The reason for this choice in methodology is clear: It is through its sacred principles that theology receives and retains its sacred identity. The body of revealed principles serves as the point of contact with the divine in this discipline. Historical narrative and sources, in and of themselves, are insufficient instruments of sacred mediation. Sources can be studied with or without the infused virtue of faith. The Bible itself can be read as human literature. However, the revealed principles from which theological science proceeds are only valid principles insofar as they are received in the light of faith. In other words, theological principles require faith in order to be true principles. Without the light of faith, they lose their certitude and the discipline forfeits

its scientific identity. Theology, in this condition, is no longer a sacred science. It is, rather, a dialectical exercise that cannot transcend the order of mere opinion. The theologian does not live by opinion and dialectics alone. And a theology compromised in this manner cannot bring people to the one God in spirit and in truth.

Theologians understandably may hesitate to embrace this principle-prioritized account of theological science. This conception of theology presupposes and requires philosophical facility.[25] The unity of faith and reason is nothing new in the history of the Catholic Church. Saint John Paul II even gave a fresh re-articulation of the lights of faith and reason in his 1998 encyclical *Fides et Ratio*. However, there generally remains (1) a lack of training in philosophy among theologians, (2) an uncertainty about which philosophical currents are fruitfully integrate-able into the Church's doctrinal teaching, or (3) a suspicion of philosophy itself. In the twenty-first century, all three of these impediments are unsurprising. First, the study of theological texts and sources requires much time and effort. Likewise, the appropriation of philosophical learning is far from easy. For Catholics who wish to offer their lives to the service of the Church, it is understandable that many would want to apply their intellectual efforts to the sources most directly associated with the Church's sacred patrimony. Second, it is no secret that the most influential philosophers have not always complimented sacred teaching. While some figures, particularly classical philosophers like Plato and Aristotle, have been famously appropriated by theologians (e.g., Augustine, Bonaventure, Aquinas, and Scotus), others have not been as easy to integrate in a fruitful way (e.g., Nietzsche, Sartre, Fichte). Third, no matter how insightful a philosopher may have been, not one can claim immunity from error. The Church has appropriated certain elements of Platonism and Aristotelianism while rejecting others, for example. Thus, a fear of philosophy

---

25. For an example of Fenton's philosophical proficiency, see his "Metaphysics Should Treat All the Categories," *Proceedings of the Eleventh Meeting* of The American Catholic Philosophical Association (1935): pp. 108–13.

arising from the lack of a *tout court* appropriation of certain philosophers does not astonish us.

Additionally, concerns remain about the relevance of particular philosophers to the disputes, needs, and priorities of the contemporary period. If philosophy is considered to be a cultural hermeneutic of a discrete period, then subsequent generations are left with philosophies that are elusive at best and anachronistic at worst. The cultural priorities of Plato, certainly, are not identical with those of the modern world. Thus, some theologians prefer to rely upon more contemporary figures who philosophize with the preoccupations of the modern world prominently in mind. The insights gleanable from these modern figures, it is thought, can perhaps best aid the Church in her current dispensation.

Students of theology also feel a professional pressure to be original and fresh in their theological research. The simple repetition of doctrinal axioms or scholastic theses rarely appeals to those who wish to work in the world of professional theology. Because of this, many attempt to find originality in either (1) placing theological figures of note in conversation with each other (comparing and contrasting various theologians, bringing out points of influence or change), or (2) placing certain theologians in dialogue with contemporary questions and non-theological disciplines. This mode of theological practice is one of horizontal dialectic: theologians placed in dialogue with each other, and theology placed in dialogue with cultural concerns. These approaches, it is hoped, engender a degree of academic freshness and represent a genuine contribution to theological literature. Fenton, however, presents another standard by which theological contributions can receive validation. In his account, theological inquiry is not evaluated, primarily, by its degree of dialectical engagement. Rather, theology's validity is located in its inherent meaning, in its essential form, in its sacred teleology. Theology's unique value lies in its contact with God. Theology is sacred because it encounters the holy God from whom it receives its first principles and to whom it tends as its end. Fenton's *What Is Sacred Theology?* presents a fresh and relevant presentation of the nature of Catholic theology. And yet he does not manifest an ideological aversion to any legitimate insights found in the newer, *ressourcement* methodologies. "We must not allow ourselves to imagine that the scholastic theologian, or the treatise in scholastic theology does not use the sources and authorities on which theological conclusions are based."[26] Readers easily recognize and appreciate Fenton's attentiveness to the questions of history and of sources.

Some theologians harbor suspicions about the rigorous scholastic (and neo-scholastic) practice of sacred theology. Fenton eschews any such misgivings. Indeed, as we have already seen, he argues that any theologian who jettisons principles from their discipline risks entry into dangerous (non-theological) territory. And the theologian "who realizes that sacred theology, by its very nature, tends to state the teaching of our Lord clearly and unequivocally will know how to answer the rather dangerous claims of those writers who wish to get away from the scientific complexity of scholastic literature and back to the limpid simplicity of Christ's own doctrine."[27] Theology's sacred, teleological nature accounts for its necessity in the life of the Church. Although the promise of an alternative presentation of Christ's message in "limpid simplicity" has a certain allure, the structures of human rationality necessitate a scientific engagement with his saving doctrine. The nature of human understanding requires such an articulation of the *sacra doctrina*. The principles proper to sacred theology actually serve human participation in the sacred simplicity of Christ's teaching: "All of the tremendous intellectual and eruditional resources of sacred theology have been concentrated on the work of expressing our Lord's teaching exactly as He gave it."[28] Of course, the scientific

---

26. Ibid., p. 216.

27. Ibid., p. 5.

28. Ibid. For more on the importance of propositions in sacred theology, see Colman O'Neill, O.P., "The Rule Theory of Doctrine and Propositional Truth," *The Thomist*, Vol. 49, No. 3 (1985): pp. 417–42; Romanus Cessario, O.P., *Christian Faith and the Theological Life* (Washington, DC: The Catholic University of America Press, 1996), pp. 62–76.

form of sacred theology is not an end to itself. It does not inhibit a fully human encounter with the teaching of the Gospel. On the contrary, it is exactly through the sacred science's very "technical apparatus," and not in spite of it, that rational creatures receive the fullness of Christ's holy teaching.

In sum, we might characterize twentieth-century Catholic theology as a gradual movement away from sacred principles to theological sources. Msgr. Fenton illustrates what a reintegrated theology might look like—a theology in which sacred principles and revered sources find fruitful harmony. In other words, this book offers a highly appealing answer to the question: *What is sacred theology?*

FENTON, THOMAS, AND THE THOMISTS

The theologian one encounters in these pages is no contrarian. Far from it. Fenton is a theologian who appropriated the tradition the Church has treasured for almost eight hundred years. Because of this, he does not hide his esteem for the teaching of St. Thomas Aquinas and the legacy of the Thomist tradition. How could he? The Church has always expressed her own esteem for Aquinas and his teaching. All theologians who work within the Church value those whom the Church herself has always valued. This has not changed in the present age. To cite but one example, the 1992 *Catechism of the Catholic Church* repeatedly reaffirms the judgment of previous councils (e.g., Vatican II, Vatican I, and the Council of Trent) that Aquinas remains a treasured resource in the Church's exposition and defense of her doctrine.

This raises a question that occupied Fenton's attention throughout his many writings: *What role can Aquinas play in the contemporary world?* In a 1936 essay published in *The Commonweal*, Fenton examined the situation of "Popular Thomism." He observed that "one of the most amiable attributes of the Thomistic philosophy is its peculiar power to inspire enthusiasm." Moreover, "the men who follow the teachings of the Angelic Doctor are more than a little inclined to be loud in the praise of their system and sanguine about its prospects."[29] Fenton generally approves of such sentiments. "The world needs to know about God and about His rights in the world, and not merely the extent but the basis of morality, and there is not a page in the 'Opera Omnia' of Aquinas that will not give a man a better understanding of God and of himself."[30]

Nonetheless, Fenton reminds his readers that Aquinas will never eclipse the influence that secular savants exercise in the world. "In the first place there is no danger whatsoever that the Angelic Doctor will ever replace men of the type of Wells, Russell and Inge. The teaching of Saint Thomas has not, and could not be made to have, that Sunday Supplement flavor requisite for that position."[31] Here the priest-essayist reminds his readers that Aquinas is not an intellectual among intellectuals. There is something specifically—even essentially—different about Aquinas's project that distinguishes his thought from that of the academy's luminaries. "The men who attain this widest popularity are those who tell their readers that men will be amused in some highly mechanized and eugenic future. Saint Thomas [by contrast] busied himself with explaining to men that they could find peace and happiness anywhere. That sort of thing is far too shocking for most men."[32] Aquinas's simplicity and his profundity both perplex the modern mind. Fenton soberly suggests that "there is not much chance that the strong old Saint of Aquino will ever become 'the fashion.'" Indeed, "there will be little room for him in the gatherings of the sophisticates, for Saint Thomas is a little too mature, and if we might use the term a little too blasé for that sort of thing."[33] Aquinas's identity as a sacred theologian helps us to appreciate Fenton's analysis. Fenton

29. Joseph C. Fenton, "Popular Thomism," *The Commonweal*, Vol. 24, No. 24 (1936): pp. 554–55 (p. 554).

30. Ibid.

31. Ibid.

32. Ibid., p. 555.

33. Ibid.

concedes that non-Catholics could "appreciate" Aquinas's teaching "or even follow it." However, he judges that "very few would be able to do so."[34] Aquinas's greatest contributions are contained in—or are inspired by—his works of sacred theology. His teaching grew out of his sacred study. His thought was a work of grace. It is difficult to be a Thomist without God—known and loved under the dual-illumination of reason and faith. "The richest sources of Thomistic lore are to be found in theological works; like the 'Summa Theologica' of the Angelic Doctor, and the commentaries of men like Capreolus, Cajetan, Bañez, Contenson, Silvius and Billuart. Naturally we cannot expect this study Catholic thought to be propounded as a rule by other than Catholic professors."[35] He concludes: "Whatever triumphs Thomism is to achieve, we can hardly expect it to be taught adequately outside of the Catholic schools even as a historical doctrine." Thomas was a thinker whose entire being was saturated with the sacredness of his religious consecration, his priestly configuration, and his theological study. Understanding and following his thought, therefore, also requires a sacred context and consecrated aid.

Fenton himself represents one such consecrated aid—an able theologian whose thought reflects the intrinsic sacredness of his discipline. He offers a vivid and compelling portrait of a theologian in possession of that sacred science whose beginning and end is God and God alone. However, Fenton—taken by himself—is insufficient for the theologian of the twenty-first century. In particular, his summary of moral theology retains the casuistic structures that dominated the science from the post-Tridentine period until St. John Paul II's *Veritatis Splendor*. Here the writings of Servais Pinckaers, Marie-Michel Labourdette, and Romanus Cessario serve as significant supplements to Fenton's account of moral

---

34. Ibid.

35. Ibid. For an insightful consideration of the life and legacy of Thomas de Vio Cardinal Cajetan, see Joseph Clifford Fenton, "The Centenary of Cajetan," *The Commonweal*, Vol. 21, No. 13 (1935): pp. 369–70.

science.[36] Fenton would hardly have taken umbrage at this claim were he alive today. Indeed, he likely would have rejoiced in the writings of the Thomists who followed him and certainly in the profound structural reconfiguration that *Veritatis Splendor* outlined for the discipline of moral theology. No theologian—and certainly no Thomist—believes that theirs is the final and sufficient word on any given doctrine. Once, in speaking of his theological mentor, Fenton remarked:

> Father Garrigou-Lagrange and the others of his schools are not in the least interested in the process of repeating the statements of Saint Thomas. They are well aware that thought is a certain possession of reality, and they realize that Saint Thomas long ago expressed an appreciation that was profound and meticulously accurate. They are interested in making that appreciation their own.... These men [of the Thomistic school] must not be looked upon as historians of philosophy. They and the school with which they are identified do not study the "Summae" and the great commentaries simply to fill out their knowledge of the progress of medieval thought, as for instance one might study the writings of William of Auxerre. The quest is not for the dicta of a philosopher, but for that grasp of reality to which the expressions of that philosopher can serve as a most valuable aid. The ideas and the system of Saint Thomas can be personal and valid in the minds of these men as they were in the mind of the Angelic Doctor. Conversely, his teaching can be assimilated by the men of the twentieth century, through his writings and the tradition of his school, just as it could have

36. Servais Pinckaers, O.P., *The Sources of Christian Ethics,* trans. Sr. Mary Thomas Noble, O.P. (Washington, DC: Catholic University of America Press, 1995); Michel Labourdette, O.P., *Cours de théologie morale: Tome 1, Morale fondamentale* (Paris: Parole et Silence, 2010); *Cours de théologie morale: Tome 2, Moral spéciale* (Paris: Parole et Silence, 2012); Romanus Cessario, O.P., *Introduction to Moral Theology,* rev. ed. (Washington, DC: The Catholic University of America Press, 2013).

been by his students at the university through the medium of his lectures.[37]

We could hardly ask for a more accurate and a more inspiring summary of that spirit which motivated the great figures of the Thomist tradition. A "grasp of reality"—not of ideas about reality—is the goal of Thomas and the Thomists. It certainly was for Fenton. And because of the example of Thomists like Fenton, theologians of the twenty-first century do not despair in the face of reality no matter what obstacles might present themselves. Even today, through his writings and the tradition of his school, students can assimilate and be transformed by Aquinas's teaching.

* * *

Joseph Clifford Fenton's *What Is Sacred Theology?* gives readers a personal glimpse of a theologian hidden behind an extensive array of speculative analysis. Although this book is not about Fenton himself, it describes the discipline which shaped his priestly and professional identity. Anyone who wants to understand the controversies in which he participated must first appreciate the sacred discipline to which he devoted his life. He was a theologian consecrated to sacred truth. And his description of the exalted nature of theology leads us to a more sublime understanding of Fenton the theologian. Designations like "conservative," "moderate," "progressive," and "liberal" often serve as default ecclesial categories. Perhaps we can attribute the renewed interest Fenton has begun to attract, at least in part, to the fact that he does not easily fit into political classifications. Fenton was traditional, certainly. But all Catholics rejoice in the tradition of the Church. A "non-traditional Catholic" is unintelligible. The Church Christ actually instituted treasures, preserves, and hands on what she received from her divine spouse. A political or ideological hermeneutic will not suffice

37. Fenton, "Modern Thomists," p. 280.

for those who wish to understand the real Msgr. Fenton—or any authentic Catholic theologian for that matter. He eludes easy classification in any one of the political categories commonly used.[38]

In a word, he was a Catholic priest and theologian. His identity and his work received their actuality and retain their intelligibility from his configuration to Christ and his Church. Only those who appreciate the sacredness of theology and of the priesthood can begin to fathom Joseph Clifford Fenton. His adherence to a certain party or his affinity for a particular camp does not fully explain Fenton's identity or his legacy. His sacramental configuration and intellectual consecration to God, alone, can do this.

Even now, over seventy-five years after its initial publication, *What Is Sacred Theology?* remains a valuable book. Why? Because "theology is necessary for the people of God, not merely as some extrinsic means for attaining eternal happiness, but as that science which teaches about the very reality in which alone men can hope to find their eternal joy."[39]

~Cajetan Cuddy, O.P.
Couvent Saint-Albert-le-Grand
Fribourg, Switzerland
The Memorial of the Blessed Virgin Mary,
Mother of the Church, 2018

---

38. Recall, for example, the criticisms he receives from some traditionalist groups for his book: *The Catholic Church and Salvation in the Light of Recent Pronouncements by the Holy See* (Westminster, MD: The Newman Press, 1958).

39. Fenton, *What Is Sacred Theology?*, p. 183.

* * *

Author's Introduction

This book is meant to aid those who are professionally and culturally interested in the science of sacred theology better to appreciate the nature and the characteristics of this discipline. Within the science of sacred theology are those lessons which will tell man how he can attain an everlasting and ineffable happiness in the next world and possess the justice, peace, and security so tragically lacking in this world in our own time. It is then a matter of the utmost importance that those who are privileged to study this science should realize its nature and its competence from the very outset of their course.

Every textbook on fundamental theology begins with some explanation of the essence and the attributes of sacred theology as a whole. Usually, however, because of the tremendous extent of the matter which must be covered in a class of fundamental dogma, the treatise on theology itself is very brief indeed. The men of our own country and of our own time, who must rely so much on the datum of sacred theology for the rebuilding of civilization, stand in evident need of some more complete exposition of the concept of theology than that which has been presented in the ordinary manuals.

There has been no book on this subject in the English language since the brilliant *Clerical Studies* of the Abbé Hogan, in which the great Sulpician described the characteristics and the dignity of each subject taken up in the regular courses offered to candidates for the priesthood and Dr. Scannel's book, *The Priests Studies*, which was intended to aid those continuing to advance in ecclesiastical science after seminary days.[†] However, since the appearance of these fine works, and since the writing of the article on "Theology" by Monsignor Pohle in the *Catholic Encyclopedia*, the literature of this science has been enriched by the methodological treatise of such men as Gardeil, Rabeau, Schultes, and Marín-Sola. It is only fitting that the American student of today should have some access in his own literature to the conclusions which have been illumined through the discussions which followed upon the production of these works.

The great effect of these discussions has been to show that theological truth expresses the very meaning which can be proved to *belong* to the body of revealed doctrine rather than merely a teaching *connected with* the divine message. The illustration and demonstration of this fact are the dominant concerns in this book. If American students of our day can be brought to realize clearly that the body of theological literature sets forth the very meaning inherent in the teaching which comes to man from the lips of our crucified Savior, then they will be able effectively to use this tremendous resource which God has given them for the happiness and the perfection of their fellow men. On the other hand, if they conclude, erroneously, that the body of theological teaching is merely a doctrine connected with divine revelation, then there is always the danger that they will seek to set aside this treasure for spurious studies which claim to bring men directly to the words and the meaning of our Lord. The setting aside of the theological

---

[†]   **Editor's Note:** Very Rev. J.B. Hogan, S.S., *Clerical Studies* (Boston: Marlier, Callanan, and Co., 1898); T.B. Scannell, *The Priest's Studies* (London: Longmans, Green, and Co., 1908).

resource today would constitute an irreparable harm to those men who stand in such great need of it.

The last four chapters of this work are, of course, not intended as even a complete outline of the history of sacred theology. As a matter of fact very little has been done in the line of a complete history of theology in post-patristic times. Monsignor Martin Grabmann's *Geschichte der katholischen Theologie* is very incomplete although it is the best work available on this subject.[†] It does little better than list and classify by schools the names of post-Tridentine theologians. Likewise the classical *Nomenclator Literarius* of Hurter, S.J., gives a resume of the lives of theological writers and classifies them by schools, but with few exceptions no attempt has been made to analyze the teaching of the masters.[††]

The present work is a development of a doctoral dissertation completed ten years ago at Rome, while the author was a student priest at the Angelicum. The author was fortunate enough to have this dissertation directed by that eminent theologian, Father Reginald Garrigou-Lagrange. Fathers Friethoff and Ceuppens were the readers, Father Michael Browne, since Rector Magnificus of the Angelicum, and Father Mariano Cordovani, now Master of the Sacred Palace, were of inestimable help by reason of their gracious counsel. It is the sincere hope of the author that this book may cooperate in some way in giving to American students a measure of that lofty and correct notion of sacred theology which these great professors expounded and realized.

The author wishes to acknowledge the kindness of his friends, the Reverend John J. Reilly, Director of the National Shrine of

---

[†] **Editor's Note:** Martin Grabmann, *Die Geschichte der katholischen Theologie seit dem Ausgang der Väterzeit* (Fribourg-en-Brisgau: Herder, 1933). Helpful books which have been published after Fenton's period include: Aidan Nichols, O.P., *The Shape of Catholic Theology: An Introduction to Its Sources, Principles, and History* (Collegeville, MN: The Liturgical Press, 1991); Ulrich G. Leinsle, *Introduction to Scholastic Theology*, trans. Michael J. Miller (Washington, DC: The Catholic University of America Press, 2010).

[††] **Editor's Note:** Hugo Hurter, S.J., *Nomenclator Literarius Theologiae Catholicae*, 5 vol. (Innsbruck: 1903–1913).

the Immaculate Conception and the Reverend Doctor Cornelius Collins, National Director of the Archconfraternity of Christian Doctrine, both of whom have been of service in the preparation of this volume.[†]

> *~ Joseph Clifford Fenton*
> *The Catholic University of America*
> *Washington, DC*
> *June 25, 1941*

[†]   **Editor's Note:** For more on the Confraternity of Christian Doctrine, see Timothy Michael Dolan, *Some Seed Fell on Good Ground: The Life of Edwin V. O'Hara* (Washington, DC: The Catholic University of America Press, 1992), pp. 126–55.

* * *

Chapter I

The Function and Necessity of Sacred Theology

A. The Ordinary Definition. A man will profit by the study of sacred theology only to the extent that he realizes exactly what theology is. For this reason most of the writers of textbooks in fundamental theology begin their works with a treatise on the nature of the science and define it acceptably. Thus Egger, Cotter, Dorsch, Pesch, and Dieckmann[1] follow Kleutgen and Scheeben in defining it as "the science of faith." Muncunill, Felder, MacGuinness, Tepe, Del Val, Hervé, Zubizarreta, Lahitton, Wilhelm-Scannell, Lepicier, and Diekamp[2] all offer modifications of a definition which Tanquerey–Bord[3] gives as "the science which treats of God and of creatures, in so far as they are referred to God, by way of revelation and of reason." Charlier, a brilliant contemporary student of the nature of theology, claims that a universally acceptable and most general definition of this subject would be "a human discipline based on revelation and developing itself in the light of that revelation."[4]

All of these common definitions of sacred theology agree in describing it in function of its source. In this description they are perfectly accurate. The theologian actually draws conclusions from principles which are true and are accepted as such with the highest degree of certitude. He proceeds in a rigorously scientific manner, and thus he develops a human discipline and utilizes the force of human reason. At the same time the principles out of which the theologian draws his conclusions are actually truths which have been revealed to the world by God through Jesus Christ our Lord. He would have no reason for accepting his conclusions as true if he did not assent to the principles from which they are drawn with the acceptance of divine faith. In so far, then, as sacred theology draws

1.   Franciscus Egger, *Enchiridion Theologiae Dogmaticae Generalis* (Bressanone, 1932), 6th ed., pp. 1 and 2; A.C. Cotter, S.J., *Theologia Fundamentalis* (Weston, MA: 1940), p. 1; Aemilius Dorsch, S.J., *Institutiones Theologiae Fundamentalis*, Vol. 1, "De Religione Revelata" (Innsbruck: 1930), ed. 2 and 3, pp. 2–4; Dr. Matthias Joseph Scheeben, *Handbuch der katholischen Dogmatik*, Vol. 1 (Freiburg im Breisgau: 1873), p. 378; Hermannus Dieckmann, S.J., *De Revelatione Christiana* (Freiburg im Breisgau: 1930), p. 4; Joseph Kleutgen, S.J., *Institutiones Theologiae* (Regensburg), p. 1; Christianus Pesch, S.J., *Praelectiones Dogmaticae*, Vol. 1, *Institutiones Propaedeuticae ad Sacram Theologiam* (Freiburg im Breisgaum: 1924), ed. 6 and 7, p. 4. Most of these authors follow Scheeben in teaching that theology is the science of faith in a double sense. Objectively the content of divine faith is the thing considered in this science. Subjectively the conclusions of theology are demonstrated from or by the truths which we accept on the authority of God revealing.

2.   Joannes Muncunill, S.J., *Tractatus de Vera Religione* (Barcelona: 1909), No. 3; Hilarinus Felder, O.M.Cap., *Apologetica sive Theologia Fundamentalis*, Vol. 1, 2nd ed. (Paderborn and Rome: 1923), p. 2; Joannes MacGuinness, C.M., *Commentarii Theologici*, Vol. 1, 3rd ed. (Paris and Dublin: 1930), p. 1; Bernardus Tepe, S.J., *Institutiones Theologicae*, Vol. 1 (Paris: 1894), pp. 1 and 2; Honoratus Del Val, O.S.A., *Sacra Theologia Dogmatica*, Vol. 1, (Madrid: 1906), p. 1; Canonicus J.M. Hervé, S.T.D., *Manuale Theologiae Dogmaticae*, Vol. 1 (Paris: 1929) p. i; Josephus Canonicus Lahitton, S.T.D., *Theologiae Dogmaticae Theses*, Vol. 1 (Paris: 1932), p. 1; Joseph Wilhelm, D.D., Ph.D., and Thomas B. Scannell, D.D., *A Manual of Catholic Theology Based on Scheeben's "Dogmatik,"* Vol. 1 (London: 1909), Introduction, p. xvii; Valentinus Zubizarreta, O.C.D., Archbishop of Santiago in Cuba, *Theologia Dogmatico-Scholastica*, Vol. 1, 3rd ed. (Bilbao: 1937), p. 9; Alexius Henricus Maria Cardinalis Lepicier, O.S.M., *Institutiones Theologiae Speculativae*, Vol. 1 (Turin and Rome: 1931), p. 18; (see also the much more extensive work of the same author, *Tractatus de Sacra Doctrina* [Rome: 1927], p. 111); Franciscus Diekamp, S.T.D., *Theologiae Dogmaticae Manuale*, Vol. 1 (Paris, Tournai, and Rome: 1933), p. 2.

3.   Adolphe Tanquerey, S.S., *Synopsis Theologiae Dogmaticae Fundamentalis*, 24th ed., entirely revised by J.B. Bord (Paris, Tournai, and Rome: 1937), p. 2; Joannes Herrmann, C.Ss.R., in his famous *Institutiones Theologiae Dogmaticae*, Vol. 1, 7th ed. (Paris and Lyons: 1937), p. 3, makes use of both definitions.

4.   Louis Charlier, O.P., *Essai sur le Problème Théologique* (Thuillies: 1938), p. 12.

out the implications and inferences contained in divine teaching, it is truly the "science of faith."

Accurate as these definitions are, they cannot be accepted as adequately expressing the nature of theology. The mere statement that this science draws conclusions from the very content of divine revelation fails, in some way or another, to touch upon that which is most characteristic of the actually existing literature of sacred theology. Years ago Rabeau pointed out the futility of attempting to explain the nature of this science merely by indicating the syllogistic process used in the production of its theses.[5] Charlier attempted to clear up the difficulty with his thesis that the traditional theologians had essayed an impossible task in trying to explain sacred theology in function of the Aristotelian notion of a science.[6] Furthermore the controversy between Marín-Sola and Schultes was sufficient indication that the textbook definitions can never serve to explain how certain theses which had once been accepted as theological conclusions could later be defined by the Church as expressing the content of divine revelation.[7]

B. The Essential Function. The answer to these modern difficulties must be sought in the direction taken by the definition of sacred theology, for this science cannot be explained adequately other than in terms of its essential function and purpose. As it is expressed in its own tradition and literature, this discipline is

---

5. Gaston Rabeau, *Introduction à l'Étude de la Théologie* (Paris: 1926), p. 218.

6. Charlier, *Essai sur le Problème Théologique*, p. 137.

7. This was one of the most enlightening theological controversies of our time. These two writers, and the others who entered into the discussion with them, debated the possibility of the Church's defining as of faith a proposition which has heretofore been received as a proper theological conclusion. In view of his contention that a proper theological conclusion is a truth which has been deduced *out of* the body of divine revelation, Schultes denied this possibility. Marín-Sola opposed him, maintaining that the theological conclusion presents a truth which is only conceptually distinct from the body of revealed doctrine. The books in which their theses are presented are, Franciscus Marín-Sola, O.P., S.T.M., *L'Évolution Homogène du Dogme Catholique*, 2nd ed., 2 Vols. (Fribourg, Switzerland: 1924). Reginaldus-Maria Schultes, O.P., S.T.M., *Introductio in Historiam Dogmatum* (Paris: 1922).

something more than a science which draws conclusions *out of* that body of teaching which we accept as true on the authority of God who has revealed it. We would fail completely to appreciate its real significance and vitality if we imagined that it was concerned with a body of truth connected with but not inherent in the message of Jesus Christ. Sacred theology is actually that science which works toward the clear and unequivocal expression of the divine message. This faithful and exact setting forth of God's teaching is the *essential* function of sacred theology. To this end all of its complex equipment, its problems and conclusions and the very procedure by which the problems are resolved and the conclusions established are orientated. The work of explaining the content of that teaching which God has given to the world through Jesus Christ our Lord, and which is proposed for the belief of men in the infallible magisterium of the Catholic Church, actually specifies sacred theology. Sacred theology is essentially a teleological discipline, and men can understand it and use it properly only when they look upon it in relation to its essential function.†

---

†   **Editor's Note: The Teleology of Sacred Theology:** In *Summa Theologiae* I, q. 1, a. 1, Aquinas explains why the human search for truth requires the *sacra doctrina* ("holy teaching"). He observes that philosophical disciplines (e.g., natural philosophy, metaphysics, et al.) are insufficient resources with regard to the sublimity of "human salvation" (*humanam salutem*). Because God is the supernatural end of the rational creature, the human person requires divine assistance to reach this end. This is true for several reasons. Human persons can only act for an end (natural or supernatural) that they first know (*praecognitum*). No one can turn their thoughts and actions to something about which they lack all knowledge or awareness. Beatific union with God in heaven exceeds all human imagination. Therefore, it is necessary for human salvation that God reveal himself to humanity as the supernatural end. Although sound philosophy can reveal many (and even profound) natural truths to man, human reason can never arrive at the supernatural truth about God himself. The human person requires God's divine revelation of himself before the human person can direct thoughts and actions to God himself. Because the human person is ordered to God as supernatural end, human persons require God's holy teaching. Theological science is essentially dependent on the *sacra doctrina* (cf. *ST* I, q. 1, a. 1, ad 2). Therefore, sacred theology also bears the teleological orientation of the *sacra doctrina*.

This supernatural teleology has always stood as the key element within the Thomist tradition's understanding of the *sacra doctrina* and of sacred theology. In his

Thus the man who realizes that sacred theology, by its very nature, tends to state the teaching of our Lord clearly and unequivocally will know how to answer the rather dangerous claims of those writers who wish to get away from the scientific complexity of scholastic literature and back to the limpid simplicity of Christ's own doctrine. All of the tremendous intellectual and eruditional resources of sacred theology have been concentrated on the work of expressing our Lord's teaching exactly as He gave it. Thus, if one

---

commentary on *ST* I, q. 1, a. 1, Thomas de Vio Cardinal Cajetan (1469–1534) considers the teleology of the *sacra doctrina* at great length. Later Thomists like Domingo Bañez (1528–1604), John of St. Thomas (1589–1644), and Reginald Garrigou-Lagrange (1877–1964) continued to consider the implications of the *sacra doctrina*'s divine teleology. The teleology of the *sacra doctrina* ensures several things. Like the *sacra doctrina* from whose principles it proceeds, sacred theology can never be separated from the source of all sanctity. Objectively, theology remains intrinsically dependent upon and ordered to God. God is the object of sacred theology. Subjectively, students of theology remain united to the God whom they contemplate. Authentic theologians participate in the sacredness of the divine object they study.

This is the only explicit reference to teleology in *What Is Sacred Theology?* However, it remains foundational to Fenton's analysis throughout. In one of his other books, *Laying the Foundation: A Handbook of Catholic Apologetics and Fundamental Theology* (Steubenville, OH: Emmaus Road Publishing, 2016), Fenton explores the formal significance of teleology in divine revelation at greater length. In *Laying the Foundation* (originally published under the title: *We Stand with Christ: An Essay in Catholic Apologetics* [Milwaukee, WI: Bruce Publishing Co., 1942]), Fenton examines the necessity of divine revelation in relation to man's supernatural end. With precision, Fenton distinguishes the order of nature from the order of grace. He explains the end of man in reference to the philosophical principles of potency and act: "It is, of course, absolutely impossible that there should be a thing without a purpose. In the case of a creature this purpose must be something distinct from its own essence. In terms of metaphysics the purpose of a thing is the good, and the good is that which is in act opposed to that which is merely in potency…. As a result the purpose of man consists *formally* in an act of understanding and *objectively* in that thing which is seen as the ultimate and perfect object of such an act, God himself" (*Laying the Foundation*, p. 56). Fenton summarizes a great deal of philosophical fundamentals in these few lines. Purposeless beings are impossible and do not exist. Every actual being has a nature, a form, an end, and a teleological orientation. Goodness is annexed to the being of a thing—purpose is fulfilled through act in reference to some good (some end). The purpose (and the good) of man consists in an act of understanding the truth of God himself. God has called man to a cognitive union with himself that exceeds the limitations of metaphysical

understands it aright, the very complexity and the austere scientific form of technical theology will appear as a mechanism by which we can focus the light of our minds on the very words and the meaning of our Lord Himself.[8] The scientific form of sacred theology is not an end to itself. It is not calculated to distract men's minds from the teaching of the Gospel. Because of that very technical apparatus, and not in spite of it, men are able to grasp and teach the actual meaning of the message which God has given to the world.

Sacred theology is organized for a definite function. It aims to set forth clearly and unequivocally the content of Christian revelation. A theological problem is a question relative to the meaning

science. Indeed, he has called us to beatific, supernatural union with him. "As far as the life of man is concerned, it must be perfected in the attainment of the supernatural end, or not at all. The alternative open to man, as far as his final lot is concerned, is God or nothing" (ibid., p. 57). "The supernatural end, which is God, to be seen in the light of the beatific vision, is by its very nature a reality which men could never come to know through the exercise of their merely natural intellectual activity.... They must derive their knowledge from some source to which this clear knowledge of God belongs by right. In other words, they must learn it from God Himself" (ibid., pp. 57–58). Fenton emphasizes the necessity of this sacred instruction God himself provides: "If God had not mercifully given to the world in a supernatural manner the doctrine about the final end which man must attain in order to have eternal happiness, this happiness could not be had by men" (ibid., p. 58). Because "this happiness is a reality" the divine revelation of the *sacra doctrina* "is absolutely necessary" (ibid., p. 58) for the attainment of real happiness.

Fenton summarizes key elements in the Thomist tradition's articulation of the great gift and necessity of the *sacra doctrina*. These passages from *Laying the Foundation* are highly recommended for anyone who wishes to piece together the teleological nature of the *sacra doctrina* from among Fenton's other writings. For more on the relationship between the philosophical principles of potency and act, and the teleology of supernatural beatitude, see Steven A. Long, "The Perfect Storm: On the Loss of Nature as a Normative Theonomic Principle in Moral Philosophy," in *What Happened in and to Moral Philosophy in the Twentieth Century: Philosophical Essays in Honor of Alasdair MacIntyre*, ed. Fran O'Rourke (Notre Dame, IN: University of Notre Dame Press, 2013), pp. 271–303; Romanus Cessario, O.P., "The Importance of Steven A. Long's *Analogia Entis* within Contemporary Catholic Thought," *Nova et Vetera*, Vol. 12 (2014): pp. 971–74. As Fenton says in this passage: "The scientific form of sacred theology is not an end to itself." God is the end.

8.   Ambroise Gardeil, O.P., *Le Donné Révélé et la Théologie*, 2nd ed. (Juvisy, Seine-et-Oise: 1932), p. 250. Charlier, *Essai sur le Problème Théologique*, p. 123.

of some portion of the message which God has given to the world through Jesus Christ. The correct resolution of such a problem, in other words a statement of what our Lord meant and what the Catholic Church understood Him to mean from the very beginning of her existence, constitutes a theological conclusion. The process by which the conclusion is proved to be the correct statement of our Lord's meaning is called the theological proof. Consequently the function which motivates the entire operation of sacred theology has a dominating influence in any adequate definition of this science.

C. The Essential Purpose Manifest in Theological Literature. The only way in which this essential function of theology can be demonstrated is through an appeal to the literature of the science itself. The student must never forget that in dealing with sacred theology, he is treating a subject which has been taught for centuries. It has an extensive and tremendously developed literature and tradition. Consequently when a man studies the nature of sacred theology, he is not considering some possible kind of knowledge about God which might be drawn from the content of divine revelation. He is speaking about a definite discipline with easily ascertainable characteristics, a subject which is taught in the universities and seminaries throughout the Catholic world today, and which has been the dominating element not only in the Catholic university tradition, but in the cultural and intellectual life of the Church since its very foundation.

It would be perfectly possible, from an examination of theological literature as a whole, to demonstrate that the science is essentially meant for a clear and unequivocal exposition of divine revelation. The theses of modern authors like Billot and Diekamp or of classical authors like Valentia and Sylvius and John of St. Thomas are obviously meant to express the content of our Lord's teaching.[9] There is no question of mere deduction for the sake of deduction in their list

---

9. Many of the propositions advanced as theses by these men are actually statements which have been defined as of divine faith by the Catholic Church.

of conclusions. Indeed, men like St. Thomas Aquinas and Melchior
Cano have insisted that "useless questions" should be excluded from
the content of theological teaching.[10] If the actually existing science
of sacred theology had been definable merely as a knowledge about
God and the things of God in so far as these could be known by a
process of inference from the content of Catholic dogma, then there
could be no question of a "useless" conclusion at all. If theology is
to be described merely in function of its principles, as a body of
knowledge deduced from divinely revealed truth, then obviously
one inference or conclusion would have the same scientific standing
as any other. In that case a man might object to a conclusion as
incorrect, but he could never logically attack it as useless. Actually a
good proportion of the theses set forth in the ordinary manuals of
theology, as well as in the classical masterpieces of this science, have
been defined as of faith by the Catholic Church.

However possible an appeal to all of the authors of theological
works might be, it is neither necessary nor highly scientific. In the
history of theological literature there have been certain key works
upon which others have depended, certain writers who have given
direction and form to the actually existing theological tradition. In
this way the *Four Books of Sentences*, written by Peter the Lombard,
a twelfth-century archbishop of Paris, were accepted as the official
textbook in the European universities from the twelfth until the
end of the sixteenth century. A good portion of the theological
literature in that period took the form of commentaries on the
Sentences.[11] The doctrine which men taught and studied as sacred
theology was obviously that which Peter the Lombard had written,
and that which we teach and study today is the same science as that
which was expounded in the great universities of long ago. As a result, that which was the characteristic function for the theology of

---

10. St. Thomas Aquinas, *Summa Theologiae* (hereafter *ST*), prologue; Melchior
     Cano, O.P., *De Locis Theologicis*, Liber XII, Caput IV, §1.

11. Cf. the articles on Peter the Lombard by Joseph De Ghellinck in the *Catholic
     Encyclopedia* (Vol. XI, pp. 768–69) and in the *Dictionnaire de Théologie Catho-
     lique* (Vol. XII, columns 1941–2019).

Peter the Lombard is likewise characteristic of the actually existing literature and tradition which stemmed from his work.

St. Thomas Aquinas has also exercised a unique influence in the life of the theological tradition. The law of the Catholic Church obliges teachers of theology in her universities and seminaries to expound their science according to the, principles enunciated by the Angelic Doctor.[12] By far the greater number of modern theological writers have claimed to teach the doctrine of St. Thomas in their own works. Hence, if we can show that both Peter the Lombard and St. Thomas Aquinas regarded the subject that they taught as essentially orientated toward the unequivocal presentation of the Christian message, we shall have reasonable grounds for assuming that the actually existing discipline of sacred theology must be defined and understood in function of this work.

D. The Concept of Peter the Lombard. We find that the Master of the *Sentences* expressed his notion of sacred theology in the Introduction to the first of the *Four Books*, and in the content of the volume as a whole. It was his intention in writing the *Four Books of Sentences*, "to defend the faith, with the shields of the tower of David, or rather to show that it is so defended... to open up the profundities of theological questions and to manifest the meaning of the ecclesiastical sacraments to the best of his ability."[13] The context of the volume shows very clearly that defense of the faith meant for Peter the Lombard an accurate statement of Catholic dogma as that dogma had been enunciated in the writings of the Fathers. The theological investigation of which he spoke consists in a statement and solution of questions raised about the meaning of the dogmatic formulae which had entered into the defense of

---

12. *Codex Iuris Canonici* (1917 ed.), canon 1366, §2. **Editor's Note:** Fenton is obviously referring to the 1917 edition of the Code of Canon Law (promulgated by Pope Benedict XV). However, the current (1983) edition of the Code of Canon Law (promulgated by Pope John Paul II) reiterates the priority given to Aquinas in theological formation. Cf. *Code of Canon Law* (1983 ed.), canon 252, §3.

13. Petrus Lombardus, *Libri Quattuor Sententiarum*, Prologus (Fenton used the edition of Quarrachi: 1916).

the Catholic faith. The treatise on the sacraments was reserved for the last of the *Four Books of Sentences*, and in this book the Master followed exactly the procedure adopted in his earlier books. Peter the Lombard made no attempt to draw out all the possible implications and inferences which might be deduced from the content of divine faith. He was satisfied to consider those questions, the improper resolution of which might result in the perversion or the loss of the faith for members of the Catholic Church. He professed to act out of a "zeal for the house of God" which is the Church of Jesus Christ. He offered his volumes as a means of overcoming the efforts of the enemies of the faith. His only concern was to remove any ambiguity which might be favorable to these enemies of the Church through a clear statement of the content of faith which would manifest the falsity of heretical opinions.

E. The Concept of St. Thomas Aquinas. The attitude of St. Thomas Aquinas, the Common and Angelic Doctor of the Catholic Church, was identical with that of the Master of the *Sentences*. In the Introduction to the *Summa Theologica*, the greatest of all his literary works, he defines his labor as that of a "teacher of Catholic truth."† It was his announced intention to "set forth those things which pertain to the Christian religion clearly,"[14] in such a way that beginners in the study of the sacred doctrine might profit from his instruction. He complains of the "useless questions" proposed in some of the texts used in his time, questions which obviously are to be eliminated because they do nothing toward bringing out the full force and clear beauty of that teaching which God has given to the world through Jesus Christ our Lord. And when the time arrived to

---

† **Editor's Note:** For more on the nature and purpose of Aquinas's *Summa Theo-logiae*, see Jean-Pierre Torrell, O.P., *Aquinas's Summa: Background, Structure, and Reception*, trans. Benedict M. Guevin, O.S.B. (Washington, DC: The Catholic University of America Press, 2005). For a historical-philosophical consideration of the *Summa Theologiae*, see Pasquale Porro, *Thomas Aquinas: A Historical and Philosophical Profile*, trans. Joseph G. Trabbic and Roger W. Nutt (Washington, DC: The Catholic University of America Press, 2016), pp. 219–35, pp. 281–304, pp. 386–87.

14. *ST*, prologue.

consider the character of sacred theology as a science, he used the deathless words of St. Augustine to declare the scientific dignity of the sacred doctrine. It was the contention of Augustine that to this science which we know as sacred theology, there could be attributed only that "by which the most salutary faith which leads to true beatitude is generated, nourished, defended, and strengthened."[15] St. Thomas Aquinas, the man who developed the thought of Augustine to its ultimate perfection, knew no other sort of sacred theology.

The most striking and forceful expression of Aquinas' concept of theology, however, is to be found in his inaugural discourse delivered on the occasion of his receiving the doctoral biretta from the hands of Aimeric of Veire in April 1256. He took as his text the words of Psalm 103, "Watering the hills from on high, the earth shall be filled with the fruit of thy works." In this magnificent sermon[16] St. Thomas saw, under the image of the life-giving water which rains down upon the hills and then flows to the fields below to give verdure and fruitfulness to the countryside, the divinely revealed doctrine which God has given to the world through Jesus Christ. The hills were the prophets and the Apostles who were constituted as the divinely appointed bearers of the divine message to the children of men. He considered the function of the teachers of Catholic truth, or, in other words, the teachers of sacred theology, since he was addressing himself to the members of that faculty which had just given him his commission to teach, to be the bringing of his divine message to the children of men in such a way that

---

15. *De Trinitate*, Liber XIV, Caput I, no. 3.

16. This opusculum is entitled, *Breve Principium Fratris Thomae de Aquino Quando Incepit Parisius ut Magister in Theologia: De Commendatione Sacrae Scripturae.* It is listed as number 40 in the order of the *opuscula* arranged by Father Pierre Mandonnet, O.P. It is found on p. 491 of the fourth volume of the set of the *opuscula* edited by Mandonnet and published at Paris in 1927. **Editor's Note:** For more information on the dramatic context of this inaugural lecture at the University of Paris, see Jean-Pierre Torrell, O.P., *Saint Thomas Aquinas*, vol. 1, *The Person and His Work*, trans. Robert Royal, rev. ed. (Washington, DC: The Catholic University of America Press, 2005), pp. 50–53. For an English translation of this lecture, see Thomas Aquinas, *Selected Writings*, ed. and trans. Ralph McInerny (New York: Penguin Books, 1998), pp. 13–17.

men could profit from its tremendous advantages. In this sermon we see very clearly that the Angelic Doctor did not consider theology to consist in any deductions which might be made out of the content of Catholic dogma. Only that work which was directed toward bringing the message of Jesus Christ to those for whom He died upon the cross was worthy of the faculty of sacred theology. The Church itself has taken official cognizance of St. Thomas' concept of sacred theology. In the Bull *Redemptionem Misit Dominus*, of July 18, 1323, the document in which the canonization of the Angelic Doctor was proclaimed to the world, Pope John XXII was able to declare that the meaning of the very text which the Saint had used in his inaugural discourse had been fulfilled in his life and in his teaching. All of the dialectical skill, and all of the tremendous erudition at the disposal of St. Thomas had been utilized in order that the little ones of Christ might receive His message as our Lord Himself had given it, and as the Church which He founded had understood it from the very beginning of her existence.

F. The Counsel of Melchior Cano. The great theologians who have developed and continued the tradition of St. Thomas have understood theology as essentially a discipline devoted to the unequivocal statement of the divine message. Thus, for instance, Melchior Cano, one of the great glories of the Thomistic school, manifested his concept of the science when he counseled his students to advert always to the dignity of their calling. "This rule will be in accord with reason and particularly in accord with the authority of the saints; that every theologian who is going to deal with the supernatural (for this is his proper field), should consider well within himself the very name of theology; should often read his own title, that is the title of theologian; should not once but frequently, that is as often as he is called upon to discuss his subject, ask himself and realize that he is to treat of no question except that which refers to the true and supernatural philosophy of Christ, the apostles and the prophets."[17]

---

17. Cano, *De Locis Theologicis*, Liber XII, Caput IV.

Christ, the Apostles, and the prophets are the vehicles and spokesmen of the divine public revelation, that which is proposed for our belief in the infallible teaching of the Catholic Church. Our Lord is the Great Prophet, and the others acted as His heralds and His ministers. The true philosophy of Christ is the Christian message which comes to men in the form of Catholic dogma. The theologian, in virtue of his position is to be concerned with no other matter, according to the teaching of Melchior Cano. The great Spanish writer is quite impatient with those who have intruded useless and impertinent matters into the field of the queen of the sciences.

G. The *Protestatio Quotidiana* of Francis Sylvius. The same preoccupation with theology in function of its inherent and essential purpose is manifest in the writings and in the daily protestation of the great Douai theologian, Francis Sylvius. The editions of his work, published after his death, carry the formula of a promise which he made to God every day, a formula which is eloquent of the lofty and exact concept of sacred theology on which the works of the outstanding theologians are motivated. "I testify this day that I desire to live and to die in the faith and in the unity of our holy mother, the Church of Rome. I wish to order all my activity and my studies to the glory of God, to the utility of the Church, and to my own salvation and that of my neighbor. I shall neither accept nor interpret Holy Scripture other than according to the unanimous consent of the Fathers. Whatever I shall say or write or teach, either on the *Summa Theologica* of St. Thomas Aquinas, or in discussions, lectures, or other exercises at any time or place, I shall say, write, and speak according to the same unanimous consent of the Fathers. And if it should happen (as it is only human to fail), that at any time I should speak, write, or teach otherwise, from this very moment I hold that statement as if it had not been said. So, may God love me."[18] The unanimous consent of the Fathers, of which the great

---

18. The translation is that of the text cited in the preface to the edition of Sylvius's Commentaries on the *Summa Theologica* (Antwerp: 1698).

Douai master speaks so carefully, is a norm for judging the content of the faith itself. It was his explicit intention to limit his teaching to that which was in accord with this criterion. Sylvius intended, then, to set forth the actual message which the Catholic Church offers to her children as the doctrine revealed to men through Jesus Christ our Lord. The content of his teaching, and the content of the standard and traditional theological literature of the Catholic Church in every age mirrors the same tendency.

H. Revelation Given to Man in a Supernatural Way. Since it is the immediate and essential function of sacred theology to set forth and explain revealed teaching, and since theology cannot be adequately understood nor defined other than in the light of this function, it is obviously necessary that we should understand exactly what sort of teaching this revealed doctrine is. We can speak of revelation as an act on the part of God. Understood in this way, or in its subjective meaning, it is that operation by which God communicates a body of doctrine to the human race, in a way distinct from and superior to the way in which man naturally acquires his knowledge.[19] Likewise we can speak of revelation objectively, that is as the body of teaching itself. Objectively, then, divine revelation is a message which God has given to the human race in this supernatural manner.[20]

---

19. Cf. the teaching of the Vatican Council, in the Constitution *Dei Filius* (Denzinger, 1785); also the explanation of this chapter in Jean-Michel-Alfred Vacant, *Études Théologiques sur les Constitutions du Concile du Vatican, La Constitution Dei Filius*, Vol. 1 (Paris and Lyons: 1895), pp. 337–43; also Reginald Garrigou-Lagrange, O.P., S.T.M., *De Revelatione per Ecclesiam Catholicam proposita*, Vol. 1, 3rd ed. of the complete work (Rome: 1929), pp. 137–63; and Joseph J. Baierl, S.T.D., *The Theory of Revelation*, Vol. 1 (Rochester, NY: 1927), pp. 20–36; also the article "Revelation," by Iung in the *Dict. de Theol. Cath.*, Vol. 13, columns, 2580–2618.

20. Dieckmann, *De Revelatione Christiana*, pp. 144–45, prefers the term "preternatural," but this is not in accord with the wording of the Vatican Council nor with the ordinary significance of "preternatural." A thing is ordinarily spoken of as preternatural when it is beyond the competence of some created nature, but within the scope of that activity which springs from another. Thus, infused ideas would be preternatural to man because, while they are outside of the scope of natural human activity, they actually belong to the intellectual processes of created pure spirits.

When we speak of revelation as supernatural with reference to the manner in which man acquires it, we obviously imply that man is capable of natural knowledge, that is of understanding something about God, about himself and the world in which he lives by the use of faculties which are founded in human nature itself.[21] Man acquires this knowledge in a natural way when he derives it by a process of abstraction from the datum presented by his senses. Man's nature is essentially orientated toward the acquisition of knowledge in this way. Consequently this manner of acquiring knowledge is natural to him, or due to the very nature which he possesses.

However, the divine revelation which sacred theology is organized to expound is acquired in a totally different way. In making this revelation, God speaks to man and teaches him. Objectively the divine revelation constitutes a body of truth which man has received from God in the way in which a disciple or a pupil accepts a teaching from his instructor. Man has no inherent right to this instruction. He does not need it in order to possess the kind of knowledge which belongs to his human nature. Consequently we say that, considered from the point of view of the manner in which it is received, the divine revelation is something supernatural. It is a free gift of God, immensely beneficial to man, but at the same time something which God does not have to give in order to fill out the perfection of human nature as such.

We must be very careful to note that a thing is not supernatural merely by the fact that it is acquired with the aid of the divine power. As a matter of fact man receives from God every bit of knowledge which he possesses, even that which is acquired in a purely natural way. God is the First Mover and the First Cause in every operation performed by His creatures, and this holds for the operation of the human intelligence as well as for any other sort of created activity. There is not and there can never be a fiber or aspect of being and reality which man does not receive from the merciful

---

21. See the Vatican Council (Denzinger, 1785), and the Anti-Modernist Oath (Denzinger, 2145).

power of his Creator. The criterion in the light of which a thing is judged to be supernatural is the fact that this particular good is not due to, nor demanded by, the nature of man. Considered from the viewpoint of the manner in which man acquires it, the teaching which we call divine revelation is then definitely supernatural.

There have been many instances in the course of history in which God has so spoken to his creatures. Sacred theology, however, is concerned with one definite, message, that which God has given to the world through Jesus Christ. That message was imparted to the human race over an immense period of time. The introductory portion was communicated to the human race by the prophets and patriarchs, who were the heralds and the forerunners of our Lord. The main body of this message fell from the lips of the divine Redeemer Himself, and the concluding portion was entrusted to the Apostles who were the ministers and the messengers of Christ. It has been and it will be preached to the world with infallible correctness by that Catholic Church which is constituted as the Mystical Body of Christ.

I. Mediate and Public Revelation. We speak of this definite doctrine as mediate and public revelation. It is *mediate* in so far as it has been communicated by God to certain individuals, to be proposed by them to their fellow men. But as mediate revelation it is just as truly the message of God when it is received by its ultimate destinaries as it is when it first comes to the prophet who is entrusted with and strengthened for the function of bringing it to the rest of mankind. It would, of course, have been perfectly possible for God to have brought His teaching directly to each of those for whom it is intended. But it pleased Him to deal with man according to the definitely social character of man's own nature. He chose to select certain men, instruct them directly, and then commission and empower these prophets to bear His teaching to their fellows.

The revelation taught and expressed in sacred theology is called *public* in that it is meant for all men, without restriction. There may be, and as a matter of fact there have been, revealed messages which were private. These communications were addressed by God to one person or group of persons and designated for the good of this limited number. The Christian revelation, explained and taught in the process of sacred theology, is meant to benefit all human beings.

J. Intrinsically Supernatural Character of Revealed Truth. Most important of all for a proper understanding of sacred theology, the revelation which is expounded in this discipline is also *supernatural in its very essence*. The truths which God has deigned to communicate to man in this message are such that they could not be known naturally by any creature, actual or possible. They are statements about the intimate life of God, or as some of the theologians put it, about God considered from the point of view of His own divinity. God knows these truths by the very fact that He is God, but there could be no creature who would be able to learn of them by the unaided force of its own created nature. These essentially supernatural truths, conveyed in Christian revelation, constitute the order of *mysteries*.[22]

God can and does offer men a clear vision of that infinite reality which is expressed in Christian revelation. In that vision the saints in heaven find their ineffable and eternal supernatural happiness. Men are placed in this world so that they may prepare themselves to receive this beatific vision. They are not meant to possess the clarity of vision here. Consequently the only way in which the men of this world can have a definite and certain knowledge of this order of supernatural reality is through the supernatural assent of divine faith. For, with divine faith, we assent to revealed truths, not because we see or understand that they must be true, but precisely on the authority of God who has revealed them, and who can neither deceive nor be deceived. In the assent of divine faith we accept with utter certitude a truth which is not evident.[†]

---

22. See the Vatican Council (Denzinger, 1795).

† **Editor's Note:** For more on the nature of the theological virtue of faith and its formal objectivity, see Romanus Cessario, O.P., *Christian Faith and the Theological Life* (Washington, DC: The Catholic University of America Press, 1996); Michel Labourdette, O.P., *La foi: « Grand cours » de théologie morale* (Paris: Parole et Silence, 2015).

K. Procedure of Theology Determined by Fact That Its Essential Purpose Is the Teaching of Supernatural Mysteries. As a result, the truths which sacred theology means to expound and defend are such that man cannot possibly learn of them through the natural exercise of his own reason. They could not be known in any way other than by the process of revelation, and they can be accepted with certainty only on the assent of divine faith. These truths which constitute the central or essential portion of divine revelation remain no less obscure, even after they have been revealed. The subject with which they are concerned is something which will be evident to man only in the glorious clarity of the beatific vision. Sacred theology, then, will never tend toward any clear and evident grasp of the mysteries themselves, considered objectively. Thus, it can never mean to prove that the mystery of the Blessed Trinity is evident naturally, nor will it attempt to show that even after revelation we can possess a clear knowledge of the Triune God.

On the contrary, this science will begin its essential work by bringing out the actual statements in which the divine message has been proposed for the belief of men. Since the Chief Prophet of this revelation is our Lord Jesus Christ, the objective and scientific sacred theology must be a Christian discipline. And because the revealed teaching is proposed to men in the authentic magisterium of the Catholic Church, and is not to be acquired independently of that magisterium, sacred theology must also be the Catholic theology. It is the business of sacred theology, as it has been understood by its great scientific tradition, to set forth the content of revelation exactly as it has been taught by our Lord, the prophets, and the Apostles and as it has been understood and expressed by the Catholic Church during all the years of its existence.

Then sacred theology must accept the task of defending this revealed doctrine. This defense is accomplished in offering a clear and unequivocal expression of its meaning, and in refuting those incorrect interpretations which might be destructive of the faith of Christians. Even though the subject described in this essentially supernatural revelation is not and will not be evident to men as long as they live in this world, the statements which contain that revelation have a definite and highly important meaning. Sacred theology, then, can set forth the correct meaning to be attached to these formulae, and then demonstrate that this is the objective meaning. In accomplishing this function, and not in merely drawing out the content of implication *from* the dogmatic formulae themselves, sacred theology fulfills the task entrusted to it, and does the work which men like Peter the Lombard and St. Thomas Aquinas understood it was to do.

L. The Purpose of Divine Revelation.[23] Since sacred theology can be defined and understood only with reference to the teaching of divine revelation, we can know theology better only in so far as we look upon it in the light of the purpose and the necessity of that revelation. It is a fact that God has given His supernatural message to man in order that man may be prepared for an eternity of perfect happiness with Him in heaven, a happiness consisting in the face to face vision, or the intuition, of the very Reality which man has believed in this world. God also intends that we should obtain this happiness in the way most fitting for man to acquire a good. God intends that we should earn it. According to the designs of divine providence, those who have enjoyed the use of reason in this world are meant to obtain the beatific vision, not only as something acquired for them by the death of Jesus Christ, but also as a reward which they themselves have merited in living the life of grace. Thus God has given us the Christian revelation in order that we may know the eternal good for which we are meant to work and to prepare in this world.

The divine message which sacred theology is meant to teach is something definitely worth having for its own sake. The revealed truths actually perfect the mind which possesses them. It is quite fitting that these truths should be known by men who are invited by God to live as His adopted children, and as the brothers of Jesus Christ. The primary and essential purpose of the divine revelation

---

23. See the Vatican Council (Denzinger, 1786).

is to direct men toward that eternal beatitude which God wills that man should enjoy as his only ultimate end.

However, there is another and a seriously important good procured through divine revelation. As a matter of fact, man, as he actually exists, is deficient in natural knowledge about God and consequently in that understanding which is consequent upon the natural appreciation of the Creator. It is a real though secondary purpose of divine revelation to supply for the shortcomings of man's natural cognition, and to offer him a knowledge about God, even in the natural order, which is available to all, easily, and without that error which would endanger or destroy man's intellectual perfection.

M. The Necessity of Divine Revelation. It is the essential function of sacred theology to explain and teach a revelation which is *physically* necessary for man. Such is the order which the providence of God has instituted in the world that man will not attain the eternal and supernatural happiness of the beatific vision, which is, as a matter of fact, the only ultimate beatitude available to him, apart from the definite revelation which God has given to the world through Jesus Christ and which He proposes and guards in the unerring teaching of the Catholic Church. A thing is said to be physically necessary when an end cannot be obtained independently of it. Since the end which will not be obtained other than with the divine revelation is the only ultimate good of man, we can realize how profound is man's need of the revelation which sacred theology is ordered to expound.

This same Christian revelation is *morally* necessary for man. A thing is said to be morally necessary for the attainment of some good which, absolutely speaking, could be obtained without this help, but which could not be obtained fitly and properly except through its influence. The Christian revelation is morally necessary for the attainment of a knowledge of God in the natural order which is available to all, with reasonable ease and celerity, and without a serious and perverting admixture of error.

There can be no understanding of theology apart from a realization of this necessity. A natural knowledge of God is, of course, that which man can obtain through the exercise of those faculties which are rooted in his own human nature. As a rational creature, man is capable of recognizing the existence of a First Cause. He can and should be able to demonstrate accurately and with perfect certitude that this First Cause is simple, spiritual, eternal, immutable, one, good, and true, resplendent with an infinite intellectual and moral perfection. As a matter of fact the perennial Catholic philosophy contains such demonstrations drawn out in their ultimate scientific complexity, and utterly beyond the possibility of any legitimate impeachment.[†]

However, the long course of history shows us very clearly that those men who have not had the advantage of the divine revelation taught in sacred theology, have never made full and perfect use of this naturally available knowledge about God. The great masses of mankind who have not possessed the virtue of divine faith have labored under the most ludicrous and dangerous misconceptions regarding the divinity. A kind of knowledge relatively far more perfect than the ordinary was included in the traditional metaphysics of the Greek philosophers, but even this science was burdened with serious errors. Certainly it was beyond the competence of the great masses of the people who had neither the time to cultivate it nor the inclination to embark upon studies of such immense technical exigency.

The Christian revelation is supernatural in the manner in which man receives it. Its primary and essential content is also

---

†   **Editor's Note:** For more information on this very important topic, see Reginald Garrigou-Lagrange, O.P., *The One God: A Commentary on the First Part of St. Thomas' Theological Summa*, trans. Dom Bede Rose, O.S.B. (St. Louis, MO: B. Herder Book Co., 1943); Romanus Cessario, O.P., "*Duplex Ordo Cognitionis*," in *Reason and the Reasons of Faith*, ed. Paul J. Griffiths and Reinhard Hütter (New York: T&T Clark, 2005), pp. 327–38; Serge-Thomas Bonino, O.P., *Dieu, « Celui qui est » (De Deo ut uno)* (Paris: Parole et Silence, 2016); Steven A. Long, "On Natural Knowledge of God: Aquinas's Debt to Aristotle," in *Theology Needs Philosophy: Acting against Reason is Contrary to the Nature of God*, ed. Matthew L. Lamb (Washington, DC: The Catholic University of America Press, 2016), pp. 74–87; Thomas C. O'Brien, O.P., *Metaphysics and the Existence of God*, ed. Cajetan Cuddy, O.P. (Tacoma, WA: Cluny Media, 2017).

intrinsically supernatural, comprising the great mysteries of the order of salvation. However, it also contains truths which are themselves essentially natural. If man does not accept the body of revelation with the assent of divine faith, he will not possess the fullness of the natural knowledge about God which is requisite for his perfect moral and intellectual life upon this earth.

We must not, however, make the mistake of thinking that apart from a supernatural revelation man could know nothing whatsoever about his Creator. Neither must we believe that whatever knowledge the human race has ever had of God is something which it has acquired by way of divine revelation. These errors, ordinarily designated as fideism and false traditionalism, have both been condemned by the Catholic Church.[24] We must never forget that the human mind is capable of finding out a great deal about God, and that men have actually learned much about God through the exercise of their natural faculties apart from any revelation whatsoever. Furthermore, some of this knowledge about God, at least the fact of His existence, is so easy to obtain that Holy Scripture justly calls the person who denies God a "fool."

In order that man may live a perfect intellectual and moral life, however, he must possess an extensive knowledge about God.[†] When, as in a modern democracy, the government of the state is dependent upon the moral and intellectual disposition of the

---

24. Both in the declarations of the Vatican Council (Denzinger, 1785), and the Anti-Modernist oath to which reference has been made, and in the instructions issued to Bautain (Denzinger, 1622–27), and Bonnetty (Denzinger, 1649–52), by Pius IX.

† **Editor's Note:** Knowledge about God (even of a natural sort) remains absolutely critical to the intellectual and moral life. There is no such thing as a robust natural law morality that lacks all formal advertence to God. For a recent consideration of these themes in light of recent theological discourse, see Cajetan Cuddy, O.P., "Thomas Aquinas on the Bible and Morality: The Sacred Scriptures, the Natural Law, and the Hermeneutic of Continuity," in *Towards a Biblical Thomism: Thomas Aquinas and the Renewal of Biblical Theology*, ed. Jörgen Vijgen and Piotr Roszak (Pamplona: EUNSA, 2018), pp. 173–97. See also Yves R. Simon, *The Tradition of Natural Law: A Philosopher's Reflection* (New York: Fordham University Press, 1999); Steven A. Long, "Yves Simon's Approach to Natural Law," *The Thomist*, Vol. 59, No. 1 (1995): pp. 125–35.

populace as a whole, naturally that knowledge of God must be widespread. Such a widespread and accurate knowledge will not be possessed other than through that Christian revelation which it is the essential function of sacred theology to set forth. The man who strives to understand sacred theology today cannot afford to overlook the real necessity of divine revelation.

N. The Necessity of Sacred Theology. The place of theology in the economy of human welfare is such that apart from it mankind will not achieve its ultimate destiny. The science of sacred theology, as distinct from the virtue of faith itself, is an absolute requisite for the human race. Obviously, however, sacred theology is not requisite for mankind in the same way that divine revelation and the faith on which this revelation is accepted are necessary. According to the great Douai theologian, Francis Sylvius, "Theology considered as the awareness of the principles of the science of theology, which principles are the articles of faith, is necessary with the necessity of means [physical necessity], for everyone who arrives at the use of reason. It is so necessary because without it the end of man which is supernatural, could not be known at all, and it is necessary that man should know this end so that he can direct all his actions toward it." With reference to theology precisely as distinguished from the content of divine faith, the same theologian writes: "Theology, in so far as it involves, over and above a knowledge of the principles (that is, of the articles of faith), the knowledge by which these principles can be in some way explained and conclusions deduced from them, is not necessary for each individual, either by way of means or by way of precept. It is, however, requisite, both with the necessity of means and by reason of precept to the Church itself, that is to the Christian republic."[25]

---

25. Sylvius, Commentaries on the *Summa Theologica*, Commentary on I, q. 1, art. 1. **Editor's Note:** For further analysis of the distinction between theological science and the content of divine faith, see Reginald Garrigou-Lagrange, O.P., *The One God: A Commentary on the First Part of St. Thomas' Theological Summa*, trans. Dom Bede Rose, O.S.B. (St. Louis, MO: B. Herder Book Co., 1943), pp. 39–92; James A. Weisheipl, O.P., "The Meaning of *Sacra Doctrina* in *Summa Theologiae* I, q. 1," *The Thomist*, Vol. 38, No. 1 (1974): pp. 49–80.

It is thus the contention of Sylvius, expressing a doctrine quite common among Catholic theologians, that in the actually existing order of divine providence the Church must have within its membership men who are endowed with the science of sacred theology. This necessity must be explained by the fact that sacred theology is essentially a discipline which tends toward the explanation of Christian revelation. If we could understand theology merely as a science which deduces conclusions from the content of divine revelation, then there would be no ascertainable reason why the Catholic Church should stand in need of this science for the accomplishment of that work which the Son of God entrusted to her care.

Sacred theology is requisite for the Christian republic precisely because it is by its very nature that discipline which sets out to expound the articles of faith, the key statements in that revelation which men must accept on the authority of God if they are to attain eternal life. Now, it was the will of God, expressed in the actual constitution of the Catholic Church as the unique authentic vehicle of revelation, that men are meant to receive divine revelation from and in the Church from those who possess the science of sacred theology. This very important truth is manifest, not only from the actual experience of the Church, as expressed in her history, but also in the words of Sacred Scripture, as these are cited by Sylvius. Sylvius notes that, according to St. Paul, the Church is so constituted that, by the will of our Lord Himself, it counts within its ranks Apostles and prophets, evangelists, pastors, and doctors for the work of the ministry and for the edification of the body of Christ.[26] In other words, the Church was to include among those who worked in its behalf teachers of the revealed word of God, distinct at once from those who were the founders of the Church and those who were the immediate destinaries of divine revelation.[†]

---

26. Ephesians 4:11–12.

† **Editor's Note:** Of course, Fenton uses the word "founders" in a broad, instrumental sense. Jesus Christ himself founded the Church.

These teachers, in so far as they employed every human resource to set forth the divine message, actually possessed and utilized the science of sacred theology.

The Apostle of the Gentiles made it a rule that the bishops who were to be set up over the faithful whom he had converted should embrace the faithful word which is in accordance with doctrine, so that they might be able to exhort in sane teaching and confute those who contradicted the word of God.[27] All human ingenuity was to be exercised in the preaching of Christian faith. The application of human reason to the task of teaching divine revelation actually constitutes sacred theology. The great science which Peter the Lombard, St. Thomas Aquinas, and their successors have expounded constitutes the sort of activity which must exist within the Catholic Church in order that the essential function of continuing the teaching of Christ may continue.

O. The Worth of Sacred Theology. It is a matter of strict and scientific accuracy to state that the study which we know as sacred theology brings to the human race blessings and benefits far greater than those which proceed from any other discipline within the competence of man. The highest and the most perfect among the other functional sciences can aid in bringing about an ordered and cultured life in this world. They can serve to remedy the ills of the body and of the mind and can contribute toward the attainment of justice for those who live within the state. Sacred theology offers and is requisite for the accomplishment of a happiness which is never ending, a blessedness which is so high above even the most perfect temporal felicity which man can find in this world that the human mind is unable to describe it.

Other disciplines may and do avert serious evils. Ignorance, suffering, and injustice may be banished from among men through certain studies which are purely natural in their scope as well as in their method. Sacred theology, however, stands alone among the sciences which men can acquire in that it is capable of averting

---

27. Titus 1:9.

the most serious failure which man can encounter, an eternity of anguish and futility. It is perfectly true that we can recognize this tremendous value of sacred theology only in the light of divine faith. The ultimate and ineffable good which can only be procured with the aid of this science, and the catastrophic evil which it co-operates to avert are realities which cannot be recognized as such in the light of merely natural evidence. They pertain to that order of reality which man could never know apart from divine reality. Nevertheless they remain realities. Men who live in a time and in a land where realism is the rule cannot neglect them.

Moreover, sacred theology has a definite function to perform, a contribution to make for our own civilization. We are quite aware that the temporal ills to which individual men and civil societies in our own time are subject can be cured or alleviated only through the practice of Christian virtue and the recognition of the rights of God. The only discipline which is competent to offer competent instruction on the Christian virtues is sacred theology itself. This science alone can give to the world the knowledge about God which is requisite for the regeneration of our social order.

The peace and the security of nations, the social and economic justice for which the men of our time strive so passionately, the stability and happiness of family and of individual life; all of these benefits are to be obtained through the agency of sacred theology. The man who takes up this study, who wills to know and to appreciate those teachings which God has given to men through Jesus Christ our Lord and which are proposed for our belief in the magisterium of the Catholic Church; the man who works to express that doctrine unequivocally and clearly is preparing for himself a glorious part in the labor of human welfare.

Naturally sacred theology is even more strikingly valuable to men in times of stress, when all of the values which civilization has cherished through the ages are endangered. We must be realistic enough to acknowledge the fact that those evils which afflict our times are never going to be overthrown by some new system, to be excogitated by some future genius. There is never going to be a

magic formula which will bring men the happiness toward which
they strive so pitiably. The doctrine which is literally competent to
save the world is that which is enclosed in the traditional literature
of sacred theology. The men who are going to make the great contributions toward human betterment are those who have the faith
and the courage to apply themselves generously to the task of mas-
tering sacred theology, and bringing its message to a needy world.

P. The Explanation of William Estius. Long ago, William Estius, another of the famous school of Douai, succeeded in bringing
out the dignity of sacred theology very forcefully. He could recognize the inherent value of the science because he did not fail to look
upon it in the light of its essential function, the objective teaching
of divine revelation. "Since the purpose and the use of theology is
that through it man should know God, and having known Him,
should love Him, and finally that he should rest in God as in his
highest Good, it is quite manifest that theology is a great good and
that its usefulness must be sought by all men. Thus rightly over all
the others this science deserves the title of queen in the realm of
living well and happily."

Because he recognized that theology cannot be understood
apart from its essential function, Estius was able to see how truly
God Himself could be called the Author of this science. "Finally its
author and Principle is God, and Christ the Son of God. God is in
heaven, revealing the mysteries—and no man knows those things
which are of God except the Spirit of God—but the only begotten
Son, who is in the bosom of the Father, He has told it." He cites
the prophecy of Baruch who states that no creature could know the
ways of God's wisdom and then adds, "He who knows all things
knows these ways and His prudence has found them. He has found
all the way of discipline and has given it to Jacob His servant and to
Israel His beloved." God is the Author of revelation.[28] In recognizing Him as the Author of sacred theology, Estius acknowledges in

---

28. Guillelmi Estii, *In Quatuor Libros Sententiarum Commentaria* (Paris: 1696),
praefatio.

this science more than a mere collection of conclusions drawn from a revealed source. He sees sacred theology for what it really is, that discipline which is essentially orientated to the clear and correct teaching of God's message to men.

$$* \; * \; *$$

Chapter II

The Subject Matter

A. The Material Object. The things treated in the science of sacred theology naturally comprise those realities about which we are instructed in that divine revelation which we Catholics accept with the assent of divine faith. The sum total of conclusions, teachings, or theses which sacred theology presents to the student constitutes what is known technically as the *material object* of the science.[1] Strictly speaking, these conclusions or theses which are characteristic of the science are expressed in that portion of it which we know as scholastic theology. All that is studied in the other departments of science, relative to its history and development, to Sacred Scripture, the councils, and the Fathers, is treated in so far as it is requisite for a proper understanding of the content of scholastic theology.

The message which God has revealed to man, and which is taught and expressed in the science of sacred theology constitutes an organized body of doctrine. It must not be considered as a collection of disparate and unconnected statements, but as a real teaching, offered to accomplish a definite function and possessed of a definite organic unity. As a matter of fact, the faith by which we accept this revelation is defined by St. Paul himself as "the substance of the things for which we hope, the conviction about that which we do not see."[2] According to St. Thomas Aquinas, the word *substance* in the definition of St. Paul signifies a beginning.[3] In other words, the faith is a very real beginning in the sense that the same object, the essence of God, the intuitive vision of which constitutes the eternal and ineffable joys of heaven actually is accepted on faith during the time of our pilgrimage in this world. The life of heaven consists essentially in the vision of the Triune God. "This is eternal life that they should know Thee, the One True God and Jesus Christ whom Thou hast sent."[4]

B. The Formal Subject of Attribution. Since the happiness of heaven consists in the vision of God Himself, the revelation which God gives us in order to prepare us for the life of heaven deals primarily with the same subject matter. Now, that object which is known primarily in a science, which is studied for its own sake and because of which all other matters treated by the science are considered, is called the *obiectum formale quod*. Thus, according to the traditional terminology of the theologians, God in His intimate life is the *obiectum formale quod*, or the formal subject of attribution in the science of sacred theology.[5] When we say that this formal

---

1.   Carolus Renatus Billuart, O.P., *Summa Sancti Thomae Hodiernis Academiarum Moribus Accomodata, sive Cursus Theologiae juxta Mentem Divi Thomae*, Vol. I (Paris: 1904), p. 13, teaches that the adequate material object of faith is all that which falls under virtual or mediate divine revelation. There is no question about the meaning of this term. **Editor's Note:** For more on the material object of faith and virtual revelation, see Reginald Garrigou-Lagrange, O.P., *The One God: A Commentary on the First Part of St. Thomas' Theological Summa*, trans. Dom Bede Rose, O.S.B. (St. Louis, MO: B. Herder Book Co., 1943), pp. 43–63.

2.   Hebrews 11:1.

3.   *ST* II-II, q. 4, a. 1; also *Quaestiones Disputatae, De Veritate*, q. 14, a. 2.

4.   John 17:3.

5.   Billuart, *Summa Sancti Thomae Hodiernis Academiarum Moribus Accomodata*, p. 13; Joannes a Sancto Thoma, O.P., *Cursus Theologicus*, Vol. 1 (Paris, Tournai, and Rome), p. 203; St. Thomas Aquinas, *ST*, I, q. 1, a. 7; the commentary of Francis Sylvius on this article. **Editor's Note:** See also Reginald Garrigou-Lagrange, O.P., *The One God: A Commentary on the First Part of St. Thomas' Theological Summa*, trans. Dom Bede Rose, O.S.B. (St. Louis, MO: B. Herder Book Co., 1943), p. 47; Cajetan's commentary on *ST* I, q. 1, a. 3, no. 9; and John of

subject of attribution is God in His intimate life, we mean God as He is known naturally to Himself alone, and not merely in so far as He can be known naturally by intellectual creatures, that is, known as the First Cause of the created universe.

Now, it is axiomatic that a man will appreciate the content and the procedure of sacred theology only in the measure in which he realizes the verification of the teaching about its object. Actually in sacred theology God Himself is alone considered for His own sake. All the other subjects dealt within this science are treated in so far as they contribute toward that knowledge of God which He wishes us to possess by way of faith in this world. A man will be a successful theologian, he will have drawn out of his study the wealth of meaning to which he is entitled, only when he sees each section of the science contributing toward an enrichment of his concept of God. In sacred theology a man learns about God, not only when he studies those sections on the unity and trinity of God and on the incarnation, but whenever he considers any portion of the sacred discipline.

C. God, the Primary Object of Sacred Theology as Manifest in the Division of the "Four Books of Sentences." The best way to prove that God in His intimate life constitutes the *obiectum formale quod* of sacred theology is to look into the various divisions of the science utilized by the outstanding authors. The great masters of theology organized their studies so as to take advantage of the fact that God is actually the central object considered in this discipline. Peter the Lombard organized his *Four Books of Sentences* in line with a concept which expressed all that is best in the western tradition of education and culture. Utilizing the terminology of St. Augustine, the Master of the *Sentences* made the basic division of his work follow upon the distinction between "things"

St. Thomas, *The Material Logic of John of St. Thomas*, trans. Yves Simon, John Glanville, and G. Donald Hollenhorst (Chicago: University of Chicago Press, 1955). For a succinct and recent explanation of the distinctions within formal objectivity, see Philip Neri Reese, O.P., "Theology, Faith, Universities: From Specialization to Specification in Theology," *New Blackfriars*, Vol. 92, No. 1042 (2011): pp. 691–704.

and "signs."[6] This division was to remain classical in the university
world for generations after Peter the Lombard had died. According to his explanations the "things" were those objects not used
to manifest something distinct from themselves. They comprised
those realities which were to be known for their own sakes and in
themselves. The "signs" were those objects which were meant to
bring to the mind a knowledge of realities distinct from themselves.

The first three of the *Four Books of Sentences* dealt with the
"things" mentioned by the author. Among those "things," Peter
the Lombard pointed out that some are to be enjoyed, others are
meant to be used, and still others are supposed to be used and
enjoyed. According to the teaching of the *Sentences*, in explaining
the master division of the work, the "things" which are meant to be
enjoyed are those things which actually make us blessed. These are
the Father and the Son and the Holy Spirit. Thus the Three Divine
Persons, or God considered in His intimate life, as He is at once
the Author and the End of the entire supernatural order, constitutes the center of sacred theology as this science was expounded
by Peter the Lombard. The actual theological literature of medieval
and modern times was intimately dependent upon the work of the
Lombard. Thus a science which centered around God as the One
who is to be enjoyed, the One who is to be sought above all others
and for the sake of whom all other agencies are expected to act, is
the sacred theology of our tradition.[†]

All the rest of the matter of sacred theology is actually gathered
about the concept of God, according to the explanation of Peter
the Lombard. The world and the created things which enter into it
constitute the things which we are meant to use for the attainment

---

6. Peter the Lombard, *Libri Quattuor Sententiarum*, Prologus. **Editor's Note:** For
    a recent translation of Peter Lombard's work in English, see Peter Lombard,
    The Sentences, Book 4: On the Doctrine of Signs, trans. Giulio Silano (Toronto:
    Pontifical Institute of Mediaeval Studies, 2010).

†   **Editor's Note:** For a masterful study of theological science as it was conceived
    following Peter Lombard, see Henry Donneaud, O.P., *Théologie et intelligence de
    la foi au XIIIème siècle* (Paris: Parole et Silence, 2006).

of God as our ultimate end. Ourselves and the holy angels of heaven are the things which are meant to be both used and enjoyed. The men with whom we are called upon to associate and cooperate in this world are meant to live a life which is a sharing of the intimate activity of God Himself. Many of them actually live this life of habitual grace. By reason of their vocation, they and the saints and the angels in heaven, together with those souls who expiate their faults in the cleansing fires of purgatory are to be loved with that same charity which is an act of benevolence and friendship toward God. We are meant to enjoy their society in heaven, where they are to live and share the intimate life of God Himself.

At the same time the saints and the men with whom we are associated in this world constitute means which we are enabled to use for the attainment of God's glory and our own salvation. This concept of our social and individual life embodies a definite consecration of human activity to God. It manifests all that is best in the cultural tradition which produced and continued the work of Peter the Lombard, and shows in sharp detail the highly developed theocentric aspect of the living sacred doctrine. For Peter the Lombard, one of the great exponents of this doctrine, was brilliant enough to realize that theology should consider all the realities of this world only with reference to God, our ultimate End. All the forces and resources of the world were looked upon as means to be employed and wealth to be expended for the attainment of the ultimate and perfect human happiness. Actually some of these material things are constituted by God Himself as "signs" or sacraments, to signify the great mysteries of our redemption, and then endowed by Him with the strength to bring about the grace which they manifest. Our fellow men are to be looked upon, in the light of the traditional theology, as brothers who are meant to live with us in the eternal light of heaven, and at the same time as forces and workers whose aid we are to enlist in our own struggle toward salvation.

D. The Master Division of the *Summa Theologica*. The theocentric character of sacred doctrine is even more strikingly manifest in the master division of the *Summa Theologica* of St. Thomas

Aquinas, the book which replaced the *Sentences* as the standard text for the theological schools of the West.[†] Every line in the theological writings of the Angelic Doctor shows his conviction that God constitutes the *obiectum formale quod* of the science to which he devoted his life and his talents. All the content of his *Summa Theologica* centers about the concept of God, and all of it contributes toward a more perfect appreciation of the Creator. "Because the principal intention of this sacred doctrine is to give a knowledge of God, not only as He is in Himself, but also in so far as He is the Principle and the End of all things, and especially of the rational creature … looking to the exposition of this doctrine we shall treat first of God, then of the movement of the rational creature toward God and third of Christ, who, as man, is the Way by which we go to God."[7]

Within these three divisions are grouped all the conclusions which St. Thomas taught as the dicta of sacred theology. In his explanation, then, God is actually the formal object of attribution for the science in the very real sense that every statement put forward in the science contributes toward a more perfect grasp of that concept of God which He has offered to the world in the content of divine revelation. St. Thomas developed his division in such a way that the master idea was never overlooked. His order is calculated to make every part of sacred theology contribute to the elaboration of the idea of God.

I. THE FIRST PART

The first of the three parts into which the *Summa Theologica* is divided deals with God as He is in Himself, and in so far as He

---

† **Editor's Note:** For more on the emergence of the *Summa Theologiae* as the standard text for the Thomist school, see Jean-Pierre Torrell, O.P. *Aquinas's Summa: Background, Structure, and Reception*, trans. Benedict M. Guevin, O.S.B. (Washington, DC: The Catholic University of America Press, 2005); Romanus Cessario, O.P., and Cajetan Cuddy, O.P., *Thomas and the Thomists: The Achievement of Thomas Aquinas and his Interpreters* (Minneapolis, MN: Fortress Press, 2017).

7.   *ST*, prologue.

is the Cause of creatures. That part of sacred theology which deals with God as He is in Himself is divided between the sections *de Deo Uno* and *de Deo Trino*. The section on the One God is subdivided into the treatises on the existence of God and those concerning His nature and attributes.

1. *The Existence of God.* Sacred Theology manifests the necessity and the possibility of rational proofs that God really exists, and then it sets forth the proofs themselves. In the light of these demonstrations, it becomes evident that a First Cause of the universe actually exists, since there could be no motion, causality, necessity, beauty, and order among the things we see in this world unless these realities had been communicated to creatures by One who is the Cause of all being, and at the same time is Himself subject to no causality whatsoever.[†] The proofs are peremptory and convincing. They utilize all of the force of human reasoning, and all of the equipment of philosophical tradition available to the science of sacred theology.[8]

2. *The Divine Attributes.* There are certain definite characteristics which we must predicate of God, whose existence is thus

---

[†] **Editor's Note:** For a classic consideration of Aquinas's proofs for God's existence, see Reginald Garrigou-Lagrange, O.P., *The One God: A Commentary on the First Part of St. Thomas' Theological Summa*, trans. Dom Bede Rose, O.S.B. (St. Louis, MO: B. Herder Book Co., 1943), pp. 93–155. For a more lengthy consideration of this topic in the light of modern philosophical objections, see Reginald Garrigou-Lagrange, O.P., *God, His Existence and His Nature: A Thomistic Solution of Certain Agnostic Antinomies*, trans. Dom Bede Rose, O.S.B., 2 vols. (St. Louis, MO: B. Herder Book Co., 1949). More recent considerations of various proofs for God's existence include Ralph McInerny, *Characters in Search of Their Author: The Gifford Lectures 1999–2000* (Notre Dame, IN: University of Notre Dame Press, 2001); D.Q. McInerny, *Natural Theology* (Elmhurst, PA: The Priestly Fraternity of St. Peter, 2005); Edward Feser, *Aquinas: A Beginner's Guide* (Oxford: Oneworld Publications, 2009); Gavin Kerr, O.P., *Aquinas's Way to God: The Proof in De Ente et Essentia* (Oxford: Oxford University Press, 2015); Thomas Joseph White, O.P., *Wisdom in the Face of Modernity: A Study in Thomistic Natural Theology*, 2nd ed. (Ave Maria, FL: Sapientia Press, 2016); Edward Feser, *Five Proofs of the Existence of God* (San Francisco: Ignatius Press, 2017).

8. *ST* I, q. 2. (The First Question of the First Part in the *Summa* has reference to the nature of sacred theology.)

manifest in the proofs expounded in the treatise *de Deo Uno*.[†] These
characteristics are called the divine attributes. As they exist in God
Himself, they are not really distinct one from the other. According to the conditions of our human knowledge, however, we must
distinguish these various characteristics in order to arrive at that
knowledge of God which He expects us to possess.

John of Saint Thomas, one of the outstanding contributors to
the literature of sacred theology, and one of the great commentators on the *Summa Theologica*, points out three orders among
those attributes of God of which St. Thomas speaks.[9] The first order embraces what are termed the *entitative* attributes, those by
which we remove from our concept of God all of those imperfections and limitations proper to created reality, and recognize in
Him that fullness of being and perfection which characterizes His
own nature. The first of these entitative attributes is *simplicity*. In
predicating this basic attribute of God, we acknowledge that He is
in no way subject to that composition which must affect all bodies,
and to a certain extent all created reality. Consequently under the
heading of the divine simplicity, the theologian who follows the
order of St. Thomas considers the spirituality of God, His absolute
independence of all other beings, and finally that prerogative which
the Thomists generally put forward as the metaphysical essence of
God, the fact that He is subsistent Being Itself, the only One in
whom the essence is not really distinct from existence. The other

---

†   **Editor's Note:** The recent and masterful book from Serge-Thomas Boni-
     no now serves as the standard Thomistic study of the *De Deo Uno* treatise:
     Serge-Thomas Bonino, O.P., *Dieu, « Celui qui est » (De Deo ut uno)* (Paris:
     Parole et Silence, 2016). With penetrating analysis and crystal clear prose,
     Bonino explains why *De Deo Uno* considerations remain essential to any
     adequate study of the *sacra doctrina*.

9.   Ioannes a Sancto Thoma, O.P., "The Isagoge" (in the *Cursus Theologicus*, Vol.
     1), p. 151. The Isagoge is the outstanding treatise on the order of the *Summa
     Theologiae*, and thus upon the inherent arrangement of theological teaching.
     Editor's Note: This masterpiece from John of St. Thomas is available in English:
     John of St. Thomas, *Introduction to the* Summa Theologiae *of Thomas Aquinas*,
     trans. Ralph McInerny (South Bend, IN: St. Augustine's Press, 2003).

seven entitative attributes, in the order in which they are treated by the Angelic Doctor are *perfection, goodness, infinity, immensity, immutability, eternity,* and *unity.*[10]

The second order of the divine attributes includes those which have reference to the knowability of God. In this section St. Thomas showed that God can never be known through the operation of any sense faculty whatsoever. The created intelligence, however, is capable of knowing God, when the rational sees Him as the necessary First Cause, upon whom all the reality of the created and finite universe depends. Here sacred theology explains this type of knowledge about God and shows that it is perfectly within the natural competence of any created intelligence. There is, however, another kind of knowledge about God which must be considered by theology. It is that which only God can possess naturally about Himself, for He alone is capable by His own power of seeing Himself as He really is. It is this type of cognition which God has decreed, in all the fullness of His mercy, to give to His creatures. Some of them possess it in the fullness of vision in heaven. Others hold it by faith in the place of preparation which is this world.

The treatment of the second class of the divine attributes is completed in the magnificent section of the Names of God. The human concepts or ideas, of which names are the signs, are, of course, incapable of expressing perfectly and adequately the infinite reality which is God. Those concepts, however, which express perfections which are in themselves unlimited, perfections which do not include within their own natures any limitation or potentiality incompatible with the divine essence, can be applied to God and can express that divine reality inadequately and analogically. The statements about God which make use of such analogy are perfectly correct, in spite of their inadequacy. This portion of sacred theology which deals with the analogy of those terms and concepts

10. *ST* I, qq. 3–11, inclusively.

which are predicated of God is one of the most important in all the extent of the sacred doctrine.[11]

The third order of attributes comprises those which are called *operative*. We predicate these of God to express His activity. Some of those acts which we must predicate of God are in themselves purely immanent, that is acts which of their very nature must begin and terminate within the same subject.

Others have reference to an activity of God, which, while it is perfectly immanent in Him, results in the production of beings distinct from Himself. Such causal activity is not entirely immanent in so far as it is found in creatures.

Among the *immanent* attributes there are some acts which belong to the intelligence alone, others which belong purely to the will, and still others which are found in the practical intellect, in which the intelligence is moved and used by the will. In the first class, among the intellectual acts, St. Thomas places the *divine science* or understanding, that *wisdom* which is perfect in itself and which is the cause of all things distinct from God. He then teaches about those *ideas* which exist in the divine mind, the archetypes which serve as primary exemplars for all created reality. There follows a consideration of the divine *truth* and of that falsity which is utterly incompatible with its perfection. The treatise on the divine knowledge is completed with the section on the *life* of God, expressed in the activity of the divine intellect.

In dealing with the *will* of God, St. Thomas teaches us that it is an act by which God tends toward a good as known by Him, an act which is sovereignly free with regard to any good other than God Himself. He considers the will of God in itself, and then in the acts of *love* and of *joy*. The treatise on the divine will terminates with the consideration of those moral virtues, which are consonant with the absolute perfection of God—divine justice and mercy.

---

11. *ST* I, qq. 12 and 13. **Editor's Note:** For more on analogy, see Steven A. Long, *Analogia Entis: On the Analogy of Being, Metaphysics and the Act of Faith* (Notre Dame, IN: University of Notre Dame Press, 2011).

In the line of the practical intellect, the order of the Angelic Doctor treats of the divine *providence*, the plan existing from all eternity in the mind of God, according to which all creatures are brought to their ultimate end. Then it deals with that particular providence of God with reference to those who are to be in His courts for all eternity, the plan of the divine *predestination*. This is treated directly, and then in terms of its scriptural metaphor, the *book of life*.[12]

Subsequent to the treatise on the purely immanent attributes of God, there comes the section on the divine *omnipotence*. The entire tract on the One God is completed with consideration of the divine *beatitude*, which consists in the perfect possession of the divine and infinite good.[13]

3. *The Blessed Trinity*. The most important portion of all sacred theology is that contained in the tract on the *Blessed Trinity*. This tract is subdivided into three distinct parts, as it is given in the *Summa Theologica*.† In the first of these parts there is a study of the divine *processions*, and of those *relations* which are based upon the processions, and which distinguish the three divine Persons, one from the others.[14] In the second part of the treatise there is a special consideration of the *divine persons* themselves.[15] St. Thomas taught first about the divine Persons in general, that is, about those things which are to be predicated of the person as such, and then he set forth the Catholic doctrine on each of the three divine Persons in particular. For the primary study he organized a consideration of the meaning of person itself, then the doctrine on the plurality of the persons in God. He followed this with a treatise on the way in

---

12. *ST* I, qq. 14–24.

13. *ST* I, qq. 25 and 26.

†   **Editor's Note:** For more on this treatise, see Reginald Garrigou-Lagrange, O.P., *The Trinity and God the Creator: A Commentary on St. Thomas' Theological Summa, Ia, q. 27–119*, trans. Frederic C. Eckhoff (St. Louis, MO: B. Herder Book Co., 1952); Gilles Emery, O.P., *The Trinitarian Theology of Saint Thomas Aquinas*, trans. Francesca Aran Murphy (Oxford: Oxford University Press, 2007).

14. *ST* I, qq. 27 and 28.

15. *ST* I, qq. 29–38.

which we are to speak of the divine Persons in accordance with the rules of the authentic Catholic tradition and one on the various notions or concepts used to designate the characteristics of the individual persons.

When the Angelic Doctor taught about the divine Persons individually, he utilized the various names which serve in Sacred Scripture and in the writings of the Fathers to designate the Father, the Son, and the Holy Spirit. The Father is also called the Principle and the Unengendered.[†] The Son is also designated as the Word and the Image. The Holy Spirit is Love and the great Gift of God. In the masterful explanation of St. Thomas, each one of these names serves to help men to understand what God has revealed about the greatest of all the mysteries.

The third and final portion of the tract on the Blessed Trinity is that in which St. Thomas takes up the various comparisons which can be made about the divine Persons.[16] He compares the Persons with the divine essence, with the relations, and with the notional acts. They are then studied in comparison with one another and finally with reference to creatures, to whom the Son and the Holy Spirit are truly said to be sent, and in whom all of the three divine Persons may dwell in a special manner. This manner of indwelling in the souls of those who live the life of habitual grace, and who are animated by the virtue of charity, is at once distinct from and superior to the way in which God is actually in all of His creatures, through His presence, His power, and His substance.[††] This last section of the tract on the Blessed Trinity is the tremendously important treatise on the *divine missions*.

4. Creation. That portion of sacred theology which, according to the order of St. Thomas Aquinas, follows immediately after the

---

†   **Editor's Note:** For more on this topic, see John Baptist Ku, O.P., *God the Father in the Theology of St. Thomas Aquinas* (New York: Peter Lang, 2012).

16.   *ST* I, qq. 44–45.

††   **Editor's Note:** See Gilles Emery, O.P., *Présence de Dieu et union à Dieu: Création, inhabitation par grâce, incarnation et vision bienheureuse selon saint Thomas d'Aquin* (Paris: Parole et Silence, 2017).

tract on the Blessed Trinity deals with God as the cause of the created universe.† The message which sacred theology is organized to
teach, that doctrine which we accept with the assent of divine faith,
contains a great deal of teaching about what God has done for the
world in which we live. This section of the divine teaching has an
obvious reference to God as the *obiectum formale quod* of the science. There is no portion of the teaching contained in this section,
even the most abstruse doctrine in the section on the angels, which
is not calculated to bring us the appreciation of God which we are
expected to gain through a science which has God in His intimate
life as its formal subject of attribution.

Under the heading of the divine causality in itself, St. Thomas
arranges the truth that God acts as a cause or principle of the universe in three distinct ways. He is at once the Efficient Cause, the
Final Cause, and the Exemplary Cause in the production of those
beings which depend upon Him for every portion and aspect of their
reality.[17] The divine causality is best expressed in the term "creation."
God *created* the world, and did not merely form some pre-existing
matter which had being in some way independently of His causality.
Thus it is absolutely impossible that there should be an aspect or
fiber of reality or goodness in the world which was not brought into
existence by God and maintained in being by His omnipotence.

After treating of creation as such, St. Thomas goes on to explain
the content of divine revelation relative to the things which God
has brought into being.[18] He divides off his matter in such a way
as to treat first of the created universe in general and then of the
various classifications into which created substances naturally fall.
With reference to the universe as such, the Angelic Doctor brings
out the divinely revealed truth that every fiber and aspect of that

---

† **Editor's Note:** For a masterful consideration of the integration between God as
Trinity and God as creator, see Gilles Emery, O.P., *La Trinité créatrice: Trinité et
création dans les commentaires aux Sentences de Thomas d'Aquin et de ses précurseurs Albert le Grand et Bonaventure* (Paris: Vrin, 1995).

17. *ST* I, qq. 39–43.
18. *ST* I, qq. 47–49.

reality which is possessed by creatures is something which has come from God. Thus the harmony of the world, and the inequality and distinction of the creatures in it must be attributed to God Himself.

5. *The Angels.* The three classes of creatures to which divine revelation makes reference are those of purely spiritual nature, called the angels, those whose nature is wholly corporeal, and those human beings who possess natures which can be classified as both spiritual and corporeal.

The *Summa Theologica* summarizes in its treatise on the *angels* all the truth which divine revelation offers to us about the purely spiritual creatures of God.[19] It describes the nature, the properties, and the natural mode of activity of the angels. The treatise terminates with an explanation of that life of grace with which these beings were endowed from the very instant of their creation. It tells of the trial which they underwent, of the eternal glory and blessedness of those who persevered, and of the sin and the ignominious punishment of those who failed.

6. *The Material World and Man.* What divine revelation has to say about the purely corporeal creatures of this world is summed up in the theological tract on the *work of the six days* which follows directly after the tract on the angels in the order of St. Thomas Aquinas.[20] Briefly, this tract explains the doctrine which is proposed for our belief in the opening chapters of Genesis. The tract on *man* opens with a description of the nature, the powers, and the natural mode of activity of human beings.[21] It passes on to the consideration

---

19. *ST* I, qq. 50–64. **Editor's Note:** For more on the angels, see Serge-Thomas Bonino, O.P., *Angels and Demons: A Catholic Introduction*, trans. Michael J. Miller (Washington, DC: The Catholic University of America Press, 2016). Bonino has subsequently published a second edition of this text, but it has not been translated from its original French. Serge-Thomas Bonino, O.P., *Les anges et les démons: Quatorze leçons de théologie*, 2nd ed. (Paris: Parole et Silence, 2017).

20. *ST* I, qq. 65–74.

21. *ST* I, qq. 75–102. **Editor's Note:** For a philosophical consideration of the nature of man and his powers, see Robert Edward Brennan, O.P., *Thomistic Psychology: A Philosophic Analysis of the Nature of Man*, ed. Cajetan Cuddy, O.P. (Tacoma, WA: Cluny Media, 2016); D.Q. McInerny, *Philosophical Psychology* (Elmhurst, PA: The Priestly Fraternity of St. Peter, 2016).

of the conditions which surrounded the creation of man, of the life
of grace with which the first man was endowed at the moment of his
creation and of the trial to which he was subjected. The treatise on
man closes with the doctrine on the sin of Adam, with its disastrous
effects for himself and for those who were to be his descendants.

7. Divine Government. The entire first part of the *Summa
Theologica* terminates in the tract on the divine government.[22] In
this treatise St. Thomas explains the revealed teaching about the
administration over creatures which is proper to God Himself and
the influence exercised by one creature upon another under the
order which the divine providence has established in the world.
The administration proper to God Himself is dealt with under the
headings of the divine conservation by which God retains all of His
creatures in existence and of the divine concursus, in which He acts
as the First Cause and the Prime Mover in all the activity carried
on by His creatures.[†] In closing this treatise, he tells us what divine
revelation has to say about the influence exercised on mankind and
upon the material universe by the angels, about the power of men
over the material universe, and finally about the influence exercised
by some corporeal creatures upon others.

II. THE SECOND PART

The second portion of sacred theology, according to the order
of the *Summa Theologica*, contains an explanation of the revealed
Catholic message about God in so far as He is the Final Cause
of man. Thus it presents the teaching of Catholic faith concerning human acts by which man advances toward God, his last end,
or turns away from Him. Because of the great complexity of the

---

22. *ST* I, qq. 103–19.

†   **Editor's Note:** The universality of God's primary causality stands as a philo-
      sophical key to all of Aquinas's theology. Nothing stands outside of God's causal
      reach. He is always the First Cause and the Prime Mover. For a magisterial
      examination of this important topic, see Steven A. Long, "Providence, Freedom,
      and Natural Law," *Nova et Vetera*, Vol. 4, No. 3 (2006): pp. 557–606.

matter involved, the second part of the *Summa Theologica* is sub-divided into two main sections. The first of these, most frequently mentioned as the *Prima Secundae*, contains the general teaching about human acts. The second subdivision, known as the *Secunda Secundae*, deals with human acts under the headings of the individ-ual virtues according to which they are classified and according to the various states of life into which they are meant to enter.

The First Division

1. The End of Man. This section opens with the consideration of the ultimate end of man as the final purpose, in the attainment of which man is to find the only perfect and eternal happiness at-tainable by him.[23] This ultimate end is God Himself, to be seen and possessed forever in the eternal and super natural clarity of the beatific vision.[†] The key to the marvelous success of St. Thomas in dealing with this most important portion of sacred theology can be found in his never losing sight of the fact that here as elsewhere, God remains the *obiectum formale quod*. Every conclusion in his moral theology is orientated toward the enlargement and the per-fection of our concept of God. When we have finished the study of what the Angelic Doctor wrote on human acts, we shall find that we have learned to know God better, in so far as we can see His ho-liness in those very operations of man which lead us toward Him.[††]

---

23. *ST* I-II, qq. 1–5.

†   **Editor's Note:** God as ultimate end of the human creature remains a complex topic that has continued to vex philosophers and theologians alike. A compre-hensive study of this topic has been conducted by Lawrence Feingold in his *The Natural Desire to See God according to St. Thomas Aquinas and His Interpret-ers*, 2nd ed. (Naples, FL: Sapientia Press, 2009). See also Steven A. Long, "On the Possibility of a Purely Natural End for Man," *The Thomist*, Vol. 64, No. 2 (2000): pp. 211–37.

††   **Editor's Note:** The significance of the formally theological nature of moral theology is difficult to overstate. God remains the formal object of theological inquiry even in considerations of the moral life of rational creatures. God is the formal subject of all of theology—even of moral theology. For more on this, see Romanus Cessario, O.P., *Introduction to Moral Theology*, rev. ed. (Washington, DC: The Catholic University of America Press, 2014).

2. *Human Acts.* All the rest of the first division of the second part in the *Summa Theologica* is taken up with a study of human acts and the principles from which these acts proceed. St. Thomas deals separately with those acts which are primarily moral and those which partake of morality but which, of themselves, are common to man and to the irrational animal. To the first class belong such operations as are performed through the spiritual or rational faculties in line with the ultimate end of man. These are studied, first of all materially as acts, and then from the formal and precise point of view of their morality.

The acts which are primarily moral are, of course, those elicited by the spiritual faculties themselves with reference to the end of human endeavor, or the means by which this end is meant to be attained.[24] The will looks to the end or purpose of human activity in acts which are designated as simple volition, fruition or enjoyment, and intention. The will and the practical intellect which is moved by the will cooperate for the achievement of those means which are ordered toward the end of man in the acts of election or choice, counsel, consent, command, and use.

Such acts derive their morality, that is are designated as good or bad, with respect to the specific object toward which they are immediately ordered, the purpose for which they are performed, and the circumstances which surround them.[25] The acts which have reference to a purpose or end alone, rather than to means which are ordered to the attainment of an end are constituted as morally good in so far as they are in conformity with the will of God or with His law, applied through the dictates of man's conscience.[†]

---

24. *ST* I-II, qq. 6–17.

25. *ST* I-II, qq. 18–21.

† **Editor's Note:** It is important to note, however, that the morality of human action is not evaluated in reference to the divine will or law as if from an arbitrary rule or regulation. The truth of the eternal law enjoys a metaphysical primacy in all of created reality and, subsequently, in all of human morality. Voluntaristic conceptions of man's relation to God have no place within Aquinas's moral theology. Goodness is understood only in reference to the truth about reality. And the truth about reality proceeds from God's wisdom—how God knows the world to be (i.e., the eternal law). Moral precepts follow the truth about human

The other acts, as choice and counsel, must be judged, not merely by reason of their own object, but also in the light of the purpose for which they are employed and the circumstances in which they are placed. This portion of sacred theology naturally must give great consideration to the nature of voluntary acts.

St. Thomas follows his treatise on the voluntary acts with that on the passions.[26] The passions partake of morality.[†] They are elicited by the sense appetite rather than by the will itself, and when they occur a bodily change takes place in the subject which performs them. They can be morally good or morally evil in so far as they are directed by reason. In themselves, however, they are of the same type as the acts performed by irrational animals. The passions, as enumerated in the order of St. Thomas are love and hatred, desire and flight, delectation and sadness, all of which pertain to what is termed the *concupiscible appetite*; and hope and despair, fear and rashness and anger, all belonging to the *irascible appetite*. With the consideration of these operations, the Angelic Doctor concluded his teaching about the acts of man in themselves.

The next section of the *Summa Theologica* has to do with those principles from which human acts proceed. The principles, as classified and explained by St. Thomas, are either intrinsic or extrinsic. He calls *intrinsic* principles those entities like the virtues, vices, and gifts of the Holy Spirit which are by their very nature sources from which human activity proceeds. The *extrinsic* sources are those which affect man's activity in so far as he is instructed by God in the law or aided by the force of divine grace.

nature and human flourishing. With regard to this point, Cessario's *Introduction to Moral Theology* offers significant clarification. For a more specific consideration of moral action, see Steven A. Long, *The Teleological Grammar of the Moral Act*, 2nd ed. (Ave Maria, FL: Sapientia Press, 2015).

26. *ST* I-II, qq. 22–48.

†   **Editor's Note:** For more on the relationship between the passions and the virtues, see Romanus Cessario, O.P., *The Moral Virtues and Theological Ethics*, 2nd ed. (Notre Dame, IN: University of Notre Dame Press, 2008). See also Robert Miner, *Thomas Aquinas on the Passions: A Study of* Summa Theologiae, *1a2ae 22–48* (Cambridge: Cambridge University Press, 2009).

3. Habits, Virtues, and Vices. In the order of St. Thomas, the section devoted to the intrinsic principles of human activity opens with a discussion of habits in general.[27] Those habits which are good, and which dispose the potencies of man for their proper operation are called *virtues*.[†] In order to teach correctly about those virtues which have reference to the moral life of man, sacred theology first considers the nature and the properties of virtues as such, and the various classes into which they fall.[28] Then it describes and distinguishes the intellectual virtues, those which perfect and dispose the mind for the proper performance of its own activity. The speculative intellect is perfected in the intellectual virtues of understanding, wisdom, and science. Art and prudence are the virtues which are rooted in the practical intellect.

The *moral* virtues perfect man's will and appetite with reference to those things which contribute to the attainment of his ultimate end. Some of these moral virtues are acquired, others are infused. The acquired virtues are of the natural order while those which are infused pertain to the life which a man leads as an adopted child of God and a brother of Jesus Christ. The *theological* virtues, faith, hope, and charity, perfect man for operation with reference to his ultimate supernatural end.

The seven gifts of the Holy Spirit, like the infused virtues both moral and theological, dispose man for activity which will lead him to God, his ultimate supernatural end.[29] However, the acts which proceed from the gifts differ sharply from those which have the

---

27. *ST* I-II, qq. 49–54.

† **Editor's Note:** The real distinction between potency and act stands as the overarching, metaprinciple of Aquinas's thought. Moreover, the dynamics between potency and act stand at the heart of his moral theology. For a penetrating consideration of potency and act in Thomistic virtue theory, see Vernon J. Bourke, "The Role of Habitus in the Thomistic Metaphysics of Potency and Act," in *Essays in Thomism*, ed. Robert E. Brennan, O.P. (New York: Sheed and Ward, 1942), pp. 103–109.

28. *ST* I-II, qq. 55–67.

29. *ST* I-II, qq. 68–70. **Editor's Note:** For a classic study of the Gifts of the Holy Spirit, see John of St. Thomas, *The Gifts of the Holy Spirit*, trans. Dominic Hughes, O.P. (Tacoma, WA: Cluny Media, 2016).

virtues as their immediate principles with reference to the manner in which they are produced. The acts which proceed from the gifts, certain acts which are designated as the fruits of the Holy Spirit and as the beatitudes, are performed in a way which is at once distinct from and superior to that way in which man naturally acts. Hence these acts are supernatural on two distinct counts—by reason of the object with which they are concerned and by which they are specified, and by reason of the very manner or way in which they are elicited.

The treatise on the intrinsic principles of moral acts ends with a consideration of those operations by which man turns away from God and places his end in created things.[30] These acts are sins. The science of sacred theology studies the sin itself, and then that by which a human act is rendered evil. A sinful act has definite causes and produces certain definite effects upon the soul.

4. *The Law and Grace.* St. Thomas deals with the *extrinsic* sources of human acts in the great treatises on the law and on grace, two of the most brilliant and important sections in all the science of sacred theology. The tract on the *law* opens with a consideration of the subject as such, and then passes on to individual studies of the eternal, the natural, and the divine positive law, both in the Old and in the New Testaments.[31] This section of sacred theology ends, with the discussion of the necessity of grace, its nature and divisions, its cause and its effects.[32]

The Second Division

In the order of the *Summa Theologica* the *Secunda Secundae* embraces that portion of the science which we know as special

---

30. *ST* I-II, qq. 71–89.

31. *ST* I-II, qq. 90–108. **Editor's Note:** For a recent study of Aquinas's treatise on law, see J. Budziszewski, *Commentary on Thomas Aquinas's Treatise on Law* (Cambridge: Cambridge University Press, 2014).

32. *ST* I-II, qq. 109–14. **Editor's Note:** Reginald Garrigou-Lagrange's study of Aquinas's treatise on grace remains the most extensive and thorough book available in English on this most important topic: *Grace: Commentary on the* Summa theologica *of St. Thomas, Ia IIae, q. 109–14* (St. Louis, MO: B. Herder Book Co., 1952).

moral theology. This section considers in detail and specifically those same acts which had been studied in their more general nature in the previous portion of the work. The first division within the *Secunda Secundae* itself is that which distinguishes the acts which belong to a Christian as such from those which pertain only to persons in certain states of life. The acts which belong to the general course of Christian life are studied from the viewpoint of the various virtues from which they proceed and in function of which they are to be classified. These virtues are, of course, either moral or theological. The intellectual virtues as such are not considered since they are in themselves indifferent to the moral excellence or evil of the person who possesses them. One intellectual virtue, namely prudence, is a subject of study in this section of sacred theology, but this is due to the fact that it is also one of the moral virtues.

1. *Faith.* St. Thomas opens his treatise on special morals with the study of the virtue of *faith*.[33] He considers first the habit of faith itself, and then the act of which this habit is the principle. The gifts of the Holy Spirit which correspond to faith are *understanding* and *knowledge*. Faith itself is opposed by the vices of infidelity, heresy, and apostasy, while the sins contrary to understanding and knowledge are culpable ignorance, blindness, and obscurity with reference to the truths which have been revealed by God. The treatise on faith closes with the study of the commands which God has given us to believe His teaching.

2. *Hope.* After defining and explaining the virtue of hope[34] the order of the *Summa Theologica* proceeds to the study of the gift of fear of the Lord, which has to do with the matter with which hope is concerned. The sins directly opposed to hope are presumption

---

33. *ST* II-II, qq. 1–16. **Editor's Note:** See Romanus Cessario, O.P., *Christian Faith and the Theological Life* (Washington, DC: The Catholic University of America Press, 1996); Michel Labourdette, O.P., *La foi: « Grand cours » de théologie morale*, vol. 8 (Paris: Parole et Silence, 2015).

34. *ST* II-II, qq. 17–22. **Editor's Note:** See Michel Labourdette, O.P., *L'espérance: « Grand cours » de théologie morale*, vol. 9 (Paris: Parole et Silence, 2012).

and despair. These are described along with the commands which God has given us relative to the matter of Christian hope.

3. Charity. The treatise on *charity* is quite extensive.[35] In the order of the *Summa Theologica* there is first of all a study of the virtue itself, and then a consideration of the principal act which proceeds from this virtue, the act of dilection. The internal effects of charity are joy and peace; the external effects beneficence, almsgiving, and fraternal correction. The examination of these precedes the study of the sins which can be committed against this most perfect of all the virtues, the one which actually gives form and perfection to all of the others possessed by man himself.

Opposed to the act of dilection is the sin of hatred of God, the most heinous of all those which can be committed by man. Opposed to that joy which follows upon charity are the sins of envy and sloth. Discord, contention, schism, war, quarreling and sedition are all contrary to peace. Men can sin against that beneficence which is consequent upon charity through the act of scandal.

In teaching about the commands with reference to charity, the order of St. Thomas considers the twofold precept for the love of God and of our neighbor. The treatise on charity ends with the study of the gift of *wisdom*, corresponding to this virtue and the sin of stultitude which is contrary to wisdom.

4. The Cardinal Virtues and Their Parts. In the *Summa Theologica*, St. Thomas considers all the *moral* virtues under the heading of four. These four are the *cardinal* virtues, in so far as all of the others may be properly defined with reference to these. The other virtues are considered as parts of the four cardinal virtues of prudence, justice, fortitude, and temperance.[36]

---

35. *ST* II-II, qq. 23–46. **Editor's Note:** See Michel Labourdette, O.P., *L'espérance: « Grand cours » de théologie morale*, vol. 10 (Paris: Parole et Silence, 2012).

36. One of the best scientific explanations of the virtues through this division into subjective and integral parts is to be found in the "*Arbor Praedicamentalis sive Generalis Divisio Omnium Virtutum usque ad Infimas Species*," which terminates the sixth volume in the 1878 edition (Paris and Brussels) of the *Collegii Salmanticensis Carmelitarum Discalceatorum Cursus Theologicus*. This work as a whole is one of the outstanding commentaries on the *Summa Theologica*.

They are parts in two different ways. The *subjective* parts of a virtue are those divisions into which the matter of a virtue naturally falls. They constitute the various species which go to make up the genus which is the cardinal virtue itself. Other parts are called *potential*. These differ from the cardinal virtue in so far as the definition of the cardinal virtue can be applied to any one of them, but not with its full force or meaning. Thus, for example, religion is one of the potential parts of justice. Justice disposes a man to render to another that which belongs to that other, and to render what is due in perfect equality. Since religion is the virtue which governs the service which we owe to God because of His supreme excellence, it is manifestly impossible to render to the One to whom service is due all that is actually due to Him. Thus religion is classified as an integral part of justice. There are still other parts of the moral virtues, called *integral* parts in the technical terminology of sacred theology. However, these integral parts are not properly virtues in themselves, but merely acts which cooperate to achieve the end of the virtue.

5. *Prudence.* The first among the cardinal virtues is *prudence.*[37] Its integral parts are memory, reason, understanding, docility, alertness, providence, circumspection, and caution, since all of these acts conspire to render conduct really prudent. Among the subjective parts of this virtue, political, economic, and military prudence are all distinguished from the quality which perfects and governs the life of the individual man. For potential parts, prudence has the virtues of eubulia, synesis, and gnome.

Corresponding to the virtue of prudence, and attached to it in the explanation of the *Summa Theologica*, is the gift of *counsel.* The vices which are opposed to prudence fall away from the proper perfection of human conduct in two distinct directions. Imprudence, inconsideration, recklessness, and inconstancy are contrary to prudence as are the opposite vices called prudence of the flesh, cunning, fraud, deceit, and over-solicitude for the future. The treatise on

---

37. *ST* II-II, qq. 47–56. **Editor's Note:** See Michel Labourdette, O.P., *La prudence: « Grand cours » de théologie morale*, vol. 11 (Paris: Parole et Silence, 2016).

prudence terminates with a consideration of the divine commands
concerning the matter of this virtue. Like every other portion of sacred theology, this treatise is orientated toward bringing out a more
perfect appreciation of God, as He has revealed Himself to us.

6. Justice. The treatise on *justice*[38] opens with a study of the
object of the virtue, the vice called injustice, which is directly and
immediately opposed to it, and the act which proceeds from it. It
contains with the consideration of its subjective parts, legal, distributive, and commutative justice. Opposed to distributive justice is
the vice which is known as the acceptance of persons. Commutative
justice is violated by those acts in which injury is done to a man's
own person, to those who are connected with him or to his property.
A man's person may be violated by murder, unjust mutilation, beat-
ing, or unjust incarceration. Injustice against those who live under
a man's protection may be perpetrated by acts of impurity like adul-
tery. Injustice can also be done through taking or destroying a man's
goods without his permission, either with or without his knowledge.

Commutative justice may also be violated by words. This may
be done by an unjust legal process, either in false judgment or in
false testimony. Furthermore, it may be done independently of any
legal process, through the acts of detraction, slander, or derision.

After completing the consideration of the subjective parts of
justice, the *Summa Theologica* goes on to study the integral parts
which cooperate to perfect the act of this virtue. The integral parts
of justice are two in number; to do good, and to decline from evil.

The potential parts of justice are those virtues in which the full
perfection of its definition cannot be realized. Since justice is that
quality by which we are disposed to render to another in perfect
equality that which is due to him, it is obvious that any virtue
which governs our relations with others can fall away from the full
perfection of the definition of justice in two distinct ways. Either
it will fail to render to that other all which is due to him in perfect

---

38. *ST* II-II, qq. 57–122. **Editor's Note:** See Michel Labourdette, O.P., *La justice: «
Grand cours » de théologie morale*, vol. 12 (Paris: Parole et Silence, 2016).

equality or it will render a good which is not due in the full and strict sense of the term. Under the first heading the order of the *Summa Theologica* lists religion, piety, and observance as potential parts of the virtue of justice. Under the second heading are veracity, gratitude, vindication, liberality, and affability or friendship.

In studying about the virtue of *religion*, the *Summa Theologica* considers first the essence of this quality and then the acts which proceed from it. The basic acts of religion are, of course, those elicited by the spiritual faculties, the act of devotion which belongs to the will, and the act of prayer, the petition of fitting things from God, which belongs to the intellect. Manifesting these are the external acts, adoration, sacrifice, the giving of tithes and offerings, the taking of oaths, vows, and adjurations. The central and social act, manifesting all the rest and expressing the full perfection of man's religion, is the act of sacrifice.

Opposed to the virtue of religion are the vices of superstition and irreligion. This irreligion results in the temptation of God, perjury, sacrilege, and simony.

The order of the *Summa Theologica* considers the virtue of *piety* as that habit by which we are disposed to render to our parents, our country, and our family that which is due to them. It is characteristic of the scientific theological doctrine that in the order of the *Summa Theologica* it is acknowledged that we owe to all of these far more than we shall ever be able to repay. It is in this category that we find the teaching on the virtue of patriotism. The *observance* which is due to legitimate superiors takes the form of *dulia* and of obedience, both of which are treated at the end of the section on piety.

With reference to the other set of potential parts of justice, *gratitude* is considered in itself and in conjunction with its opposing vice, ingratitude. *Veracity* is opposed by lying, by hypocrisy, boastfulness, and irony. Adulation and quarrelsomeness are contrary vices, both of which are opposed to that *affability or friendship* which should characterize the man who is called upon to live with God for all eternity. The *liberality* of the morally good man is opposed at once to avarice and to prodigality. The treatise on justice concludes with the study of the gift of *piety* which corresponds to this virtue and which must be considered in the light of it.

7. *Fortitude.* The third among the cardinal virtues considered in the order of the *Summa Theologica* is *fortitude.*[39] After studying the nature of this virtue, sacred theology looks at the vices which are opposed to it. These vices take the forms of timidity and a reckless lack of fear, on the one hand, and over-boldness and a lack of any daring whatsoever, on the other. The integral parts of fortitude consist in attacking difficulties and sustaining evils. The potential parts are magnanimity, magnificence, patience, and perseverance. Among the gifts of the Holy Spirit, that of fortitude corresponds to the virtue of the same name.

8. *Temperance.* The fourth and last among the cardinal virtues is *temperance.*[40] The order of the *Summa Theologica* considers respectively the nature of this virtue, the vices directly opposed to it, which are those of intemperance and insensibility, and the subjective parts of the virtue, which are abstinence and chastity. The potential parts of temperance are the virtues of continence, meekness, clemency, humility, and modesty.

9. *The Charisms and the Diversity of Works.* The second section of the *Summa Theologica* ends with the consideration of those acts which pertain only to those who occupy a special position or have attained a definite place in the spiritual life. This last portion of the second part is divided into three sections.

In the first, St. Thomas considers the acts which are consequent upon the diversity of functions assigned by God in the propagation of His teaching.[41] To those men who were called upon to assist in the first dispensation of the revealed teaching, God gave certain favors or charisms, gifts which were beneficial to the Church as a

---

39. *ST* II-II, qq. 123–40. **Editor's Note:** For a consideration of the virtue of fortitude in relation to psychology, see Craig Steven Titus, *Resilience and the Virtue of Fortitude: Aquinas in Dialogue with the Psychosocial Sciences* (Washington, DC: The Catholic University of America Press, 2006).

40. *ST* II-II, qq. 141–70.

41. *ST* II-II, qq. 171–78.

whole rather than to the immediate recipients. Such charisms are prophecy, the gift of tongues, the power of the word, and the grace of miracles. Much of that which is considered in modern treatises on revelation is treated by St. Thomas in his section on prophecy.

The second portion of this last section in the second part deals with the diversity of works, those which are assigned to the active and to the contemplative life.[42] The last deals with the diversity of ministrations, and under this heading the *Summa Theologica* considers the episcopate and the religious life as states of perfection.[43]

III. The Third Part

The third and last great section of the *Summa Theologica* studies God as the Cause restoring to man those supernatural benefits lost through the sin of Adam. As such it is a treatise about Jesus Christ our Lord, who, as Man, constitutes the Way by which we are to return to God. It is subdivided into three sections. The first of these considers our Lord Himself. The second deals with the sacraments, by means of which we are united with Christ. The third considers the effect produced by the passion of Christ, namely, the resurrection and the eternal glory which men are to enjoy in their capacity of adopted children of God in heaven.

1. *The Incarnation.* According to the order of the *Summa Theologica*, there is, first, a study of the fitness and the necessity of the Incarnation itself. This is followed by a consideration of the actual union through which a created human nature belongs to the uncreated person of God the Son. Then St. Thomas goes on to give the revealed doctrine about the extremes involved in this hypostatic union. The second Person of the Blessed Trinity, and He alone, has assumed this human nature as His own. Furthermore, He assumed

---

42. *ST* II-II, qq. 179–82.

43. *ST* II-II, qq. 183–89. **Editor's Note:** For a study of Aquinas's teaching on the episcopacy and the state of perfection, see Michael G. Sirilla, *The Ideal Bishop: Aquinas's Commentaries on the Pastoral Epistles* (Washington, DC: The Catholic University of America Press, 2017).

a perfect human nature, complete with all of those parts and attributes which should naturally belong to the children of men.[44]

Next, there is a study of the perfections and imperfections assumed with the human nature of Christ, qualities which contributed toward the achievement of that purpose for the sake of which the Incarnation was accomplished. The perfections were those of grace, of science, and of power.[45] The imperfection was the passibility of Christ's sacred body, his ability to suffer and to die for the redemption of man.[46]

2. The Grace of Christ. The grace of Christ is considered under a twofold aspect. St. Thomas first studies the habitual grace in the human soul of our divine Savior, through which His human nature was rendered connaturally able to perform the works of the supernatural order. After treating of the nature and the fullness of this grace in Christ, the Angelic Doctor describes that grace with which the human nature of our Lord was endowed in virtue of His position as the Head of the human race.

3. The Human Knowledge of Christ. There are three kinds of science or knowledge in the human mind of Christ. First of all, there is the blessed science, which is nothing more or less than the act of the beatific vision itself. Then there is the infused knowledge, that which proceeds from species imprinted in the human intellect of Christ by God, independently of any human process of acquiring cognition. Finally, there is the acquired knowledge, that which our Lord obtained in the same way as that by which men naturally come to possess knowledge in this world. In explaining the content of God's message to man, sacred theology tells us about all these types of knowledge, as well as about the unlimited power which was possessed by Christ even according to His human nature.

---

44. *ST* III, qq. 1–6. **Editor's Note:** For a modern Thomistic commentary on the Christology of the *Summa Theologiae*, see Reginald Garrigou-Lagrange, O.P., *Christ the Savior: A Commentary on the Third Part of St. Thomas' Theological Summa* (St. Louis, MO: B. Herder Book Co., 1950).

45. *ST* III, qq. 7–13.

46. *ST* III, qq. 14, 15.

The *Summa Theologica* proceeds to explain what are termed the consequences of the hypostatic union. Under this heading comes the study of the relationship of our Lord's human nature to the divine essence, to His being and to His operation, the relations of Christ with reference to His eternal Father, and our own relations to Christ.[†]

4. *Communication of Idioms.* Because the Second Person of the Blessed Trinity has assumed a human nature and subsists in it, it follows that the characteristics of both the divine and the human natures may correctly be attributed to the Person who possesses both. The characteristics of one nature, however, must not be predicated of the other. Moreover, all explanation of the doctrine about the Incarnate Word must be such as to stress the truth that there is only one being, one subsistence, that of the Person who is both God and man, since He subsists in both the divine and the human nature. At the same time the operations of the two natures remain distinct one from the other. Thus our Lord has two wills, the one divine, and the other human. The human will retains its own operation, the real activity of which it is the connatural source.[47]

5. *Our Lord's Subjection to His Father.* By reason of the human nature which He has freely assumed out of love for men, our Lord is really subject to His divine Father. He can and does pray to Him on our behalf. Our Lord is constituted as a priest, as a mediator between God and man. However, He must not be thought of as an adopted Son of God, because sonship is the attribute of a person rather than of a nature and the Person who has assumed the human nature is and remains forever the natural Son of God. However, by reason of His human nature, Christ is actually predestined to eternal glory by His divine Father.[48]

6. *Our Relation to Christ.* The study of the communication of idioms, as the doctrine on the relationship of the human nature

---

†   **Editor's Note:** For a recent study of these themes, see Dominic Legge, O.P., *The Trinitarian Christology of Thomas Aquinas* (Oxford: Oxford University Press, 2017).

47. *ST* III, qq. 17–19.

48. *ST* III, qq. 20–24.

to the divine essence in Christ is called, and the study of the relations of Christ to the Father are followed by the exposition of the
revealed doctrine about our relations to Him who is our Savior.
Under this latter heading the Angelic Doctor considers our duties
toward Christ, and His activity on our behalf. Our duties with
reference to our Lord are brought out in the question on the adoration of Christ, while His activity in our favor is summarized in
the question on His mediation. These questions bring to an end the
basic treatise on the incarnation.[49]

7. *The Redemption and the Life of Christ.* The other portion
of the theological doctrine about our Lord is brought out in the
treatise on the redemption. This involves, in the order of the *Summa Theologica*, a masterly treatise on the life of our Lord. It opens
with a study of the revealed doctrine relative to Christ's entrance
into this world. Included in this section is a summary of what
God has told us about the life and the prerogatives of the Blessed
Mother of God. There follow treatises on the various mysteries of
our Lord's life, on His birth and legal sanctification, His baptism,
public life, and His passage out of this world. The section dealing
with our Lord's passion and death considers both the cause of His
suffering and the effects which that suffering produced. In the passion of Christ God's justice was satisfied through a sacrificial and
meritorious action which redeemed man and thereby efficaciously
brought about man's reconciliation with God.[†] The treatise on the

---

49. *ST* III, qq. 25, 26.

† **Editor's Note:** For more on the nature of Christ's satisfaction, see Romanus
Cessario, O.P., *The Godly Image: Christ and Salvation in Catholic Thought from
Anselm to Aquinas* (Petersham, MA: St. Bede's Publications, 1990); Emmanuel
Perrier, O.P., "L'enjeu Christologique de la Satisfaction (I)," *Revue Thomiste*,
Vol. 103 (2003): pp. 105–36; "L'enjeu Christologique de la Satisfaction (II),"
Revue Thomiste, Vol. 103 (2003): pp. 203–47; Rik Van Nieuwenhove, "'Bear-
ing the Marks of Christ's Passion': Aquinas's Soteriology," in *The Theology of
Thomas Aquinas*, ed. Rik Van Nieuwenhove and Joseph Wawrykow (Notre
Dame, IN: University of Notre Dame Press, 2005), pp. 277–302. See also
Nieuwenhove's earlier essay: "St. Anselm and St. Thomas Aquinas on 'Satis-
faction': Or how Catholic and Protestant Understandings of the Cross Differ,"
Angelicum, Vol. 80 (2003): pp. 159–76.

redemption in the order of the *Summa* ends with a consideration of Christ's descent into hell, His resurrection, ascension, and His eternal glory and dignity in the kingdom of heaven.[50]

8. *The Sacraments.* The second portion of the third part deals with the sacraments of the Catholic Church, first in general and then individually.[51] The general treatise on the sacraments looks first to the nature of a sacrament as a sign and then to the necessity, the cause, the effects, and the number of the sacraments. Among the effects it distinguishes between that sacramental grace which is signified and produced by all of them and the sacramental character which is signified and produced by three only.[†]

Each one of the seven sacraments is studied individually. The nature of each is treated as it has been explained in the course of divine revelation. Likewise there is an explanation of the minister who is competent to administer each of these sacraments, the effects produced, the subjects who can receive them, and the

---

50. *ST* III, qq. 27–59.

51. The treatise on the sacraments in general extends from *ST* III, qq. 60–65. The work was never completed. The last question St. Thomas wrote in the *Summa* was the ninetieth of the third part. What was to follow according to the order already described by him was taken from his Commentary on the *Fourth Book of Sentences* and added as a Supplement to the third part of the *Summa*. This Supplement, arranged by Reginald of Piperno, contains the rest of the treatise on penance and the other sacraments which are treated subsequent to this and all of the doctrine on the last things. There are 99 or 101 questions in this supplement, according to the disposition followed in the ordinary texts.

† **Editor's Note:** The nature of the sacraments and their true and proper causality has suffered grave neglect in contemporary theology. For an insightful analysis of the state of sacramental theology after the Second Vatican Council, see Romanus Cessario, O.P., "The Sacraments of the Church," in *Vatican II: Renewal within Tradition*, ed. Matthew L. Lamb and Matthew Levering (Oxford: Oxford University Press, 2008), pp. 129–46. In recent years, theologians have once again turned their attention to sacramental causality. See the penetrating analysis of Reginald M. Lynch, O.P., *The Cleansing of the Heart: The Sacraments as Instrumental Causes in the Thomistic Tradition* (Washington, DC: The Catholic University of America Press, 2017). See also Roger W. Nutt, *General Principles of Sacramental Theology* (Washington, DC: The Catholic University of America Press, 2017). Together, these two texts distinguish themselves for their eminent readability and for the timely assistance they provide to contemporary students interested in the Church's teaching about the sacraments.

individual characteristics of each. Thus it is the business of theology to show how the sacrament of the Holy Eucharist is likewise the sacrifice of the Mass, the great act of worship for the people of the New Law. It is the act of Christ's Mystical Body and at the same time the sacrament about which all the others are grouped, and by which they are explained and finalized.

9. *The Last Things.* The *Summa Theologica* is an unfinished masterpiece. St. Thomas died while he was still working on the portion of the work which dealt with the sacrament of penance. However, the order of the *Summa* is something intrinsic to the volume itself. At the very outset of the third part the Angelic Doctor had made it clear that the entire work was to be completed with the end of that third part. In the last portion of this part he intended to explain the revealed doctrine dealing with the effect achieved by the passion of Jesus Christ.

This portion of sacred theology includes the treatises on the condition of the soul after death, the doctrine about purgatory, hell, and heaven, and the teaching on the particular and the general judgments. It concludes with the doctrine on the general resurrection which will immediately precede the last judgment.

10. *Theology Actually Organized Around God as the Formal Subject of Attribution.* Each portion of sacred theology in the order of the *Summa Theologica* has evident reference to God. Not only is the general outline of the work directed toward an understanding of the doctrine which God has revealed to us about Himself, but each individual treatise, question, and article keeps to this central and dominating work of sacred theology. This concern with God so dominates the *Summa Theologica* that it is perfectly correct to denominate, not only the science of sacred theology as such, but even this particular work of theology as having God Himself for an *obiectum formale quod.*

The order of the *Four Books of Sentences* and that of the *Summa Theologica* are manifestations of a perennial tradition in the field of Catholic thought. They follow along the general lines set down centuries before in the *De Fide Orthodoxa* of St. John Damascene, and even earlier in the *De Principiis* of Origen. Another exemplification of the same trend in the teaching of sacred theology is to be found in the ordering of the content of this science along the lines of the three theological virtues of faith, hope, and charity. This order is found in the *Enchiridion* of St. Augustine and in the remarkable *Compendium Theologiae* of St. Thomas Aquinas.[52]

The great modern manuals of dogmatic and moral theology stress this same theocentric character. There is no portion of sacred theology which can properly be understood until it is seen as a device for bringing us to understand something of that message which God has revealed to man about Himself. There is no process in sacred theology, however abstruse it may be, which is not centered upon the task of bringing to the student, and through him to the Christian world, the ineffable beauty and simplicity of the message of Jesus Christ, the truth about God.

---

52. This division is mentioned at the beginning of the *Enchiridion* although the matter of the book is not arranged very strictly in function of this division. The *Compendium Theologiae* is another of the unfinished masterpieces of St. Thomas. The second section, on hope, which is arranged according to the nature and the petitions of the Lord's Prayer is not complete. The third section was never begun.

* * *

Chapter III

The Light of Sacred Theology

The teaching which sacred theology offers is set forth under the form of theses, known as theological conclusions.
Theological conclusions refer to the very same subject matter which
is expressed and described in those propositions which we accept
with the assent of divine faith. However, a man accepts a statement
on divine faith for one reason or motive and assents to a theological
conclusion for another reason.

**A. Formal Reason for Acceptance of a Proposition Received
on Divine Faith Is the Authority of God Revealing.** The proposition of divine faith is one which we receive precisely because of the
authority of God who has revealed it. That proposition is included
in the deposit of doctrine which God has given to man through our
Lord Jesus Christ. It comes to us in the form of Catholic dogma,
that teaching which the infallible Church of Jesus Christ presents
as having been revealed by God to be believed by all men.[1] When it
has been thus presented, it is accepted solely because God Himself
has taught it.[2]

**B. A Theological Conclusion Is Acceptable as Such Only
When It Has Been Demonstrated.** The theological conclusion as
such, however, is not accepted in the same way. Such theses are

63

accepted only because it is demonstrably evident that they express the correct meaning of that message which constitutes divine public revelation. The motive for their acceptance is not precisely the authority of God revealing, as is the case with propositions of faith, but the demonstrated evidence that these theses present the objective and traditional significance contained in the divine teaching. This element of proof differentiates sacred theology from that deposit of faith which it is organized to expound. There can be no theological conclusion apart from discursive rational activity, a demonstration in function of which the conclusion or thesis is acceptable.[3]

Now, it must be understood at the outset that the same proposition can be at the same time accepted with the assent of divine faith and established as a theological conclusion. A glance through any competent textbook for this science will show that the theologian takes Catholic dogmas and demonstrates that these propositions

---

1.   Vatican Council (Denzinger, 1792).

2.   Vatican Council (Denzinger, 1789).

3.   A thesis thus demonstrated as true is said to be seen in the light of virtual or mediate revelation. Cf. *ST* I, q. 1, a. 3. St. Thomas speaks of all things which are divinely revealable (*divinitus revelabilia*), as communicating in the one formal reason of this science. Among the commentators, Sylvius (commentary on the above article), says that while the Deity is the formal object that is known in theology (*obiectum formale quod*), the formal object by which or under which the things of theology are known (*obiectum formale quo vel sub quo, id est ratio formalis sub qua*) is being revealed (*esse revelatum*). He reasons thus, "That is the formal object *sub quo* of any science which is the reason of its assent. But the reason (or cause) of theological assent is revelation, by which the principles are immediately revealed, and the conclusions mediately; in so far, that is, as they follow by means of discursive reasoning from revealed principles." John of Saint Thomas (*Cursus Theologicus*, Vol. 1, p. 377), speaks of this virtual revelation as the formal reason under which the theological conclusion is rendered intellectually acceptable. Billuart (*Summa Sancti Thomae Hodiernis Academiarum Moribus Accomodata*, p. 13) speaks of the *obiectum formale quo* of theology as virtual and mediate revelation. Among recent authors Dorsch prefers to speak of the *obiectum formate quo* of theology as "demonstrability from the word of God." He considers the term "virtual revelation" too closely bound up with the theory of Father Schultes, which he chooses to ascribe to Billuart (*Summa Sancti Thomae Hodiernis Academiarum Moribus Accomodata*, p. 12).

actually express the meaning which has always been conveyed in the divine message. A good number of the theses set forth in the ordinary manuals of sacred theology are dogmas of faith. Many of them are set down as theses in the very terminology in which they have been defined by the solemn magisterium of the Church.

Naturally there is nothing to prevent the theologian from showing that a proposition actually accepted with the assent of divine faith is a part of the revealed message. Again he may establish as his thesis a proposition which has never been defined at all, and in this case the thesis is merely a theological conclusion. In any event he must demonstrate that his proposition really manifests the meaning which Jesus Christ our Lord attached to the message which He gave the world. In the clarity and force of that demonstration lie the motive and the light which specify the science of sacred theology.

A proof or demonstration can, of course, be resolved into a syllogistic process. Thus any proper theological conclusion can be presented as the resultant of a syllogism expressing the process in which this conclusion is shown to be true. Many of those who have written about the science of sacred theology attempt to explain it merely or mainly in terms of such a syllogistic process. These men consider the statement that the theological conclusion is correctly drawn from two premises, at least one of which is a truth of divine faith, as an adequate explanation of sacred theology.

C. Opinions of Schultes and Marín-Sola on Definability of a Theological Conclusion Consider This Conclusion Merely in Terms of Its Syllogistic Foundation. Now, to essay an adequate explanation of the theological conclusion *merely* in terms of a syllogism is to engender a dangerous confusion about the very nature of this science. The syllogism as such is organized to give knowledge of a new truth, a statement quite distinct from the principles out of which it has been deduced. For this reason Father Schultes maintained that the true theological conclusion could never be defined as of faith since it was necessarily distinct, as a truth, from the propositions of faith which had served as premises in the theological demonstration.[4] Father Marín-Sola, on the other hand, held that the true theological conclusion could actually be defined as a proposition which must be held on divine faith since this conclusion was only conceptually distinct from the premises out of which it had been inferred.[5]

D. A Conclusion Extrinsic to the Content of Revealed Truth Can Never Be Defined As of Divine Faith. Now, only that doctrine which has actually been revealed by God can be defined by the Church and proposed to her children as something which must be accepted on the word of God. Father Schultes was perfectly correct in teaching that a proposition actually inferred *out of* the content of divine revelation could not be considered as intrinsic to the deposit of God's message. On the other hand, his doctrine that propositions once considered theological conclusions and later defined as of faith by the infallible magisterium of the Church were never really conclusions in the proper sense at all, could never be considered as satisfactory. According to his teaching, the proposition which has once been defined turns out to have been the resultant of a process of investigation which was never a real demonstration. Writers of one period in the history of the Church might have supposed that they were demonstrating a conclusion. The men of a later time would certainly see that they had done nothing of the sort.[6]

---

4. *Introductio in Historiam Dogmatum*, pp. 195–203. The two conclusions given here by Father Schultes express his doctrine most accurately. They are: (1) theological conclusions as such (*quoad se*), that is doctrines which are only virtually revealed, cannot be defined as dogmas; (2) theological conclusions which are such with regard to us only (*quoad nos tantum*) can be defined as dogmas in so far as the doctrine asserted in them is concerned, and even according to the mode and the formulae by which the doctrine is expressed. However (they are not definable) precisely in so far as they are known through syllogistic reasoning, but in so far as, according to the judgment of the Church, they are contained in the extent and the comprehension of formal revelation.

5. Marín-Sola, *L'Évolution homogène du Dogme Catholique*, pp. 154–202.

6. Schultes, *Introductio in Historiam Dogmatum*, p. 197, actually cites a passage from Tanquerey to this effect. "Sometimes it happens that a truth which was first thought to be only virtually revealed, afterwards, the affair having been better considered, is seen as formally and implicitly revealed." Cf. Tanquerey, *Synopsis Theologiae Dogmaticae*, 19th ed., p. 109.

They had merely examined into the content of Catholic dogma and restated the revealed truth in their own terminology. Consequently, according to the teaching of Father Schultes, these later writers could merely conclude that their predecessors had never actually performed the work of scientific theology.

E. As Manifest in Its Own Literature, and as Described in the [First] Vatican Council, the Theological Demonstration Is a Complex Process and the Theological Conclusion Is Not Extrinsic to the Body of Actually Revealed Doctrine. Just as white light is composed of radiations of many diverse colors, the crystal splendor of sacred theology is the resultant of processes far too complex and diversified to be expressed adequately even under the heading of the syllogism. We can begin to appreciate the inherent order and perfection involved in the theological process only when we have looked into the actual content of the existing literature of the science. For St. Augustine, St. Anselm, Peter the Lombard, and St. Thomas Aquinas the theological conclusion was never classified merely as an inference drawn from the content of revealed truth. These men, like the great commentators of the golden age and like the able writers of our own time, understood that there were different kinds of intellectual activity which entered into the process of sacred theology, and that this science could never be considered and treated accurately except in function of all these procedures.

In the dogmatic constitution, *Dei Filius*, the [First] Vatican Council drew up a schedule of this multiplex theological activity. "When sedulously, piously and soberly it seeks from God some understanding of the mysteries, reason, enlightened by faith, attains that understanding which is most fruitful, both from an analogy with those things which it knows naturally, and from the connection of the mysteries among themselves and with the last end of man."[7]

When we look into the actually existing literature of sacred theology, we find that the conclusions are established after processes

7.   Denzinger, 1796.

of analogy and comparison. The analogy is employed in the choice of those terms which are to enter into the theological conclusion while the proposition or thesis itself is developed through the process of comparison. Out of this complex activity comes the statement which expresses clearly and unequivocally the real meaning of divine revelation. The proper theological conclusion is seen as acceptable in the light of this demonstration.

   1. *Analogy in Sacred Theology.* [8] We speak of a term as *analogous* when it applies to two objects which are primarily different but which have a certain unity of reference or proportion.[†] In this way it differs from the *univocal* term, which conveys the same meaning whenever it is employed, and from the *equivocal* term which is merely the same word applied to two divergent and unrelated realities. Thus the term *animal* is univocal when it is used with reference to man and to a horse. The term *bank* is equivocal when it is applied to a financial institution and to the side of a stream. The word *healthy* is analogous when it is used with reference to a human being in good physical condition and to a location which is conducive to the acquisition of that condition by man.

   The formal subject of attribution in the science of sacred theology is, as we have seen, God Himself. Now, there is no term which could possibly apply univocally to God and to creatures. Whatever there is in the way of goodness and perfection in the created universe exists as something dependent upon God. In Him all perfection subsists simple and immutable. Purely equivocal terms are, of course, quite incapable of contributing the progress of knowledge. As a result the only kind of term which can serve for the work of sacred theology is that which we call analogous.

---

8. For a competent explanation of analogy in sacred theology read M. T.-L. Penido, *Le Rôle d'Analogie en Théologie Dogmatique* (Paris, 1931). **Editor's Note:** See Stephen A. Long, *Analogia Entis: On the Analogy of Being, Metaphysics and the Act of Faith* (Notre Dame, IN: University of Notre Dame Press, 2011), pp. 97–106.

† **Editor's Note:** For a contemporary study of Cardinal Cajetan's classic treatise on the analogy of names, see Joshua P. Hochschild, *The Semantics of Analogy: Rereading Cajetan's* De Nominum Analogia (Notre Dame, IN: University of Notre Dame Press, 2010).

Not only are the terms which enter into those judgments which form a part of man's natural knowledge about God thus analogous, but actually the propositions in which the divine message itself is expressed are made up of these terms. As we have seen, the message which we accept on divine faith is a mediate revelation that is one which we receive through the ministrations of our fellow men. The doctrine itself is supernaturally acquired. As a matter of fact, it is essentially supernatural, something over and above the natural competence and power of any creature, actual or possible. But the terms in which this doctrine is couched are words intelligible to any man.

In the course of explaining the meaning inherent in the divine message, the theologian is forced to examine many terms and expressions which might be used with reference to God. Thus for example, long ago when the exigencies of the controversies about the Blessed Trinity impelled the defenders of the Catholic faith to say that there were three Persons in God, these theologians had to show that the connotation of the term *person* was such as to bring out the actual meaning contained in the divine message.[†] They were perfectly aware that there was a world of difference between the created human person and the uncreated Son of God. They were careful to insist that all of the limitations which were associated with the individual human beings ordinarily designated as persons were in no way to be attributed to the divinity. But at the

---

†   **Editor's Note:** The metaphysics of personhood and the analogical proportionality between human, angelic, and divine persons has justly received much attention from prominent figures in the Thomist tradition. In this context, one can recognize the benefit that accrues to the Christian contemplative when sound philosophy serves sacred theology. See Thomas U. Mullaney, O.P., "Created Personality: The Unity of Thomistic Tradition," *The New Scholasticism*, Vol. 29, No. 4 (1955): pp. 369–402. This essay from Mullaney remains one of the most erudite and breathtaking examples of Thomistic metaphysics serving the *sacra doctrina*. Additionally, the author identifies unifying speculative threads that reveal an essential continuity among the great Thomists of history—Capreolus, Cajetan, John of St. Thomas—on the topic of personhood. As an inheritor of the great luminaries within the Thomist tradition, Mullaney himself illustrates why the true Thomist theologian must also always be a master metaphysician.

same time they pointed out that the objective meaning of the term *person* was such that it could serve to designate the Father, the Son, and the Holy Spirit, not, of course, with perfect adequacy but still correctly. The theologians investigated the essential connotations of the word and then looked to see if this meaning had been ascribed to God in the actually existing literature of the Catholic faith.

2. *The Process of Comparison.* The process of *comparison* completed the theological operation. A question is asked about the meaning inherent in one of the dogmatic formulae. The answer can be given only after an inquiry into the content of Catholic teaching as it is found in the inspired Scriptures and in the organs of tradition. The statement to the effect that the procession of the Son of God from the Father is an intellectual generation is shown to express the actual meaning of the divinely revealed message only after an examination into that literature in which the Catholic teaching is contained and expressed. To be exact, the process does not involve drawing a conclusion *out of* the content of revealed truth. It serves merely to manifest that content in such a way that there can be no chance for ambiguity and error. It operates to bring out the meaning which is *within* the content of Christian teaching. In manifesting the errors which disfigure and destroy divine faith, sacred theology actually defends the content of that faith in the course of its traditional procedure.

The light of sacred theology, that is, the motive through which the characteristic utterances or theses of sacred theology are rendered acceptable, involves erudition as well as mere reasoning. The parallel between the process of metaphysics and that to which sacred theology is consecrated by its very nature, a parallel suggested by Father Marín-Sola, is certainly not extensive. The metaphysician is devoted to the investigation of a naturally observable reality. In the pursuit of his studies he naturally avails himself of the resources supplied by the great human literature of his own science. However, the best that this literature can afford is a certain aid or direction toward the more effective observation of the reality itself. The essential task remains the study of this naturally observable reality, and in the final analysis the metaphysician will be judged by his understanding of this object rather than in function of his appreciation of the literature pertaining to his science.

On the other hand, the theologian is consecrated to the study of a message. It is his business to express the content of this definite teaching in such a way that the danger of ambiguity is removed. It is the message taught by Jesus Christ our Lord. It is contained only in Holy Scripture and in the apostolic tradition of the Catholic Church. This Church is given the privilege and the duty of declaring that message with infallible accuracy until the end of time. As a result the theologian can hope to find the objective meaning of the message, or what is the same thing, the correct resolution of the problem with which he is confronted, only in and through the literature of the Catholic Church. Consequently his is a task for the accomplishment of which a definite erudition is absolutely necessary.

The theologian can never hope successfully and scientifically to resolve the problems with which he is confronted apart from the resources of his own literature. When a question is asked about the meaning of the dogmatic formulae, he cannot respond after an observation of the Object to which these formulae have reference. He must seek enlightenment from the content of the message itself. He will find that message in the authentic sources of Sacred Scripture and tradition and in the pronouncements of the Catholic Church and of its teachers. In order to act as a theologian, then, he must know that literature.[†]

---

†   **Editor's Note:** As I suggested in the Introduction, the general trend of Catholic theology in the twentieth century might be typified as a movement from principles to sources. Certainly the neo-scholastic theologians of the nineteenth and twentieth centuries were adept in discursive movements from principles to conclusions. The philosophical and theological "manuals" of this period serve as intellectual artifacts of this period. Unsurprisingly, many students of theology in the early twentieth century found the almost absolute formalism of the manual-approach to theological education cumbersome at best and repugnant at worst. It is important to observe at this point that the "manuals" and the "manualists" were not all created equal. The theological manual was, primarily, a pedagogical tool. It outlined the discursive structure that informed the many and important doctrinal conclusions educed from the theological first princi-

F. Theological Demonstration Exemplified in Writings of Peter the Lombard. One of the finest examples of the way in which the light of sacred theology actually works is to be found in the procedure of Peter the Lombard in his *First Book of Sentences*. The Master began his work by expounding the revealed teaching about the Blessed Trinity. Thus, after the opening chapters in which he sets forth the nature and the divisions of his theological work, he proceeds immediately to state exactly what God has revealed and what the Church proposes to us about this central mystery of our faith. He announces that his teaching must neglect neither the ineffable unity of the divine nature nor the perfect distinction of the divine Persons and then he brings out the order which governs his scientific procedure. He uses the words of St. Augustine himself in the declaration of that order. These words are so perfectly illustrative of the light of sacred theology, both considered in themselves and in so far as they are explained by the actual teaching of Peter the Lombard, that it is well worthwhile to cite them.

> First it must be demonstrated, according to the authorities of the Holy Scriptures, that the faith is actually what it is claimed to be. Then we must use *Catholic reasons* and *apt analogies* for the defense and the assertion of the faith against those garrulous reasoners who are stronger in confidence than they are in ability, in order that, resolving their problems, we may more perfectly instruct the docile man. Our instruction must be such that the enemies of the faith may lay the blame for their failure upon their own minds rather than upon the truth itself or upon our exposition of it, should they fail to find what they seek.[9]

ples contained in the *depositum fidei*. However, as in all literary genres, some manualists were more effective than others. Moreover, of course, not all manuals reflected the Thomist tradition to the same degree and in the same manner. Diocesan priests and religious of various congregations frequently penned their own philosophical and theological manuals.

9.   *The First Book of Sentences*, Dist. II, Caput 3.

Thus the great Master of the *Sentences* proposes to divide off his actual theological investigation into three distinct steps. First of all, there is to be the consultation of the "authorities of the Holy Scripture." In the *First Book of the Sentences* this step turns out to be a combination of the "proof from Scripture" and the "proof from tradition" so popular in later manuals of this science.[10] Peter the Lombard alleges from both the Old and the New Testaments texts referring to the mystery of the Trinity. However, he offers his citations with the interpretations of the Fathers themselves in such a way that his teaching represents the scriptural doctrine as it is taught by the Catholic Church itself. The two chapters which he devotes to this task tend to show that the dogmatic formulae, as they have already been set down, are contained in and taken from the authentic sources of revelation, Scripture, and tradition.

The "apt analogies" which Peter the Lombard promised to integrate into his theological exposition turn out to be the famous "trinities" of St. Augustine.[11] There are certain vestiges of the Blessed Trinity found in the created mind or soul. In explaining these Peter the Lombard, like Augustine before him, shows the aptness of the terms used in Sacred Scripture and in the teaching of the Catholic Church to serve as instruments for teaching about the Triune God. All the expositions of theological analogy which have ever been written have been explanations of that traditional procedure which Peter the Lombard incorporated into his volume.

The "Catholic reasons," however, form the crowning points in the theological activity of Peter the Lombard. In them the light of sacred theology completely attains its object. Hitherto the matter of the *Books of Sentences* has been merely declarative. Now the note of inquiry is introduced. Certain misconceptions about the content of Catholic dogma and certain objections against it are brought forward. Actually the objection is based upon a misconception.

---

10. Ibid., Chaps. 4, 5.
11. Ibid., Dist. III, Chaps. 1–3.

The Master of the *Sentences* sets his first objection in the form
of a dilemma. It was an argument which aimed at the very heart
of the doctrine about the Blessed Trinity, a contention that the
teaching about the generation of the Divine Son from the Father
would involve a denial either of the Trinity itself or of the teaching about the divine Unity. He resolves that dilemma and then
brings forward an objection against the validity of his response,
again couched in the form of a dilemma. This second objection is
triumphantly resolved and the resolution stands as a statement of
the doctrine of the Blessed Trinity which utilizes the resources of
the scientific tradition in the interests of accuracy and clearness.

This statement, however, is challenged in the name of the opponents of Christian doctrine. This last objection is, in turn, resolved and the entire question again summarized. The treasures of
patristic teaching are investigated, and the meaning of the Fathers
is shown from the context of their own writings.

> Behold from these and from many other authorities it is
> evidently shown that we must say and concede that the One
> God is the Trinity and that the one substance is the three
> persons as conversely the Trinity is said to be the One God and
> the three Persons are said to be the one substance.... Now let
> us return to the previous question, where we inquired whether
> God the Father begot Himself God or begot another. To this we
> answer that neither alternative can be accepted.

One last objection must be overcome, an objection taken from
the terminology of St. Augustine himself. "Still Augustine says in
his letter to Maximus that God the Father begot Himself another
God, using these words. 'The Father, that He might have a Son of
Himself, did not lessen Himself, but He so begot of Himself another Self that He would remain whole in Himself and would be as
much in the Son as He is alone.'"

Peter the Lombard then concludes this portion of the discussion. "This can be understood to mean that He has begotten of

Himself One other than Himself, but another Person, not another God, or to mean that He begot Himself another, who is what He is Himself. For although, with reference to the Son, the Father is another Person, He is not another thing, but one and the same."[12]

Throughout the course of Peter the Lombard's reasoning there is an appeal to the actual content of Christian faith as that faith is contained in its proper sources and vehicles. The Master uses as principles the articles of faith themselves. These articles, according to the terminology of St. Thomas are the various points which enter into the divine message and bring with themselves some special difficulty. They are the various headings under which the content of divine revelation is classified. Peter the Lombard appeals now to the teaching on the unity of God, and now to the doctrine on the distinction of the three divine Persons. Out of these articles of faith he reasons with cold scientific accuracy to the establishment of his own conclusions. And this conclusion is certainly not to be assigned to what we might call the penumbra of divine truth. The conclusion has to do with the actual meaning of the divine message and, of course, with the manner in which this objective meaning must be expressed.

We have seen that the Master construed this process as a defense of the Catholic faith. The theses which he established were set forth as contradictions to certain misconceptions, which incidentally were prevalent and dangerous in his own time. Some of these false interpretations of the divine message were such as to destroy or pervert the faith of those who were deceived into accepting them. Others would at least becloud and obscure the belief of men. In destroying these misconceptions through the establishment of legitimate theological conclusions the Master of the *Sentences* succeeded in protecting the faith of those who were the recipients of the message of God.

G. The Process of St. Thomas Aquinas. The two processes mentioned by the [First] Vatican Council and employed by Peter

---

12. Ibid., Dist. IV, Chap. 2.

the Lombard are also to be observed in the theological works of
the greatest of the Doctors, St. Thomas Aquinas. With matchless
success he pointed out the "apt analogies," the analogies with those
things which we know naturally, and which can be of service to us
in expressing the message which God has given to us through Jesus
Christ. In the portion of the *Summa Theologica* in which he covers
the same matter as that set forth in the section of the *First Book of
Sentences* to which we have had reference, the Angelic and Common Doctor of the Catholic Church makes use of doctrinal history
for the establishment of this thesis. His was characteristically the
genius of order. Thus he was able to divide off his matter more
effectively than his predecessors had done and to deal with each
point with more perfect accuracy and precision. While his method
was quite superior to that of Peter the Lombard, the direction of his
inquiry was exactly the same. He reasoned from the articles of faith
to ascertain the objective meaning of that divine message which
we hold on faith. He asked questions about the content of divine
revelation, and then resolved these questions by an examination of
the terms involved and finally through a recourse to the authentic
declarations of Catholic dogma.

   **H. The Contradictory to a Demonstrably Erroneous State-
ment About the Content of Christian Doctrine Is a Proper
Theological Conclusion.** In considering the light of sacred theology we must not lose sight of what we might term the *negative*
process through which many of its theses are evolved. The proper
theological conclusion is very frequently set forth explicitly as the
response to a question. The improper response is studied, and is
seen as improper precisely in so far as it involves a denial of some
article of faith. Since such a statement is obviously false, its contradictory is obviously true. The demonstration that proposition "A"
involves a contradiction of an article of faith is by that very fact
the establishment of proposition "B," its contradictory, as a proper theological conclusion. Such a conclusion is obviously *intrinsic*
to the divine message. It could never be properly construed as a
mere inference drawn from the content of Catholic dogma. It is a

statement which the Church could define as revealed truth if the opportunity or the necessity were to arise.

I. Theses Actually Proposed as Theological Conclusions Have Reference to the Meaning of the Divinely Revealed Message. The intrinsic character of the proper theological conclusion can be seen quite plainly through an examination of post-Tridentine writings in this science. Such men as Suarez, Sylvius, the Salmanticenses, and Billuart, to name only a few of them, set forth very clearly the theses they intended to demonstrate as theological conclusions. Some of their conclusions were set down as opinions, as statements which only probably expressed the meaning of the divine message. Others were named as certain. These latter theses, which alone are theological conclusions in the strict and perfect sense of the term, are always shown to state the meaning actually conveyed in divine revelation and actually propounded by and in the Catholic Church. The processes of analogy and comparison are utilized to show first the significance of the terms which enter into the thesis and then the fact that this particular thesis actually conveys the meaning of God's teaching.

J. Importance of a Proper Concept of the Motive Which Dominates Sacred Theology. It is vitally important that the students of our own day and of our own country appreciate the nature of this light of sacred theology. There has never been a time when men were more sorely in need of the treasures contained in the traditional Catholic science. It is imperative that they should realize that it contains, not merely a complexus of statements reasoned, as it were, out of the content of divine revelation, but actually the teaching of the living God. The labors of the scholastics, the immense treasures of erudition and insight which enter into the literature and the equipment of this science are ordered so that through them the little ones of Christ may hear His voice, and through His words may find the peace and the happiness they desire.[†]

---

†   **Editor's Note:** This "traditional Catholic science" of sacred theology is not something impersonal. As Fenton says here, sacred theology touches on the "actual

There would be little point in attending to the study of sacred theology in our days if its light merely shone out upon certain
statements associated with the content of God's message, statements which constituted a sort of penumbra for divine revelation.
The light of sacred theology actually shines upon the very truths
which God has revealed to us. We understand a truth precisely as
a theological conclusion when we can demonstrate clearly that this
statement actually belongs to the content of that message which
God has given to the world through Jesus Christ. A man should
be willing to work and to utilize the resources of this greatest of
the sciences, to apply all of the exact precision of which the human
mind is capable when he knows that through this study he can state
exactly what fell from the lips of his Savior.

---

teaching of the living God." Therefore, even the most erudite and, admittedly,
abstract reflections from theologians do not terminate in mere ideas about God.
The discursive movements of their arguments are directed to God himself. The
rational formality of their writings assists the rational creature in finding real
union with the living God. See Romanus Cessario, O.P., *Christian Faith and the
Theological Life* (Washington, DC: The Catholic University of America Press,
1996), pp. 49–83. See also the note above (on pp. 4–6): "The Teleology of
Sacred Theology."

* * *

Chapter IV

Certitude in Sacred Theology

Sacred theology is a *certain* discipline because the propositions which it puts forward as its theses or conclusions
are offered firmly and objectively as true. There is neither fear nor
danger that the strictly theological conclusion might turn out to
be erroneous. Furthermore, precisely because of its nature and its
functions, sacred theology is able to endow its conclusions with a
sureness definitely superior to that possessed by the dicta or the
theses of any other science. Consequently we say that the certitude
of sacred theology is higher than that offered by any other science
which man can obtain.[†]

A. The Designation of Theological Theses. Naturally we are
speaking of the certitude offered by sacred theology by reason of its
own proper characteristics and processes. There are certain theses
listed as proper theological conclusions which still possess a certitude quite superior to that which pertains to sacred theology as a
science. A glance at the list of theses set forth in any manual of this
discipline will show that some of them are put forward as *of faith*.
Other conclusions again are offered as *proximate to faith*. Still other designations are *certain, more common, common teaching, more
probable*, and *probable*. The intrinsic certitude of sacred theology

as such is shown by the fact that there are conclusions which are certain merely by the force of theology itself.

B. The Thesis "*De Fide.*" The propositions listed as *of faith* are those which the Catholic Church has infallibly declared to have been revealed by God to the world through Jesus Christ our Lord. As such they are statements which must be believed firmly and constantly by all the faithful. These statements are accepted as true, not because they constitute the object of any demonstration but because of the authority of God Himself, who can neither deceive nor be deceived. Neither the declaration of the Church nor, *a fortiori*, any theological reasoning, enter into the motive of divine faith. However, the Catholic Church has exclusive infallible authority to teach the divine message. When she chooses to exercise that infallible power and to declare that this particular truth was actually revealed by God as something to be accepted by all men with the assent of divine faith, the proposition which she sets forth is accepted on the authority of God who has revealed it, and for no other reason. As a result the assent with which these propositions of faith are received and professed by the faithful is stronger and more certain than the acceptance given to any other sort of proposition which can be formulated by man in this world. The strength of that certitude which faith enjoys proceeds from the very mind of God.

In spite of the fact that they possess a degree of certitude far superior to that which can proceed from sacred theology itself, the *de fide* propositions can be, and actually are, legitimate theological conclusions. Both the function of theology and the status of the dogmatic formulae make this clear. It is the work of sacred theology accurately and unequivocally to express the content of divine public revelation. To the accomplishment of this end it considers problems or questions about the meaning of the divine message

---

†   **Editor's Note:** For more on the themes considered in this chapter, see William A. Wallace, O.P., *The Role of Demonstration in Moral Theology: A Study of Methodology in St. Thomas Aquinas* (Washington, DC: The Thomist Press, 1962).

and resolves these problems scientifically in such a way as to prove that the solutions offered actually are intrinsic to the content of revelation.

The propositions of faith have been set forth by the Church precisely to resolve questions about the meaning and content of the divine message definitively. Obviously, then, there is nothing to prevent the theologian from raising the same problem and setting forth the same solution, demonstrating clearly that this proposition really expresses the meaning of that message which our Lord preached to the world as divinely revealed. The proposition is eminently capable of theological proof, even though it is above the realm of theology in so far as it has been defined by the Church. The theological exposition of this proposition is something which belongs to the technical equipment of the man who is charged with the privilege and the duty of teaching Christian doctrine. Thus the propositions *of faith* are rightly set forth as theological theses in the actually existing literature of this science.

C. The Thesis Not Presented as Certain. On the other hand, a statement which is merely *probable* or *more probable* is not the resultant of a perfect theological demonstration. It is not completely evident that this proposition actually expresses the meaning of divine revelation because the proof of the proposition is not perfectly cogent. However, there are conclusions which can be set down as certain even though they have not been defined as such in the solemn teaching of the Church. The certitude attaching to such propositions is distinctly and solely theological.

D. The Thesis Presented as Certain Solely by Reason of Theological Demonstration. The theologically certain conclusion is one which men accept, not solely on the authority of God revealing, but precisely because this science demonstrates clearly that it expresses the actual and objective meaning of the divine teaching. Because it is demonstrably a part of the divine message, it rejoices in a certitude higher than that which accrues to the theses of any other science obtainable by men. But precisely because a human process of demonstration is requisite to show that this proposition is the correct expression of the divine teaching, its certitude is essentially inferior to that of the faith itself.

The theological demonstration, the analogies and the comparisons enter into the very motive of the theological conclusion. If a man should be asked why he assents to the proposition "the Son of God became Incarnate," he could only answer that he accepts it on the authority of God who has revealed it. This statement is presented to man as a part of the divine message, and moreover as obviously pertaining to the body of revealed doctrine. But, on the other hand, should a man be interrogated as to why he assents to this proposition, "the generation of the Son from God the Father is an intellectual generation," he would have to answer that he accepts this teaching because it is scientifically demonstrated that it expresses the actual meaning contained in the divine message. After examining the meaning of the terms involved in this proposition, the theologian can show that the statement expresses the meaning of Holy Scripture according to the unanimous interpretation of the Fathers. However, the Church has never officially proposed this statement as something divinely revealed, and so, as it stands, it is acceptable only in function of the theological demonstration from which it proceeds.

E. The Individual Theologian and Corporate Character of Sacred Theology. As a result the individual theologian necessarily disclaims any sort of infallibility for his own conclusions as such. Like Peter the Lombard and St. Thomas Aquinas before him, he submits his writings to the Church herself for correction, explicitly disavows any teaching of his which might be opposed to the doctrine of the Church, and welcomes any objective criticism and correction which might come from contemporary or subsequent authors. Obviously the theologian does not consider the formulas of faith themselves as subject to correction of any type whatever. However, he is convinced that it is possible for him to explain the content of that faith in an inept or unfortunate manner. He can be mistaken in considering an inadequate demonstration as something adequate. His very willingness to accept correction constitutes a testimony that the proof alleged for the conclusion actually enters in to the *obiectum formale quod* of sacred theology.

We must not forget that sacred theology is a social and not merely an individual discipline. It is, so to speak, the property of the Catholic Church as a whole, a discipline which has developed in and for the Church with the passing of the ages. As a result, although the individual theologian might be inexact in some of his theses and statements, the science as such is endowed with a perfect certitude. The theologians of the world, at any one time, and through the ages as well, constitute what might be called the corporate faculty of sacred theology for the Church. At the hands of this corporate faculty, the theological conclusion is demonstrated clearly and evidently to be the traditional teaching of the Catholic Church. This corporate faculty has at its disposal resources adequate to demonstrate clearly that the conclusions which it proffers are actually expressions of the message which God gave to the world through Jesus Christ. Furthermore, it possesses a living and evident rule of faith with which the theological conclusion can be compared, and in function of which it can be established as an accurate statement of the divine teaching. Thus for the science as such, the possibility and the legitimate fear of error are entirely eliminated.

F. The Catholic Rule of Faith Alone Explains the Objective Certitude of the Theological Conclusion. Seen in its proper perspective, the teaching on the certitude of sacred theology stands as a projection of the doctrine on the Catholic *rule of faith*. By the rule of faith we mean the standard in function of which a man can judge the actual content of that message which he is willing to accept on the authority of God who has revealed it. Man wishes to believe all that God has taught to the world through Jesus Christ and nothing else on divine faith. However, he must have some way of knowing exactly what is contained in that message in order to distinguish the real content of faith from the various counterfeits with which he might well be faced. Now, the Sacred Scriptures and the apostolic traditions contain all the content of divine public

revelation, unmixed with any element of superstition. Consequently they constitute a rule of faith, which, however, is not immediate,
since these sources are not meant to be interpreted by the individual Christian authoritatively.

The living magisterium of the Catholic Church is alone competent to present infallibly to those who seek it the content of the
divine message which was preached by our Lord. As a result this
magisterium, available to all of those who are willing to utilize it,
stands as the immediate rule of faith, the immediate and practical
standard by which men can discern the true content of Christ's
message.

Precisely because men have at their disposition this competent,
clear, and immediate rule of faith, the science of sacred theology
can offer a grade of certitude superior to that with which the other
sciences are endowed. Once the theologians have ascertained the
exact meaning of the terms in which their problem is couched,
they have a standard with which they can compare this problem,
and in the light of which they can most surely resolve it. Like any
other science, sacred theology depends upon the evidence inherent
in its own demonstrations. And that evidence is forthcoming precisely because of the nature of the Catholic rule of faith. In other
words there can be a science of theology endowed with a lofty and
firm certitude because God has chosen to present His message to
the world in the living, evident, and available magisterium of the
Catholic Church.

G. Evidence in the Theological Demonstration. We cannot
be too careful in describing the evidence which pertains to the science of sacred theology. We must never allow ourselves to imagine
that the Object with which sacred theology is primarily and essentially concerned becomes evident in function of the involved logical
processes which pertain to the operation of this science. Actually,
of course, as long as we remain in this world, that Object, God
Himself in His Own divinity, must remain the Object of faith. But
sacred theology, *fides quaerens intellectum* seeks and finds evidence
of the meaning of that message in which the doctrine about God is

contained, the message which we accept on the word of God with the assent of divine faith itself.

The point is that there can be evidence of the meaning and the content of that message. The body of divine revelation is so organized that through and in it we shall not be able to see the Triune God. But in and through that message, in accordance with the principles and the procedure of sacred theology we shall be able to know that the generation of the Son of God from the Father is really an intellectual generation. The meaning of that message is clear. Misconceptions which could pervert or destroy the act of faith itself are avoidable precisely because the message is presented to us through an available, living, and competent authority. It is only the clarity with which the Catholic Church presents the divine message to men that makes possible a certitude for scientific theology superior to that which characterizes the findings of any other human discipline.

H. A Proposition Extrinsic to and Merely Connected with the Content of Actually Revealed Truth Cannot Be Theologically Certain. The certitude proper to sacred theology is, of course, strictly limited to those propositions which convey the actual meaning of divine public revelation, to those statements in other words which are "intrinsic" with reference to the content of divine faith. The conclusion that "the generation of the Son from God the Father" is a legitimate theological conclusion and enjoys the fullness of theological certitude precisely because it can be proven clearly that this expresses the actual meaning of Sacred Scripture and the teaching of the Fathers in proposing the word of God. Occasionally, however, the literature of sacred theology will contain statements or theses which have not this legitimate place and dignity in the fabric of the discipline. For instance, there is the thesis, found in a certain number of manuals, to the effect that the souls in Purgatory are able to pray in our behalf. Those who put this teaching forward never go so far as to say that this doctrine was contained in the actual sources of revelation. The most that can be said for the proposition, according to the demonstrations which are alleged in its favor, is that it is not contradicted in scripture and tradition. In the literature of sacred theology this thesis can be traced back to the refusal of certain theologians, most notably Richard of Middleton[1] and Juan de Medina[2] to accept the explanation of St. Thomas Aquinas on this particular portion of sacred doctrine.[3]

Thus the thesis that the souls in Purgatory are able to pray for us can never be, in the strict and perfect sense of the term, a theological conclusion. Neither can it ever possess the sort of certitude with which the characteristically theological thesis is endowed. In the last analysis it is quite incapable of receiving the type of theological proof which men like Peter the Lombard and St. Thomas Aquinas described and exemplified in their writings. Again, since such a proposition does not constitute a part of the content of divine revelation, it can never be defined as of faith by the Catholic Church.

I. The Ultimate Source of Theological Certitude. According to the teaching of St. Thomas, sacred theology derives its superior certitude from the light of the divine mind itself. "Other sciences have their certitude from the natural light of human reason, which can err." Sacred theology, on the other hand, "has certitude out of the light of divine knowledge, which cannot be deceived."[4] Since the certitude of theology is of divine knowledge, it cannot be explained merely in function of the syllogistic process by which its conclusions are derived. Seen by virtual revelation, as the light of sacred theology is commonly termed, the thesis in sacred doctrine is demonstrated as an expression of the actual meaning contained in divine revelation. The content of this divine and *intrinsically*

---

1.   Richard of Middleton, O.F.M., *Commentary on the Fourth Book of Sentences of Peter the Lombard*, dist. 45, a. 7, q. 2.

2.   Ioannis Medinae, *De Poenitentia, Restitutione et Contractibus* (Ingolstadt, 1581), Vol. 1, p. 348.

3.   Cf. Joseph Clifford Fenton, *The Theology of Prayer* (Tacoma, WA: 2017), pp. 191–98.

4.   *ST* I, q. 1, a. 5.

supernatural revelation is something which is *seen* naturally by God alone. As a result the characteristic process of sacred theology results in the demonstration that this particular conclusion or thesis is a truth which has been seen and expressed by God. Such a truth, and only such a truth can properly be said to derive its certitude from the divine mind rather than from the natural light of any created intelligence. The very terminology and conclusions of the prince of the theologians are sufficient evidence that he thought of the theological conclusion in function of the purpose to which the science itself is dedicated, the expression of the true doctrine of Jesus Christ our Lord.

Vincent Contenson gave as the reason why sacred theology possesses a certitude superior to that enjoyed by the other sciences which are naturally attainable, the fact that it utilizes a medium or means "more infallible"[5] than any found in a purely natural domain. This more infallible medium is, of course, divine revelation itself, proposed to us in the articles of faith which are the proper principles of sacred theology. The articles of faith, proposed to us in the infallible magisterium of the Catholic Church are so evident that, in resolving problems about the significance of divine revelation in their light, the theologian can arrive at a certitude far greater than any he could possess through the examination of naturally observable realities. The certitude that the proposition "the Son of God is less than the Father" is at variance with and contradictory to the content of the divine message is stronger than the certitude he can have about an erroneous proposition in any other science. The meaning of the divine revelation, as it is proposed in the infallible magisterium of the Church is so clear that demonstrations directed toward bringing out that meaning can possess a superior certitude.

J. Theological Problems Not Yet Resolved. Naturally there can be, and there actually are, problems which have not as yet been resolved in the light of those articles of faith which are infallibly guarded and proposed by the Catholic Church. But the fact that

5.   Vincent Contenson, O.P., *Theologia Mentis et Cordis* (Lyons, 1687), Vol. 1, p. 7.

a problem is not as yet solved in no way implies an imperfect cognizance or proposition of divine revelation by the Church. Rather it is an indication that the meaning of the problem has not as yet been made perfectly clear. The solution of theological problems, and the resultant gaining of theological certitude may, in a sense be said to involve an advance for the Church, and for her corps of theologians as a whole, as well as for the individual or the individuals who have labored toward a solution of the problem. The beautiful citation which the [First] Vatican Council has made from the *Commonitorium* of Vincent of Lerins applies to advance toward theological certitude as well as to the history of dogma, properly so called. "The understanding, the science, the wisdom, of individuals and of all men, of one man and of the entire Church, should grow and progress vigorously by degrees of times and of ages, but only in its own genus, in the same dogma, in the same meaning, and in the same proposition."[6]

K. The Certitude of Sacred Theology in the Life of the Catholic Church. We can never begin to appreciate the force of theological certitude until we examine it in the light of Catholic history. In face of the lives and the activity of the great defenders of the Catholic faith, the high certainty of sacred theology is not merely a vague sort of ideal which it might be well for men to possess. It has characterized the demonstrations and the conduct of traditional theologians throughout the life of the Catholic Church. It was precisely the certitude of sacred theology which led to the unmasking of the various heresies which have appeared during the course of Christian history. Thus St. Athanasius, the theologian, was perfectly certain that the terminology and the teaching of Arius constituted a denial of the Christian faith. This certitude antedated the pronouncement of the Church in the Council of Nicaea, which officially condemned the doctrines of the heresiarch. In function of this theological certitude St. Augustine was able to detect the destructive errors inherent in Pelagianism and Semi-Pelagianism. In

---

6.   Denzinger, 1800.

the same way Cajetan, Latomus, and Eck were perfectly certain of the heresies contained in the teaching of Martin Luther while Francis Sylvius was absolutely sure in his denunciation of Jansenism.[†] These men were endowed with a certitude unquestionably more convincing than any other scientific sureness which this world can know because they had at their disposal the articles of faith clearly and unequivocally interpreted in the living magisterium of the Catholic Church.

---

†   **Editor's Note:** For a translation of selections from Cajetan's writings relevant to his engagement with incipient Lutheranism, see *Cajetan Responds: A Reader in Reformation Controversy*, ed. and trans. by Jared Wicks, S.J. (Washington, DC: The Catholic University of America Press, 1978).

* * *

Chapter V

The Equipment of Sacred Theology: Part I

A. The Theological Places. In the prosecution of its end, the clear and unequivocal statement of the meaning inherent in the divine revelation, sacred theology has at its disposal certain definite resources. According to the terminology of Melchior Cano, O.P., who wrote the first great scientific treatise on this particular portion of sacred doctrine,[1] these are commonly referred to as theological sources or "*loci theologici*." These are the forces which the theologian can utilize in forming conclusions which are seen as perfectly certain in the light of virtual or mediate revelation.

According to the teaching of Cano, which is still classical in this portion of sacred theology, these sources are ten in number:

1. The authority of Holy Scripture, which is contained in the canonical books.

2. The authority of the traditions of Christ and of the Apostles which, since they have not been written, but have come down to us orally, are rightly called oracles of the living voice.

3. The authority of the Catholic Church.

4. The authority of the Councils, especially of the general Councils.

5. The authority of the Roman Church, which is, and is called by divine privilege, apostolic.

6. The authority of the ancient Fathers.

7. The authority of the scholastic theologians, to whom the teachers of canon law are joined.

8. Natural reason, which appears in all of those sciences naturally acquired.

9. The authority of the philosophers who follow the natural light of human reason, and with them the masters of civil law.

10. The authority of human history, either written by trustworthy authors or expressed in serious national tradition.

Melchior Cano, in drawing up this list, adverted explicitly to the fact that sacred theology, unlike any other science naturally obtainable by man, makes its supreme appeal to authority rather than to the evidence of the matter with which it is concerned.[2] Obviously this fact must influence all of the procedure of sacred theology, and the choice of resources which are to be exploited in attaining the end to which this science is consecrated.

B. Classification. The divine message, which sacred theology sets out to teach accurately and clearly, is contained in Scripture and in tradition as in its proper sources. There is not, nor will there ever be, any portion of that public revelation which it is the

---

1.   Melchior Cano, O.P., *De Locis Theologicis.* The edition used in this work is the three volume set of the *Opera Omnia Melchioris Cani, Episcopi Canariensium, ex Ordine Praedicatorum,* issued at Rome in 1900.

2.   Liber I, Caput 2.

business of the theologian to express, that is not to be found in that collection of truth contained in Scripture and in tradition.

This divine message is taught and defended infallibly by the Catholic Church, both through its ordinary magisterium and in its solemn definitions and declarations. The organs of this solemn magisterium are the Holy Father, speaking *ex cathedra* and the various ecumenical councils of the Church. The Fathers of the Church, and the scholastic theologians who have been entrusted with the expression of her teaching are authentic witnesses and proponents of Catholic teaching, even though they are not individually endowed with infallibility.

In this way the first seven among the *loci theologici* enumerated by Melchior Cano are *proper* to this science. They do not pertain to the equipment of any other discipline available to mankind. The last three are *common* to theology and to other sciences as well. These are subsidiary instruments which, however, can and must be utilized in order to attain the purpose which is essential to sacred theology.

Each of the ten theological places contributes in its own way to the perfection of that process which we know as virtual or mediate revelation. Out of the radiance of all these sources there is fused the proper light of sacred theology. Naturally an introduction to the science must consider each of them individually.

I. THE SCRIPTURES IN SACRED THEOLOGY

A. The Inspired Writers and the Inspired Books. Sacred Scripture, or the Holy Bible consists of those authentic writings which enter into the Catholic Canon and are recognized by the Church as divinely inspired. These writings are divided into seventy-three books.[3] The first forty-six of these books constitute the Old Testament, written before the birth of Jesus Christ and containing that portion of divine public revelation which was given

---

3.   Cf. the Council of Trent, Session IV (Denzinger, 784).

to the world progressively in preparation for the coming of the Savior. The New Testament, written after the death of our Lord, and embodying a portion of His message, is composed of the final twenty-seven books.

In saying that the books of the Bible are *inspired*, we use the word *inspiration* in a special and highly technical sense. Such inspired works are actually written by God Himself. He is the principal Cause in the production of these volumes, and the human authors who have produced them have acted as instruments of God.[†] Pope Leo XIII, in his encyclical *Providentissimus Deus*, has described the process of inspiration and its effect in these words. "By His supernatural power He [the Holy Spirit], so aroused and moved them [the inspired writers] to write, and so was with them while they wrote, that they conceived correctly, wished to write faithfully, and aptly expressed with infallible truth all and only what he wished to have them do."[4]

The words of Pope Leo XIII indicate the formal effect of inspiration upon the person and the faculties of that man who has been chosen by God as His instrument in the production of a book which is to have God Himself as an Author. However the place which Scripture occupies in the schema of sacred theology is best understood when we look at the effects of inspiration in the inspired work itself. It is Catholic teaching that the content of the inspired book includes all that God willed should be written therein, and nothing else. It is in this sense that the book is ascribed to God as to its principal Cause.

[†]   **Editor's Note:** For more on the instrumental causality of the Scriptural authors, see John F. Boyle, "Authorial Intention and the *Divisio textus*," in *Reading John with St. Thomas Aquinas*, ed. Michael Dauphinais and Matthew Levering (Washington, DC: The Catholic University of America Press, 2005), pp. 3–8; Timothy Bellamah, O.P., "*Tunc scimus cum causas cognoscimus*: Some Medieval Endeavors to Know Scripture in Its Causes," in *Theology Needs Philosophy: Acting against Reason is Contrary to the Nature of God*, ed. Matthew L. Lamb (Washington, DC: The Catholic University of America Press, 2016), pp. 154–72.

4.   Denzinger, 1952.

B. The First Cause and the Principal Cause. Now, we must understand at once that when we say that God is the principal Cause of Holy Scripture, we do not mean merely that all of the movement and the activity by which these books were produced were derived ultimately from Him. We are aware, of course, that God is actually the First Mover of the Universe, First not merely in the order of time but really in the order of nature. As such he is the First Mover in every activity which takes place in the created universe. The very movement of the pen upon this paper as I write is something which comes from Him, here and now. A creature may cause the activity of other creatures, as I cause the motion of my pen. However, in every instance the creature who acts as a cause is himself moved in his very operation of causing. All movement comes from God. Every fiber and aspect of being, of truth and goodness and beauty must emanate from Him. He is the One upon whom every being distinct from Himself depends absolutely and entirely. He acts in the activity of every creature. This realization of the place of God as the First Cause of the universe is essential for a correct notion of the divinity.[†]

God is the *First Cause* of all things, but He is the *Principal Cause* and the Author of those books which compose the Holy Scripture. The notion of a first cause is quite distinct from that of a principal cause. The First Cause is, as we have seen, the source of all activity and goodness. It is the Pure Act, Subsistent Being Itself. The principal cause, on the other hand, is that which is adequate to the effect which is produced, or to be more exact, it is that to which the effect produced is proportioned and ascribed. Thus, while God is the First Cause of every effect which is brought into existence, a creature may truly be said to be the *principal* cause of some of these effects, in so far as these effects lie within the sphere of the creature's competence. Naturally, where a creature is said to be the

---

† **Editor's Note:** Fenton's original text says "for a correct motion of the divinity." This appears to be a typographical error, so the text has been adjusted here to say: "for a correct notion of the divinity."

principal cause of an effect, the word *principal* has no reference to the position of God in the performance of this activity. Every creature, in every portion of activity, real or possible, is subordinate with reference to God. The principal cause is so called with respect to another cause which is not adequate for the production of the effect which it really produces. Such a cause which moves and acts only in so far as it is moved by the principal cause toward the production of an effect which surpasses its natural powers is called an *instrumental cause.*

C. God the Author of the Inspired Books. Applying these definitions to the matter of Sacred Scripture, it is evident at once that the sacred books lie altogether outside the categories of ordinary literary works. As a rational animal, competent sensibly to express intellectual concepts, man is quite capable of writing books. Thus the ordinary book, even one which treats of God or which proposes revealed doctrine, is to be referred to man as to a principal cause. In the production of this book man utilizes instrumental causes, a pen or a pencil or a typewriter or even another person who is employed as an amanuensis. However, the finished volume is the message of this individual man, the author. It is a message which he is quite capable of delivering in virtue of the natural powers with which he is endowed.

Obviously, then, it would be exceedingly improper to refer to any ordinary book as one which has God Himself as an Author. Yet this is perfectly true of Holy Scripture. These books express a message which God Himself wishes to convey to mankind. Obviously it is beyond the natural power of any creature to act as the principal cause in the expression of a divine document. What is conveyed, for example, in the gospel according to St. John, is exactly what God wished to propose to the children of men just as truly as what is contained in the *Summa Theologica* is the teaching which was expressed and given to the world by St. Thomas Aquinas. God is, then, the Author and the Principal Cause of the books of Holy Scripture just as really as Peter the Lombard is the author and the principal cause of the *Four Books of Sentences.*

D. The Human Instruments in the Writing of the Inspired Books. The inspired books had also, of course, their human authors. Sts. Matthew, Mark, Luke, and John all wrote the gospels ascribed to them just as truly and actually as any other men ever wrote the volumes which have appeared as their own. Unlike other authors, however, these men and the other inspired writers wrote the books of Sacred Scripture precisely as instruments of God.

Yet it is perfectly true that these men did not write merely in the capacity of stenographers, setting down material which had come to them by way of simple dictation. In His infinite wisdom and power, God is enabled to exercise a control over the intelligence and the will of man such as no creature can ever possibly possess. He alone can act and does act upon the spiritual faculties of man in such a way as infallibly to bring about the effect which He wills, while at the same time He causes rather than impedes or prevents the very freedom and spontaneity of human activity. In utilizing the sacred writers as His instruments in the production of the inspired books, God caused them to write as freely and spontaneously as any other men ever acted in the production of literary works. These inspired writers contributed as much toward the production of their books as any other men have ever contributed toward the writing of noninspired texts.

It would, then, be the ultimate in anthropomorphic confusion to imagine that God was in some way limited to the use of nonvital instruments in the production of the inspired books of Holy Scripture. The inspired writers chose what they wished to write, investigated their own material, and actually expressed what they wished to say. They employed those characteristics of style and composition which belonged to their own times and to their own peoples, as well as those qualities which were proper to them as individuals. But, in utilizing all of the resources of their own nature and of their own background, they were being moved by God, freely and infallibly to write books which presented the very message which He intended to communicate to men. With all the freedom and the perfection of their activity, they acted as instruments of the living God.

E. The Question of Verbal Inspiration. In the process of considering the place of Holy Scripture in the economy of sacred theology, it is pertinent to inquire whether the actual words which go to make up the books of the Bible were chosen by God or whether the message alone is from Him and the actual words which convey that message were chosen by the human authors, as competent to express the ideas involved in the message itself. In this latter supposition the choice of the individual words would have been made by the human authors under the direction of a divine assistance in some way distinct from the actual process of inspiration itself. This is the famous question on verbal inspiration, a question which has important repercussions in the field of theological methodology. On its resolution depends the use which must be made of Sacred Scripture in the production of the theological conclusion.

Teaching that inspiration itself does not extend to the choice of the individual words which enter into the text of Holy Scripture are such writers as Cardinal Franzelin,[5] Hurter,[6] Pesch,[7] Dorsch,[8] Felder,[9] Vacant,[10] and Egger.[11] Pesch goes so far as to speak of the opposite teaching as having been proposed, not only by early protestant writers, but even by theologians of the first class, as for example Bañez. He contends, however, that the doctrine which holds that the process of inspiration extends to the choice of the words which compose the text of the sacred books is rapidly losing ground. Egger considers his own thesis so strong that the opposite

5. Ioannes Cardinalis Franzelin, S.J., *Tractatus de Divina Traditione et Scriptura*, 4th ed. (Rome: 1896), pp. 322ff.

6. Hugo Hurter, S.J., S.T.D., Ph.D., *Theologia Generalis Complectens Disputationes Quatuor*, 2nd ed. (Innsbruck: 1878), thesis 27.

7. Christianus Pesch, S.J., *Institutiones Propaedeuticae ad Sacrum Theologiam*, 6th and 7th ed. (Freiburg im Breisgau: 1924), pp. 450ff.

8. Dorsch, *Institutiones Theologiae Fundamentalis*, Vol. 3, *De Inspiratione Sacrae Scripturae*, pp. 202–12.

9. Felder, *Apologetica sive Theologia Fundamentalis*, Vol. 1, pp. 298–301.

10. Vacant, *Études Théologiques sur les Constitutions du Concile du Vatican, La Constitution Dei Filius*, Vol. 1, p. 472.

11. Egger, *Enchiridion Theologiae Dogmaticae Generalis*, pp. 314–18.

doctrine is devoid of probability. However, this doctrine of verbal inspiration is found in the works of such modern writers as Mangenot,[12] Herrmann,[13] Schultes,[14] DeGroot,[15] Tanquerey,[16] Van Noort,[17] Hugon,[18] Diekamp,[19] Zubizarreta,[20] Bainvel,[21] and Hervé.[22] Actually it is the more common teaching in the schools despite the fact that as eminent a modern writer as Bartmann[23] opposed it and Berthier[24] refused to pass judgment on the matter.

The doctrine that the individual words as they stand in the text of Holy Scripture are inspired by God and thus chosen through the process of inspiration itself, is alone competent to explain the function of Scripture in the process of sacred theology. It is, moreover, the explanation which is clearly in harmony with the teachings of the Church, as manifested in *Providentissimus Deus* and elsewhere. Ultimately, of course, the books of Holy Scripture are the things inspired. Men are said to be inspired in so far as they are moved by God to write these books which have God Himself for an Author.

---

12. Mangenot, article *"Inspiration de l'Écriture"* in the *Dictionnaire de Théologie Catholique*, Vol. 7, columns 2192–2207. The position of Mangenot and of Bainvel is not as strong on this question as is that of other writers cited.

13. Herrmann, C.Ss.R., *Institutiones Theologiae Dogmaticae*, pp. 557–59.

14. Schultes, O.P., *De Ecclesia Catholica* (Paris: 1931), p. 528.

15. J. V. DeGroot, O.P., S.T.M., *Summa Apologetica De Ecclesia Catholica ad Mentem Sancti Thomae Aquinatis*, 3rd ed. (Regensburg: 1906), pp. 696–98.

16. Tanquerey, Vol. 1, *Synopsis Theologiae Dogmaticae Fundamentalis*, p. 770.

17. G. Van Noort, *Tractatus de Fontibus Revelationis necnon de Fide Divina*, 3rd ed. (Bussum, Holland: 1920), p. 47.

18. Edouard Hugon, O.P., S.T.M., *La Causalité Instrumentale dans l'Ordre Surnaturel*, 2nd ed. (Paris: 1924), pp. 51–72. This is one of the best theological treatises on the matter in modern literature.

19. Diekamp, *Theologiae Dogmaticae Manuale*, pp. 38–41.

20. Zubizarreta, *Theologia Dogmatico-Scholastica*, pp. 483–85.

21. J. V. Bainvel, *De Scriptura Sacra* (Paris: 1910), pp. 133–34.

22. Hervé, *Manuale Theologiae Dogmaticae*, pp. 592–93.

23. Monsignor Bernard Bartmann, *Précis de Théologie Dogmatique*, translated from the 8th German edition by Marcel Gauthier, 2nd French edition (Mulhouse, France: 1935), p. 39.

24. Joachim Joseph Berthier, O.P., *Tractatus de Locis Theologicis* (Turin: 1900), p. 80.

If the concepts and the judgments expressed in the books of Holy Scripture had come by way of inspiration while the words by which they are externally expressed had not been chosen through this process, it would be very difficult to see how the book itself could be called inspired. There is a world of difference between the part played in the production of a book by the man who is responsible for most of the ideas expressed in the book and that of the man who actually writes the volume itself. Boswell wrote his *Life of Johnson*, in order to publicize the ideas of the great lexicographer. But, although the ideas which fill the book are those of Johnson, no one would attempt to claim that he was the author of the book in which these ideas are expressed.

One could never be called properly the author of a book when he merely conveys certain teachings to another and then leaves to his associate the task of selecting the words in which these doctrines are to be expressed. If a man should claim authorship of such a document, the modern American would say that he had made use of a "ghost writer." This sharp Americanism, with its wealth of contemporary connotation, should be of some service to the theologian in demonstrating or illustrating the inadequacy of any doctrine which claims that God is the Author of the books of Holy Scripture and then denies verbal inspiration. A person is actually the author of a book only when he has conceived what he is to write, has decided to write it, and has then given external verbal expression to the concepts which he desires to communicate.

There are opponents of the doctrine of verbal inspiration who have professed to see in it a certain trace of anthropomorphic error. They conceive of verbal revelation as involving a process in which God would speak orally to the sacred writer while this latter merely set down on paper the words which he had heard God dictating to Him. This concept of the doctrine of verbal inspiration is a sort of straw man set up for polemic purposes exclusively, since no proponent of the traditional teaching ever advances any such explanation of his doctrine. It is true, however, that Bañez, to whom Pesch refers, actually makes use of the term *dictate* in explaining the process by which God produces the books of which He is the Author.[25] So does Francis Sylvius,[26] and so, for that matter does Pope Leo XIII in *Providentissimus Deus*.[27]

There is nothing misleading or anthropomorphic about the term itself. Considered in its formal meaning, as it enters into a statement objectively describing the process of inspiration, the term *dictation* signifies an operation by which a person can become the author of a document or book in utilizing another person as an instrumental cause. This is, of course, exactly what God has done in the production of the books of Sacred Scripture. The connotation of uttering words orally, and the limitation of instrumental activity to the bare material side of writing belong to the human rather than to the divine field of conduct. The whole context of the older writers, and most certainly the text of Pope Leo's encyclical show that such a connotation never entered into the traditional teaching on verbal inspiration. As a matter of fact, Sylvius and the writers with whom he is associated in his defense of the traditional teaching are at special pains to explain that all of the faculties and the spontaneity of the human writers enter into the composition of the inspired books. The essential point of their teaching is, however, that these human writers, acting freely, were moved by God to produce a book which brought to the children of men a message which He had conceived and thus a book of which He is properly the Author.

It is also a common practice of the opponents of verbal revelation to cite in favor of their own theses certain passages from the Fathers of the Church, distinguishing between the study of the words and the consideration of the meaning in the investigation of

25. Dominicus Bañez, O.P., *Scholastica Commentaria in Primam Partem Sancti Thomae Aquinatis* (Madrid and Valentia: 1934), commentary on the eighth article in the first question.

26. Franciscus Sylvius a Brania Comitis, *Controversiarum*, Liber I, q. 1, a. 3 (p. 150 in the edition of the *opuscula* edited at Antwerp in 1698 by Father Norbert D'Elbecque, O.P.).

27. Cf. Denzinger, 1951.

Holy Scripture. Invariably, however, we find that the texts cited, seen in their proper background, have no reference whatever to the problem of verbal inspiration. The sort of attention to the words of Holy Scripture which the Fathers compared unfavorably with a study of its meaning was obviously one which shut out any fruitful and properly theological consideration of the inspired text. It was, and for that matter it still is, perfectly possible for a man so to limit his attention to the poetic or the grammatical structure of the sacred books as to forget entirely the meaning conveyed in them. It was, and is still possible for men to attempt an explanation of these words contrary to that which is expressed in the living and infallible magisterium of the Catholic Church. This was the sort of word consideration against which the Fathers so justly protested.

At the same time, however, the Fathers and the common tradition which they expressed recognized clearly the divine authorship of the written words which composed the various books of the Bible. In their common way of citing the content of the Scriptures, the expression "It is written," they did not refer to any mere mental word, communicated by God to the mind of the inspired author. They meant the actual words written in the inspired books, words that men might read.

F. Revelation and Inspiration. For a proper understanding of Sacred Scripture as one of the theological places, it is absolutely requisite that we appreciate the distinction between revelation and inspiration. The act of revelation, considered formally, consists in God's speaking to man in such a way as to teach him. Considered in its objective meaning, it signifies the actual message or doctrine which God has communicated to man. This revelation, then, constitutes a body of truth which man has received from God in a way at once distinct from and superior to the natural manner in which man derives his knowledge. Revelation, then, involves the actual communication of truth not previously known by man.

Quite distinct from this is the concept of inspiration. As authentically described by Pope Leo XIII, inspiration involves the use of a man by God in the process of writing a book of divine authorship. The human writer who is inspired, who is used as an instrument by God in the production of one of those books which enters into the canon of Holy Scripture, need not necessarily have received by way of revelation those truths which are expressed in the book which he writes as the instrument of God. He may very well set down matters which he has known by purely natural means. Thus the writers of the historical books in both the Old and the New Testaments told of happenings which they had seen themselves or about which they might well have learned through conversation with actual eyewitnesses. The writers of the doctrinal or sapiential books might very well have set down material which was the common teaching among the faithful of their own time. Thus while no revelation would be made immediately to the inspired writers in setting down such truths, the books which they wrote as instruments of God naturally would convey a message to mankind at large.

Revelation and inspiration also differ by reason of the varying effects which they produce in the person who is acted upon by God. A man cannot, of course, receive a revelation from God without knowing very well that he is receiving a divine communication. However, it would be perfectly possible for a man to be utilized by God as an inspired instrument for the production of a book which has God Himself as an Author without knowing the resultant volume was really the work of God. If the book has God as an Author and contains something of that message which man must possess in order to attain the perfect happiness which should be his for all eternity, it is only requisite that mankind should know that this particular volume actually has God as an Author. This knowledge must, of course, come by way of revelation. However, it is quite evident that this revelation need not necessarily be made to the one who is employed by God as an instrument in the production of the inspired book.

As we have seen, the inspired writer need not receive any immediate revelation for the truths which he is to set down in the volume which he writes as an instrument of God. However, the one to whom an immediate revelation is made can receive this communication from God in many different ways. By virtue of His infinite power, God is able to speak immediately to man either by way of external objects or by acting directly upon the human cognitive faculties. In dealing with external things God can certainly make use of the oral or printed word, as well as other signs which are fitted accurately to convey to the recipient of the revelation the content of that message which God wishes to communicate. When God acts directly upon the cognitive faculties or powers of man, He can produce His effect either upon the senses, external or internal, or upon the intellect itself. Obviously when God chooses to act immediately upon man's intellect, neither the spoken nor the written word is employed in the process.

When God wishes to have the recipient of an immediate revelation communicate the divine message to the rest of mankind, the choice of words in which this message is to be expressed is not necessarily involved in the revelation itself. But, when that revealed message is expressed in one of the books of Holy Scripture, then the very words in which the message is conveyed are selected according to the process of inspiration which brought about the production of a book which has God as its Author. Thus the characteristics which the opponents of verbal inspiration predicate of the process of inspiration itself are actually verified when they are applied to a noninspired exposition of revealed truth to the children of men.

G. Infallibility of Holy Scripture. Precisely because they have God as an Author who has selected the actual words of which they are composed the books of Holy Scripture are absolutely free of error.[†] Obviously the presence of any mistake, even the least consequential, in the pages of Holy Writ, would be directly contrary to the infinite wisdom and veracity of God. As a result, the theologian has at his disposal a group of infallible documents which convey some of that divine message which it is his business to express

---

†   **Editor's Note:** For a more recent examination of this and related topics, see David P. Bolin, "On the Inerrancy of Scripture," *The Aquinas Review*, Vol. 8, No. 1 (2001): pp. 23–178.

and teach with unequivocal perfection. Those books which God Himself has written, which manifest the truth which God Himself wishes the world to know, express the content of the Christian message accurately, although they by no means express all of it.

H. Scripture Explained by the Church. Although the text of Sacred Scripture, as a volume of which God Himself is the Author, stands as absolutely free from error, it is unfortunately possible to use and explain that text erroneously. Moreover, some parts of Holy Scripture are, according to the testimony of the inspired writings themselves, quite difficult to understand and interpret. However, God has chosen to present these books to the world at the hands of a qualified teacher which alone is competent infallibly to explain the message conveyed on the inspired pages. That infallible teacher is the Catholic Church. As a result, Holy Scripture is utilized correctly by the theologian when it is explained in terms of that objective meaning which its divine Author attached to it, and which is expressed in the unerring magisterium of the Catholic Church. The meaning which the Church predicates of one or another passage in Holy Scripture is not to be looked upon as an outside interpretation of a document which is in some measure common property. It is not one of the many possible accurate interpretations of the inspired pages. Actually it is the statement of that meaning which God the Author gave to the message which He conveyed upon the inspired pages. It is one which the theologian must utilize for his correct interpretation of the revealed truth.

So complete is the supervision over the matter of Sacred Scripture with which the Catholic Church has been endowed by God that it is her duty and prerogative to assert which books have actually been inspired by God. Only through the divine and public revelation with which she is entrusted could it be known that books like the Epistle of St. Jude, for example, were inspired while others were not. Furthermore, it is the duty and the prerogative of the Church to watch over the various translations which are made of the inspired writings. Thus she accepts as authentic and useful, not only for preaching but for scientific theological disputation, the ancient Latin version of the Bible which we know as the Vulgate. She forbids any one to reject it.

I. The Use of Sacred Scripture in Theology. The theologian, then, is expected to utilize Sacred Scripture for the attainment of his own purpose. It consists of a set of documents containing a message which has come from God, a message which He has expressed in a book which comes from Him to the children of men. In the same sense that an ordinary book contains what some author wishes to say to the world, the books of which God is the Author obviously contain what God Himself wishes the world to accept as His teaching. Although the Bible by no means contains the entirety of the divine message which God intends to have accepted by all men, it differs from the other agency in which that message is contained in that as the very terms in which the doctrine is expressed are chosen by God. The Bible is thus one of the resources at the disposal of sacred theology. It is properly also a source of divine revelation. The teaching which it contains is that which comes from God as His message. It is not merely the divinely guided interpretation of that message.

In the investigation of these sacred books, according to the living and ever available magisterium of the Catholic Church, lies the great triumph of sacred theology. The man who begins the study of the sacred doctrine will advance more perfectly in so far as he is aware of this. Thus, for example, the scientific perfection of that portion of the *Summa Theologica* which deals with the processions and the relations in God can be seen in all of its beauty and in all the perfect profundity of its meaning only when a man realizes that it is meant to explain the significance of the words of our Lord, contained in the Gospel according to St. John. "I have come forth from God."[28]

---

28. John 16:28. **Editor's Note:** For more on Aquinas's doctrine of the Trinity in relation to the Gospel of John, see Gilles Emery, O.P., "Biblical Exegesis and the Speculative Doctrine of the Trinity in St. Thomas Aquinas's *Commentary on John*," in *Reading John with St. Thomas Aquinas*, ed. Michael Dauphinais and Matthew Levering (Washington, DC: The Catholic University of America Press, 2005), pp. 23–61.

II. Divine Apostolic Tradition

The second among the theological places is, like Holy Scripture itself, also a source of divine public revelation. It is the only other point at which we may look for the teaching which God has given to the world through Jesus Christ. In other words, all that God put into that revelation which He wills that all men should accept in order to attain the only eternal and perfect felicity which is available to them is contained either upon the inspired pages of Holy Scripture or in the divine apostolic tradition itself.

A. Traditions Within the Church. This divine apostolic tradition is the unwritten teaching of the apostolic college, the doctrine which they taught and presented to the Church as having been the message of our Lord Himself, and thus divinely revealed to man. The standard theologians of the Catholic Church recognize, as distinct from this divine apostolic tradition, certain other traditions which are merely apostolic and others again which are merely ecclesiastical. The merely apostolic tradition is teaching given to the Church by the Apostles themselves, either individually or collectively. It is, however, doctrine which the Apostles offered precisely on their own authority, as the first teachers within the Church of God. The ancient ecclesiastical traditions come from early leaders within the Church, but again they rest upon the authority of those leaders alone. They are not offered as having been taught by Jesus Christ as a part of that divine message which all men are called upon to accept with the assent of divine faith. The divine apostolic tradition differs from these in that it was given to the Church by the Apostles precisely as expressing the content of divine public revelation.

B. The Priority of Tradition to the New Testament Books. For the first few years in the life of the Catholic Church, this divine apostolic tradition was the only source from which the characteristically Christian teachings, defended and propounded by that Church, were available to men. The first of those inspired books included in the New Testament did not make its appearance until the Church had been in existence for more than a decade. The

other books which go to make up the New Testament were written
before the end of the first century. However, all of these books
expressed the then existent fund of divine tradition, although, of
course, from time to time, truths which had not hitherto been
communicated to man were set forth upon the sacred pages. No
one of these books claimed, singularly or collectively, to express the
entire content of Christian revelation. Actually, as is the case in St.
Paul's Second Epistle to Timothy, they pointed to an already existing and well-known deposit of divine apostolic tradition.[29]

**C. The Existence of Divine Apostolic Tradition as a Source
of Revelation Distinct from Sacred Scripture.** It is of faith that
not all of the public revelation which God has given to the world
is actually expressed and contained on the pages of Sacred Scripture. For example, the truths of the Immaculate Conception and
of the perpetual virginity of Our Lady form a part of the content
of Christian revelation, although they are not taught explicitly in
any inspired book. Those truths which constitute this *unwritten
tradition* enter into the rule of faith in the same way as does Sacred
Scripture itself. Like the revealed truths set down on the inspired
pages of the Bible, these unwritten verities are infallibly taught,
guarded, propounded, and explained by the Catholic Church. Like
the truths contained in Sacred Scripture, these facts which are stated in divine apostolic tradition are to be defended and expressed in
the science of sacred theology.

D. The Unwritten Tradition. Naturally the theologian must
know where to find those truths which are contained in the divine
apostolic tradition. They are said to be unwritten merely in the
sense that they are not proposed on the pages of inspired Scripture.
However, they have been committed to writing in noninspired
works long ago. We can find this tradition expressed in the works
of the Fathers, in the documents of the councils, and in the formularies of faith adopted and utilized by the Catholic Church. A

---

29. "Hold the form of sound words, which thou hast heard of me in faith" (2
     Timothy 1:13).

doctrine can be recognized as a component part of this oral tradition when a moral unanimity among the Fathers who deal with this matter set down as something which has been revealed to the world by God through Jesus Christ our Lord, a truth which is not conveyed in the inspired words of Sacred Scripture.

What the Fathers and the councils mention as the content of Catholic faith naturally includes all of the truth which has been brought to the world through our Lord. That portion of this public revelation which has always been proposed as such by the Catholic Church, but which is not contained in inspired Scripture constitutes the body of truth which is taught and is to be sought in the divine and apostolic tradition. Naturally this body of doctrine includes the authentic interpretation of those truths which are conveyed in Scripture itself. The sense or meaning of the Scriptures is something which the Church has possessed from the very beginning. The Scriptures would be useless as a practical rule of faith apart from the divine and apostolic tradition by which they are explained and understood. But with the Scripture, this tradition constitutes the great source in which all of the truth which is to be expounded in the process of sacred theology is contained.

* * *

Chapter VI

The Equipment of Sacred Theology: Part II

III. THE CATHOLIC CHURCH

Only the first two among the theological places are spoken of as sources of divine public revelation. All of those truths which Christians accept on the word of God who has revealed them are either set down on the inspired pages of Holy Scripture or contained in that deposit of doctrine which constitutes the teaching which the Apostles gave orally to the Church as having been communicated by God to man. The Scriptures and the divine apostolic tradition are the agencies through which the divine revelation has actually come to the human race. The message which God gave to the world through Jesus Christ is to be found only in these as in its proper sources.

A. The Function of the Church as Compared with That of Scripture and Tradition. The next among the theological places, according to the listing of Melchior Cano, fulfills a different function in the process of sacred theology. Scripture and tradition contain divine revelation. The Catholic Church teaches and defends it. Scripture and tradition together constitute a definite rule of faith, but one which is mediate and remote. The living magisterium of

the Catholic Church, on the other hand, constitutes an immediate
or proximate rule of faith. It is an agency through which men may
have presented to them the actual content of divine revelation, in
such a way that they may be preserved from error and accept all
and only that which God has actually revealed in His public message to men. The Church is the one divinely appointed force by
which the truths contained in Scripture and tradition are to be
proposed correctly to the minds of men.

Because the Church has a different function with regard to revelation than that exercised by Scripture and tradition, there follow
certain consequences of importance for understanding the role of
the magisterium of the Church in the process of sacred theology.
The canon of Sacred Scripture is closed once and for all. There never will be another book included in the Holy Bible. Furthermore,
the content of the divine apostolic tradition was, of course, closed
with the death of the last Apostle. Since that time there has not
been, nor will there ever be, another truth communicated by God
to man as something which all men must accept with the assent of
divine faith.

However, the Catholic Church, the infallible defender and
proponent of the divine revelation, will go on until the end of time
in the successful accomplishment of her task of bringing this divine
teaching to the children of men. She will take that body of truth
which is expressed in Scripture and in divine apostolic tradition,
resolve correctly the problems which arise about its interpretation,
and unerringly condemn the teaching which denies or misjudges
revealed truth. Hers is a magisterium, a teaching office, unique in
the history of mankind.

B. The Constitution of the Church. Naturally the teaching
function of the Catholic Church is exercised in accordance with the
constitution which this divinely instituted society received from its
Founder. The Church is a real and definitely visible society which
Jesus Christ our Lord founded while He lived upon this earth. He
founded this society by first of all gathering the first members and
then organizing them properly for the attainment of an end which

He pointed out to them. The men chosen by Jesus Christ as the first members of the Church and the bearers of the organization to their fellow men were the Apostles.

Our Lord established the Catholic Church as an hierarchical and monarchical society. Its visible head in this world is the Bishop of Rome who, as the successor of St. Peter, the prince of the Apostles, is the Vicar of Christ. Under his direction the bishops, who are the successors of the Apostles, govern and instruct the churches confided to their care. These bishops, with the priests and ministers subject to them, take the active part in the great work of sanctification which is proper to the Church and constitute as such the hierarchy of orders.

The members of this Church are those possessors of the baptismal character who have not broken the bond of ecclesiastical unity by heresy, apostasy, or schism and who have not been expelled from the society through the incurring of the fullness of excommunication. Only these are actually members of the Catholic Church. Occasionally in our own times there have been misunderstandings about the nature of membership within this organization, misunderstandings engendered by a faulty use and explanation of the term "soul of the Church." The soul of the Church is not a kind of organization, in some way distinct from the "body of the Church," which is the visible organization of the Catholic society. Actually the Soul of the Church is God the Holy Spirit. Those said to belong to the soul of the Church are those who are in the state of habitual grace, who enjoy that friendship of God which they could not possess without at least intending to pertain as members to the organization which our Lord instituted for the salvation of men.

C. The Two Ways in Which the Church Teaches Infallibly. Now, this visible Catholic Church teaches the content of divine revelation infallibly in two distinct ways. First there is the solemn magisterium, the solemn definition or declaration which the Church may propose. Such a solemn declaration or definition takes place when the Roman Pontiff speaks *ex cathedra*, utilizing the fullness of his power in teaching the universal Church on matters of faith or morals, or when an ecumenical council together with and subject to the same Roman Pontiff speaks definitively to the entire Church on the matter of public revelation.

The second way in which the Church can teach infallibly that doctrine which was revealed to the world through Jesus Christ our Lord is through the processes of her ordinary magisterium. This ordinary magisterium or teaching office is exercised in the continuous daily instruction given in the Church throughout the world, by the competent authorities of the Church. These competent authorities are the bishops, each in his own territory and united under the supreme leadership of the Roman Pontiff.[†] The bishops carry on this instruction personally as well as through the priests and the other qualified teachers subject to them.[1]

D. The Teaching Church. Thus the Holy Father and the other bishops of the Catholic Church, in communion with and subject to him, constitute the *ecclesia docens*, the teaching Church. The priests who preach and instruct in the various parishes, and in the schools, seminaries, and the universities of the Church exercise their ministry precisely as helpers to the bishops and as carrying on in a work which is entrusted to the bishops in their capacity as pastors of souls. All of the other members of the Church, that is those below the grade of bishop, constitute the *ecclesia discens* that is the Church which learns or is instructed.

The individual bishop, of course, is not endowed with the prerogative of personal infallibility. It is possible for him to teach

---

[†]   **Editor's Note:** For more on Aquinas's teaching on the episcopacy, see Michael G. Sirilla, *The Ideal Bishop: Aquinas's Commentaries on the Pastoral Epistles* (Washington, DC: The Catholic University of America Press, 2017).

1.   The ordinary magisterium is the continuous and, as it were, positive exposition of divine revelation which the Church has conducted from the moment it began its corporate activity. The solemn judgment, on the other hand, is a decision by which the Church settles some problem which has arisen about the meaning inherent in this divine message, a decision made either by the Holy Father speaking *ex cathedra* or by an ecumenical council. Cf. the [First] Vatican Council, the Constitution *Dei Filius* (Denzinger, 1792), and the commentary in Vacant, *Études Théologiques sur les Constitutions du Concile du Vatican, La Constitution Dei Filius*, Vol. 2, pp. 84–89.

erroneously on matters of faith and morals. He can assert that some doctrine has been revealed by God through Jesus Christ when, as a matter of fact, the teaching was not a part of the divine message at all. On the other hand, it is possible for him to deny the divine origin or the truth of a statement which actually forms a part of the deposit of divine public revelation. Furthermore, he can misconstrue or misstate dogmatic formulas which are indicative of the content of that revelation.

However, the episcopal college considered corporately and in union with the Vicar of Christ on earth actually is endowed with infallibility. When the *ecclesia docens* as a whole proposes a statement as something which has been communicated by God to man as a part of public revelation, then there is no possibility of a mistake. In this ordinary universal teaching the infallibility which belongs to the Catholic Church as such is actually exercised.

E. The Ordinary Magisterium. As a matter of fact this ordinary and universal magisterium has been the means by which many of the heresies which have attacked the faith of Jesus Christ during the course of the centuries have been recognized and destroyed. It was this teaching which quelled the threats of Sabellianism, Montanism, and Pelagianism, to mention only a few. Even in the numerous cases where the Church has spoken in solemn judgment and definition, the heresy or evil which she had set out to eradicate had long since been recognized as such in the competent teaching of the universal episcopate.

In the listing of Melchior Cano's *De Locis Theologicis*, each of the two organs of the Church's solemn magisterium is recognized and treated as a distinct theological place. The explanation of the infallible teaching activity of the Church as such, together with the manifestations of that activity which are peculiar to the ordinary magisterium, falls under the heading of the third among the theological places.

We must understand clearly that the expressions of the ordinary magisterium of the Church which the theologian has at his disposal fall under many different headings. This teaching is to be found in the liturgical prayers of the Catholic Church, in the great symbols or formularies which state the essentials of her belief, in her canonical decisions, in the doctrine of the approved catechisms and texts of sacred theology, in the pastoral instructions of the bishops, and, of course, in those pontifical documents in which the Holy Father does not choose to use the fullness of his apostolic power in teaching revealed truth to the children of men. In all of these fashions the teaching of the universal episcopate comes to the *ecclesia discens*. All are resources which can and should be exploited by the theologian for the accomplishment of his task. These must enter into the scheme of studies of the theologian in order that he may possess the erudition and training so requisite for the attainment of his purpose.

F. The Prayer of the Church. The authentic liturgical prayers and practices of the Catholic Church are, of course, infallibly expressive of the content of divine public revelation. Prayer is essentially the petition of fitting things from God. The fitting things which are asked of God in prayer constitute our own ultimate and supernatural end and those benefits which can and should be of service to us in the attainment of that end. Because they pertain to the supernatural order, that is, to the category of those things which are intrinsically and essentially beyond the competence of any created nature as such, the only authentic information about these fitting things is contained in the doctrine which God has revealed to the world through Jesus Christ our Lord. God has told us about the nature, the possibility, and the efficacy of our prayers as well as about their direction and object. Finally, the standard upon which all the petitions of the Catholic Church are based is the formula which our Lord Himself taught to His Apostles, the Lord's Prayer.

As a result the content of those petitions which the Church, the mystical body of Christ, makes to God is an expression of the revealed doctrine itself.[2] The petition asks for those things which we hope to possess through the merciful omnipotence of God. The

---

2.   Cf. Fenton, *The Theology of Prayer*, p. 146.

things for which we hope are precisely those about which we are informed in that doctrine which we accept with the assent of divine faith. Since it is the infallible Church of Jesus Christ which offers the prayers and which therefore teaches the content of the faith in the formulas of those petitions, the official or liturgical prayers of the Catholic Church unerringly express the content of divine public revelation. For, after all, the act of prayer is expressed, not for the benefit of God, but precisely for the benefit of those human beings in whose favor the act of prayer has been instituted and integrated into the religion of Jesus Christ. It is expressed for the benefit of man in so far as man, through an appreciation of the formulae in which the petitions of prayer are manifested, may come to realize the object of his own hope.

As a result, the theologian can accept as the product of the ordinary magisterium of the Catholic Church the liturgical formulae and directions. He can accept those prayers as infallible indications of the meaning conveyed by Jesus Christ in the message which He gave to mankind as divinely revealed truth. Such prayers belong to the Church as a whole, and definitely proceed from the universal magisterium.

G. The Symbols. The symbols or creeds in which, from the earliest years of her existence, the Catholic Church has expressed the elements of her divine message must be received as infallible utterances of the universal Church. There are many of these authentic acts of the Catholic faith in existence. Some of them, as a matter of fact, are in common use in the devotional and liturgical life of the Church. One of these symbols is that ancient profession of faith which we know as the Apostles' Creed. Another is the Creed of the First Council of Nicaea, and still another the closely related Creed of the First Council of Constantinople, which is sung and recited at the Mass.

In the breviary and in the rite for the process of exorcism, the Catholic Church makes use of that magnificent formula which is known as the Athanasian Creed. There are available, furthermore, the Anti-Priscillianist symbol, sometimes called the "*Fides Damasi*," the creed of Toledo, the profession of faith of the Council of Trent and in more recent times the anti-modernist oath. All of these are at the disposal of the theologian as infallible statements of the universal Church on the content of divine revelation.

H. Catechisms and Authoritative Theological Manuals. Catechisms and other approved books of Christian doctrine, in so far as they are adopted by the ordinaries of the various dioceses for teaching the content of the faith to the people of these dioceses, may be said to express the ordinary magisterium of the Catholic Church. Naturally, of course, not all of these catechisms have equal value in declaring the content of God's message. Some of them have had a very restricted use. Others, like the old standard *Baltimore Catechism* in our own country, have really been important factors in teaching the faith to the Catholics of an entire nation. Others again, like the *Roman Catechism* or the *Catechism of the Council of Trent* have had world-wide popularity and use. The unanimous teaching of these catechisms can rightly be considered by the theologians as an indication of the ordinary and universal magisterium of the Catholic Church. The doctrine that is universally or unanimously proposed in these doctrinal books, in such a way that it is presented to practically all of the Catholics of the world as revealed truth, is certainly a verity taught and exposed infallibly in the ordinary and universal magisterium of the Catholic Church.[†]

Another class of books closely associated with the catechisms in expressing the content of the Church's ordinary magisterium is the theological manual or monograph. Those which are adopted and utilized officially in the training of candidates for the priesthood within the Catholic Church have naturally more authority along this line than others. In so far as they are adopted and utilized by the episcopate, they may be said to express the teaching of the bishops about the matters they treat. To this extent, the manuals and the monographs of sacred theology may be said to express in

---

[†]   **Editor's Note:** Of course, Fenton wrote this book before St. John Paul II's 1992 promulgation of the *Catechism of the Catholic Church.*

some way the ordinary magisterium of the Church.[†] The authority of the Scholastic theologians actually constitutes a separate and distinct theological place. However, the theological works to which we made allusion must also be considered in their place as manifestations of the teaching of the bishops throughout the world. In this light they appear as manifesting in some way the ordinary magisterium of the Catholic Church. In this way the testimony of the entire body of theological works utilized by the bishops of a country or, *a fortiori* of the world, to the effect that this certain statement is contained in the deposit of faith is good evidence that such is the doctrine of the universal episcopate, or at least of those bishops who authorize the use of these textbooks.

I. Hierarchical Instructions and Allocutions. Naturally the doctrine taught commonly in the pastoral instructions of the bishops, in the diocesan synods, and in the plenary and the provincial councils falls under the heading of the ordinary magisterium of the Catholic Church. So, too, do the letters and the allocutions of the Roman Pontiff in which he does not choose to exercise the fullness of his apostolic power. Likewise the rescripts and the decisions of the various Roman congregations, both in matters of doctrine and of discipline. This same ordinary magisterium is expressed in the ordinary preaching from the Catholic pulpit and even in the nontechnical Catholic writings on religion and spirituality. Obviously these nontechnical writings have considerably less influence in expressing the ordinary magisterium of the Church than have those works which are actually utilized in the course of Christian instruction. A lesser degree of competence is expected, and, unfortunately, far too frequently found in the writers of such nontechnical works.

J. The *Ecclesia Discens*. The effects of this ordinary magisterium of the Catholic Church are to be found in the *ecclesia discens* itself. For this reason many of the theologians of the Church have

---

[†] **Editor's Note:** For a recent reconsideration of the manual tradition, see Brian Besong, "Reappraising the Manual Tradition," *American Catholic Philosophical Quarterly*, Vol. 89, No. 4 (2015): pp. 557–84.

appealed to the faithful themselves several times in the course of
Christian history in favor of the correct interpretation of Catholic
doctrine. For example, St. Augustine was able to point out triumphantly that the teaching of the Pelagian heretics ran counter to
the Christian convictions of the faithful themselves.[3] Naturally no
one would claim that the *ecclesia discens* has an authority distinct or
separate from that of the Church teaching. Its authority, its competence to recognize the true interpretation of the Christian message and to repudiate a denial or misconception of this teaching is
simply an effect produced within the membership of the Church
by the doctrinal work of the hierarchy itself. The *ecclesia discens* is
very definitely not something to which the theologian might appeal against any pronouncement of the ecclesiastical hierarchy. As a
matter of fact, it has no active or positive authority in the doctrinal
line whatsoever. It is cited by the theologians of the Church as it
was long ago by St. Augustine, simply to show that some doctrine,
proposed by an innovator, is in obvious contradiction to the tenets
of that faith which the Christian people have ever received from
their competent authorities.

K. The Field Upon Which the Church Can Teach Infallibly.
It is essential for the theologian to realize that this living and continuous teaching of the Catholic Church which he is able to utilize for
the correct interpretation of the message of Jesus Christ is exercised
primarily and essentially on the content of that message. In whatever field the pronouncements of the Catholic Church may fall, the
primary intent of her teaching is always to propound the content
of the divine public revelation. It is her divinely given commission
to guard the content of God's revelation faithfully and well, and to
teach it infallibly to the children of men until the end of time.

The process of guarding and teaching the doctrine which Jesus
Christ proposed to the world as divinely revealed involves not only

---

3.   Cf. St. Augustine, *Contra Iulianum*, Liber I, Caput 31; *Opus Imperfectum Contra
     Iulianum*, Liber II, Caput 2. There is an excellent explanation of this point in
     Thomas Stapleton, *Principiorum Fidei Doctrinalium Demonstratio Methodica*,
     Liber VII, Caput 17.

decisions about the meaning of this message, but also resolutions which have to do with the fields of sciences other than sacred theology, declarations about what are known as dogmatic facts, and the decisions which are incidental to the canonization of a saint or the approval of a religious order. In all of these fields the Church is able to speak infallibly in line with her essential and central task of declaring the content of divine public revelation. This extensive competence of the Catholic Church guarantees the theologian a living and perfectly available standard by which to judge the proper meaning which is contained in the message of Jesus Christ.

The domain in which the Church is competent to speak infallibly, then, is exactly coextensive with the field of sacred theology itself. The Church proposes and explains the content of the divine message as a whole. She explains the significance of the dogmatic formulae in which that message is expressed in two ways. First of all she acts positively and sets forth the true meaning, the doctrine which has actually been contained in the authentic sources of divine revelation. Again she may act in a negative manner, in condemning or reproving a statement as a misinterpretation or a denial of Christ's teaching.

In other words, the Church is perfectly competent to deal, not only with truths already defined as having been revealed by God, but also with those verities which are set forward merely as true theological conclusions. She can, if she wishes, take the very terminology of the theological conclusion as it stands in the writings of an individual author, and then utilize this terminology in order to define clearly and unequivocally a truth which has been revealed by God. She has actually followed that procedure in the case of St. Thomas Aquinas[4] and Peter the Lombard.[5] On the other hand, she can condemn as heretical or erroneous certain theses which

---

4.   Compare the text of the [First] Vatican Council, the Constitution *Dei Filius*, Chap. 2 (Denzinger, 1786), on the necessity of revelation with the terminology of St. Thomas Aquinas in *ST* I, q. 1, a. 1.

5.   The Fourth Council of the Lateran employed the terminology of Peter the Lombard explicitly in its declaration of faith in the Blessed Trinity (Denzinger, 432).

other men have put forward as theological conclusions or even as theological opinions, as she did with the theses of Jansenius[6] and Fenelon.[7] The important point for the theologian to remember is this. The Catholic Church enjoys a competence and an infallibility with reference to the theological conclusion as such. She can accept or reject a statement precisely as a theological conclusion rather than as a definition or a definitive resolution on matters of faith. She can state that a proposition is acceptable precisely as a theological conclusion, and she can act in this way utilizing the infallibility with which she has been endowed by her divine Founder.

Because she is empowered and commissioned to expound infallibly the content of Holy Scripture, the Church is competent to teach unerringly about theses which pertain primarily to sciences other than sacred theology. Thus she can condemn a theory or an hypothesis advanced, let us say, by an anthropologist or an astronomer if this theory contradicts the doctrine advanced in Holy Scripture. She can reprove a statement put forward in the name of economics or sociology when such a statement involves a denial or a misinterpretation of revealed truth.

The Church is aware that in the Bible there are statements which, while they contribute to the integrity of the revealed message found in Holy Scripture, yet have implications in the direction of other fields of learning. This eruditional, historical, or scientific matter is, of course, not her primary concern. Her primary and essential purpose is to guard and expound the revelation which God has given to the world through Jesus Christ. Part of that revelation, however, is to the effect that the books of Sacred Scripture are inspired by God and that as a result it is absolutely immune from error. Consequently it is in the line of the Church's power and

---

6. The five errors contained in the book *Augustinus*, by Cornelius Jansenius, were condemned by Pope Innocent X in the Constitution *Cum Occasione* of May 31, 1653 (Denzinger, 1092–96).

7. Twenty-three errors taken from the book *Explications des Maximes des Saints sur la Vie Intérieure*, by Fenelon, were condemned by Pope Innocent XII in the Brief *Cum Alias* of March 11, 1699 (Denzinger, 1327–49).

duty to warn her children against untruths which contradict the teachings of Holy Scripture, even if these untruths are put forward in the name of some secular science. The fact of the matter is that, since one truth cannot contradict another, any statement which contradicts the content of Holy Scripture, as this is authentically and infallibly set forth in the magisterium of the Church, is false. In denouncing the error, the Church does a favor to the profane science which is dedicated to the cause of truth. The Church can recognize and denounce a statement which contradicts the evidence of Sacred Scripture even when such a statement has not an immediate religious connotation.

L. Dogmatic Facts. The theologian has also at his disposal the authority of the Church on the matter of what are called *dogmatic facts*. These are actions, circumstances, or conditions attendant upon or connected with the teaching of divine revelation in such a way that the revelation itself could not be taught properly apart from the knowledge of the facts. Thus, for example, when the posthumous book *Augustinus*, by Cornelius Jansenius, made its appearance in 1640, and met with ecclesiastical censure and condemnation, the partisans of Jansenius taught that, while the condemned propositions listed as having been taken from the book in question actually were false, still they had never been written by the author or contained in the book, at least with the meaning which the Church attached to them in condemning them.[†] In 1656 and again in 1664 the Church, through the constitutions of Pope Alexander VII, declared infallibly that the five propositions had been condemned in that sense in which they had been intended by Jansenius himself, and furthermore that the propositions had been expressed in the *Augustinus* in the same sense as that for which they had been reproved by the Church.[8]

---

† **Editor's Note:** For a recent study of the controversy surrounding the *Augustinus* of Jansenius, see Sylvio Hermann De Franceschi, *Entre saint Augustin et saint Thomas: Les jansénistes et le refuge thomiste (1653–1663): à propos des 1ᵉ, 2ᵉ et 18ᵉ Provinciales* (Paris: Classiques Garnier, 2017).

8.   Denzinger, 1099.

These dogmatic facts lie within the competence of the infallible teaching of the Catholic Church precisely because the Church could not exercise the primary and essential function which God has assigned to her without the power of judging infallibly about circumstances connected with the actual proposition of revealed truth. The very fact that she possesses and actually exercises infallible authority in teaching about these dogmatic facts is an excellent indication of the nature of that magisterium which the Church enjoys in the exposition of revealed doctrine. She is not sent merely to superintend the teaching of a dead and remote message. Her authority is over instruction in a living doctrine, a body of truth which is addressed to the minds of all men. She can judge that truth, not merely in so far as it appears on the consecrated texts of her own inspired books. She can recognize, guard, and propound this teaching as it appears on the pages of any document at any time.

M. The Approval of Religious Orders and the Canonization of Saints. Not only can she recognize and guard the divine teaching which has been entrusted to her care when that teaching appears on the pages of doctrinal works, but the Church is competent to judge about the truths which she is commissioned to teach in the matter of approving religious orders and canonizing saints. The message entrusted to the care of the Catholic Church is a doctrine of perfection. It tells of the way in which a man may advance in perfection by loving God ever more and more efficaciously. Consequently the Church is quite competent to decide that this particular rule or constitution is fitted to engender and increase Christian perfection in the souls of those who are to live under its direction. Furthermore, she can judge competently that this particular man whom she raises to the honors of the altar as a saint has actually directed his life successfully in accordance with the precepts of that revealed message which she is commissioned to teach. Sacred theology can make use both of the rules which are followed in the process of canonization and of the results obtained in each particular inquiry.

N. The Use of a Living and Infallible Magisterium. Thus the Catholic Church offers to its theologians the inestimable advantage of a teaching which presents the doctrine of Jesus Christ our Lord infallibly and clearly to the men of all ages and of all lands. Her unerring declarations contain no revealed message subsequent to that which came from God through Jesus Christ, and which was completed with the death of the last Apostle. She takes this divine revelation and presents it to the men of the various lands and ages in such a way that these men may realize exactly what our Lord included in the content of his preaching and exactly what the men who heard our Lord Himself understood and knew Him to mean.

Obviously, then, since the purpose of the theologian is to state clearly and equivocally that same message which the Catholic Church is privileged and commissioned to teach infallibly, it follows that the theologian can resolve any of the problems which are presented to him in the light of the Church's doctrine. The Church has always understood and has always taught faithfully the entire content of the message which came to men through Jesus Christ. As a result the theologian, who seeks the resolution of the problem with which he is confronted, a problem about the meaning inherent in the teaching of Christ, can always find the resolution for which he is looking in the authentic literature of Catholic teaching. Naturally he must reason carefully and accurately in order to show how the resolution of his own problem is expressed in the pronouncements of the Catholic Church. But his reasoning is successful in the measure in which he succeeds in bringing out the infallible teachings of the Church in such a way that men can grasp their real import.

IV. THE AUTHORITY OF THE ROMAN PONTIFF

A. The Primacy. As the Bishop of Rome, the Sovereign Pontiff is the successor to St. Peter and the Vicar of Christ on earth.[†] By virtue of his office he possesses all of the power which St. Peter

---

†   **Editor's Note:** For a concise study of papal authority in light of the Thomist tradition, see Ulrich Horst, O.P., *The Dominicans and the Pope: Papal Teaching Authority in the Medieval and Early Modern Thomist Tradition*, trans. James D. Mixson (Notre Dame, IN: University of Notre Dame Press, 2006).

enjoyed in his capacity as visible head of the Catholic Church. There were, of course, certain charismatic powers and certain privileges which St. Peter possessed as an individual Apostle and which consequently were never transmitted to his successors. But the primacy of jurisdiction which our Lord conferred upon St. Peter when He established him as prince of the apostolic college and as the leader of the Catholic Church is something which comes to every man who has followed St. Peter as Bishop of Rome.

In this primacy of jurisdiction are included the supreme powers to govern and to teach the members of that Church which was founded by Jesus Christ. The Sovereign Pontiff is commissioned to rule over all of the members of the Church, his fellow bishops as well as the faithful throughout the world, in the way of eternal salvation. This power comes to the successor independently of the consent of the other members of the ecclesiastical hierarchy and, of course, independently of any authority of a state.

B. The Teaching Power of the Roman Pontiff. The primacy of jurisdiction with which the Holy Father is endowed constitutes him as the supreme teacher and guardian of the divine public revelation. Since he is the visible head and leader of the Church, all of the doctrinal power inherent in this institution is centered in his person. The infallibility which he enjoys in setting forth the teaching of Jesus Christ is actually the infallibility of the Church herself. In the words of the [First] Vatican Council, the teaching power of the Holy Father is such that "when he speaks *ex cathedra*, that is when, using his function as pastor and teacher of all Christians, he defines in his supreme apostolic authority a doctrine on faith and morals to be accepted by the universal Church, through the divine assistance promised to him in St. Peter, he possesses that infallibility with which the divine Redeemer wished His Church to be equipped in defining doctrine on faith and morals." Thus, according to the proposition of the same Council, "such definitions of the Roman Pontiff are irreformable of themselves and not by reason of the consent of the Church."[9]

---

9.   Denzinger, 1839.

The pontifical definition of which the Council speaks consists in a solemn judgment of the Holy Father terminating with absolute finality some question which has arisen about the content of revealed truth. It is addressed to all those who accept the message which Jesus Christ gave to the world as divinely revealed. The science of sacred theology can avail itself of such definitions as perfectly correct statements of God's teaching. The doctrine which is asserted in the pontifical definition is not some new teaching which God has revealed to the Church as a whole or to its visible head. It is the unerring statement of matter conveyed in that same divine message which was complete with the death of the last Apostle. The assistance which God gives to the Holy Father in preserving him from the possibility of error in his definition of revealed truth does not constitute a new revelation at all. The Holy Father utilizes all of the resources of sacred theology in coming to his decision. He has the guarantee from God Himself that he will not define erroneously.

C. The Positive Definition. The infallible and solemn definition of the Holy Father may take the form of a positive statement or it may be proposed as the condemnation of an heretical teaching. The formula incident to the positive statement is exemplified perfectly in the bull *Ineffabilis Deus*, in which Pope Pius IX adverts explicitly to the use of his supreme apostolic power in defining the doctrine on the Immaculate Conception of our Lady.

> For the honor of the holy and individual Trinity, for the honor and the glory of the Virgin Mother of God, for the exaltation of the Catholic faith and the growth of the Christian religion; by the authority of our Lord Jesus Christ, of the holy Apostles Peter and Paul and by our own authority, we declare, pronounce, and define that the doctrine which holds that the most blessed virgin Mary was at the first instant of her conception, by a singular grace and privilege of almighty God preserved free from all stain of original sin because of the merits of Jesus Christ the Savior of the human race, is revealed by God and therefore is to

be believed by all the faithful firmly and constantly. Therefore, should any persons presume, which God forbid, to think in their hearts otherwise than as we have defined, let them know and realize that they are condemned by their own judgment, that they have suffered shipwreck about the faith and that they have fallen from the unity of the Church. Moreover, if they dare to manifest what they think by word, in writing or in any other way externally, they are subject to the penalties prescribed by law for that very fact.[10]

The various aspects of the solemn definition are brought out in the words of the *Ineffabilis Deus*. In the first place, the *purpose* which motivates the pronouncement as an ultimate final cause is the glory of the Triune God. This is to be accomplished through the exaltation of the Christian faith and in the growth and perfection of that worship which the Church of Jesus Christ offers to the Creator. The faith is exalted in so far as an erroneous judgment about its content is exposed for what it is. The salvific teaching of Jesus Christ, so ineffably beneficial to man, is brought to him in such a way that there is no further danger that the full meaning and beauty of one pronouncement contained in it may be obscured. Every pontifical definition tends to the accomplishment of this purpose. It was the privilege of the *Ineffabilis Deus* to bring about this result in manifesting one of the privileges of our Blessed Mother and thereby to pay her a special honor and reverence.

The *power* by which the Sovereign Pontiff acts in formulating this infallible definition is ultimately the authority of our Lord Himself. This authority was given by our Lord to St. Peter when He confided the care of His lambs and of His sheep to the prince of the apostolic college. Precisely because it is a power which was meant to be exercised until the end of time, it was given through St. Peter to all of those who were to follow him in the see of Rome. Commissioned as he is, then, to watch over and expound the teaching which Jesus

---

10. Denzinger, 1641.

Christ presented to the world as divinely revealed, the Holy Father speaks by the authority of St. Peter and as his successor.

In the formula of the definition the name of St. Paul is associated with that of St. Peter. This is not, of course, intended to imply that the Apostle of the gentiles was the equal of St. Peter in the ecclesiastical hierarchy. He was not the head of the apostolic college nor was he the recipient of any primacy of jurisdiction over the universal Church. He was, however, associated with St. Peter during the early days of the Church in Rome. As a result he is, and always will be named with the prince of the Apostles as patron of the eternal city. Speaking as the head of that Church, and as the successor to St. Peter, the Holy Father also teaches with the authority of St. Paul himself.

By *nature* the solemn exercise of the apostolic power by the Holy Father is a declaration, a pronouncement, a definition. The Holy Father declares, again infallibly, that the particular dogmatic truth, expressed in the definite formula utilized in the pronouncement, was actually revealed by God and forms a part of that Christian message which all men must accept with the assent of divine belief if they are to be joined to God in the bonds of faith. Furthermore, the [First] Vatican Council speaks of the solemn declaration of the Catholic Church, in contradistinction to that ordinary teaching which is likewise infallible, as a *judgment*. Both the Holy Father and the ecumenical council are the organs of this solemn judgment.

This judgment differs from the ordinary course of Catholic teaching in the employment of a definite dogmatic formula. The Holy Father, as well as the general council which is subject to and united with him, can declare with infallible accuracy that a definite truth, exactly as it is expressed and conveyed in this particular statement, has been revealed by God and must be believed by all Christians. The individual organ of the ordinary magisterium within the Catholic Church does not possess this competence.

Such is the force of the definition set forth infallibly in the solemn magisterium of the Church that the man who refuses to accept the declaration sins against divine faith and loses the virtue of faith itself, even though his refusal to accept the teaching of the Church be secret. However, we must remember that when the Holy Father asserts that the man who secretly refuses to accept the solemn judgment of the Catholic Church fails in or falls from the unity of the Church, he does not state that such a man ceases to be a member of that Church. The Catholic Church is, after all, a definitely visible organization. A man enters its communion through the visible sacrament of Baptism. He ceases definitely to be a member of this Church only through the visible processes of heresy, apostasy, schism, or through the full measure of excommunication. Still, however, faith in the teaching of Jesus Christ is one of those bonds of unity which brings together the members of this Church. The man who sins against this faith even in a secret manner casts off the perfection of this unity. Open rejection of the solemn pronouncements of the Church naturally constitutes that manifest heresy by which men are separated from the communion of this society.

D. The Condemnation of Heresy. When the Holy Father does not exercise the fullness of his apostolic power in defining a doctrine positively, he can utilize it in condemning some teaching as *heretical*. When a statement is reproved as being heretical, the Sovereign Pontiff in that very act defines the contradictory to this pronouncement as something which is contained actually in the deposit of divine public revelation and which must be accepted by all on the word of God Himself. The contradictory to any statement comprises, of course, the flat denial of this pronouncement rather than the assertion which is most opposed to it. Thus the statement that "all men are good" is contradicted in the contention that "not all men are good." The contrary, or extreme opposite pronouncement would be that "all men are evil." When a statement is condemned as heretical, the contrary is not thereby defined as of Catholic faith.

The statement which is stigmatized as heretical need not necessarily have been the contradiction to a formula previously defined in the solemn magisterium of the Church. It suffices that the teaching denied in the condemned proposition should have been that which was proposed as divinely revealed in the ordinary magisterium. In any case, however, a teaching is qualified as heresy only when it stands as a *direct and immediate* contradiction to revealed truth thus set forth. It is a direct and immediate contradiction to Catholic dogma when it denies a truth which has been asserted by the Catholic Church as revealed, and not merely when it objects to some resolution of a theological problem which the Church herself has not settled.

E. The Qualification of Error. Now, when a condemned proposition denies, not an actual statement which the Church has presented to the world as divinely revealed, but a correct explanation of the dogmatic formula, then the offending statement is said to be *erroneous.* An error about the meaning of revealed teaching is something distinct from and decidedly less than the contradiction or rejection of the faith itself. When the Sovereign Pontiff reproves a proposition as erroneous, he teaches authoritatively that the contradictory to this statement has at least the status of a real and therefore certain theological conclusion. The student of sacred theology can thereby utilize it as such.

The erroneous proposition contradicts, not the Catholic dogma itself, but a conclusion drawn correctly from that dogma according to the ordinary textbooks. As we have already seen, such a conclusion, in order to enter into the status of the theological thesis and consequently in order to justify the attention of the Catholic Church, must have to do with the meaning of the revealed message itself. It must be propounded as the solution to a problem about the significance of the dogmatic formulas, and thus about the content of the revealed message.

When such a solution has been advanced by the theologians, but not as yet officially by the Church herself, then the denial of this solution constitutes a theological error, and can be reproved as such with infallible accuracy by the Catholic Church and by the Holy Father who is the visible head of that Church. At another time, should circumstances warrant it, the teaching authority of the Church could infallibly declare that this error is actually heretical. In this statement the Church would state unerringly that the offending proposition contradicted the meaning actually inherent in the revealed doctrine and thus formally constituted a denial of matter which must be accepted on the word of God.

F. The Other Doctrinal Censures. During the course of the centuries the Roman Pontiffs have utilized a great many designations other than those of heresy and error in reproving teaching which is at variance with the Christian message. The man who is interested in the study of sacred theology should know the technical implications of these theological censures. Most of them, as a matter of fact, were utilized in the condemnation by Pope Clement XI of the one hundred one propositions taken from the works of the Jansenist, Quesnel. In the bull, *Unigenitus*, issued on September 8, 1713, Pope Clement declared and condemned Quesnel's listed doctrines as "respectively false, captious, ill sounding, offensive to pious ears, scandalous, pernicious, rash, injurious to the Church and to its practice, contumelious not only with respect to the Church but also toward secular authorities, seditious, impious, blasphemous, suspect of heresy, savoring of heresy, favoring heretics' heresy and schism, erroneous, proximate to heresy, often condemned, and also heretical and manifestly renewing various heresies and especially those which are contained in the notorious propositions of Jansenius, taken in the sense in which they were condemned."[11] Each of these qualifications has its own definite technical significance.

The first and by all means the most important group of theological censures have reference to the untruthfulness of the doctrine contained in the reproved propositions. Naturally the most serious of these is the qualification *heretical* attached to any teaching. The next in importance is the designation *proximate to heresy*. The statement which is proximate to heresy denies a proposition which, in the present status of dogmatic development, could actually be

---

11. Denzinger, 1451.

defined as having been divinely revealed to man, in other words, a thesis which is proximate to faith. The proximate to faith proposition, however, has not as yet been proposed as divinely revealed in either the ordinary or the solemn magisterium of the Church. Again we must realize that the truth once revealed by God through Jesus Christ has been taught perfectly by the Church since the beginning. The proposition which expresses the meaning of this truth, the proposition in this case which is proximate to faith, has been formulated as the response to a question about the meaning inherent in the divine message. Hitherto this proposition has been demonstrated and recognized by the theologians of the Church as the correct expression of that meaning which was inherent in the dogmatic deposit. Now, the Church herself is proximately prepared to pronounce that this thesis actually represents and expresses what God Himself conveyed in His message. The pronouncement that a proposition is *proximate to heresy* constitutes a declaration by the magisterium of the Church that the contradictory statement has been sufficiently demonstrated, and that the preliminary theological labor has been completed.

The qualification *savoring of heresy*, on the other hand, marks a statement as dangerously ambiguous. Such a proposition is capable of explanation or at least interpretation in an orthodox sense. But in view of the historical background of religious teaching, as it actually exists, the proposition could very well be taken as the expression of a heresy, especially when it has been used by a heretic in summing up his own teaching. Consequently the use of such a proposition, without proper distinctions and explanations, to explain the content of Christian revelation would be such as to mislead the hearer and perhaps influence him to deny Catholic dogma. When the Holy Father stigmatizes a statement as *suspect of heresy*, he declares that the heretical interpretation of the ambiguous proposition was most probably intended by the author in the work from which the proposition was taken.

A statement marked as *rash* or *temerarious* denies a thesis which has not as yet attained the full and perfect status of a theological conclusion in the schools of the Catholic Church, but which at the same time is so well grounded and so widely known that any denial of it is improper. Such a qualification is less condemnatory than the censure *erroneous*. This is manifest by the fact that it has been the practice of the Sovereign Pontiffs to specify certain teachings *as erroneous or at least rash*. The temerity of such a condemned proposition may be either positive or negative. It is said to be positive when this proposition contradicts or involves the denial of a widely known and well-established theses. It is negative when some proposition is advanced as an explanation of Christian revelation without any valid reason being adduced in its behalf.

The censure which states that a certain doctrine *cannot be taught safely* is, of course, equivalent to the qualification of rashness. This terminology is employed, among other places, in the condemnation of propositions relative to the sort of knowledge which our Lord possessed by virtue of His human nature and to the errors of the Ontologists. Furthermore, the Roman Pontiffs have frequently designated statements as *false*. A false proposition is not only erroneous, but at the same time the designation of falsity implies that the condemned proposition is a counterfeit of a true teaching, and as such liable to lead Christians into serious evil by way of deception.

Besides those censures which stigmatize a condemned statement for doctrinal incorrectness, there are others which have reference to the form in which the offending doctrine is expressed. Thus when Pope Pius VI censured as *captious* a proposition advanced by the false synod of Pistoia, he pointed out that the statement in question had been so formulated as to mislead the Christian people. The qualification *offensive to pious ears* which has been frequently used by the Pontiffs designates a proposition as one which is set forth in such a way as to run counter to the established convictions of the faithful. This censure was used, with others, when the doctrines of Baius, Molinos, and Fenelon were condemned. Many of the propositions so qualified pretended to set up higher standards of morality and perfection than those which were accepted and propounded by the Church itself. Such teachings could not but offend loyal Catholics, since they continually derided those doctrines which had always been presented by the Church. Offensive teachings of this type are sometimes qualified with the censure *ill sounding*.

There are still other doctrinal censures which stress the evil effects which the condemned proposition tends to bring about. In this class are allocated the censures of *seditious, pernicious in practice, derogatory to the practice of the Church*, and the like. Other qualifications designate the proscribed statements as definite sins against faith or charity. Such are the censures of *blasphemous, scandalous, impious*, or *schismatic*. A proposition can also be stigmatized as *new*, as *already condemned* or as *reviving an error which is already condemned*. The *new* proposition is, of course, a statement set forth as an expression of Christian doctrine without any warrant on the part of the traditional literature of sacred theology.

G. The Organs of Pontifical Teaching. The Roman Pontiff exercises his teaching authority in many different ways. Sometimes, of course, he teaches in and with an ecumenical council in such a way that the doctrine advanced is given to the world as that of the Holy Father rather than that of the council itself. Thus the profession of faith of the Council of Trent was included in the, Bull, *Iniunctum Nobis* of Pope Pius IV. At other times, and far more frequently, the Vicar of Christ teaches through letters emanating from himself, documents known as encyclicals, bulls, pontifical constitutions, and the like. At other times he teaches orally, by means of the various allocutions which he grants to those whom he wishes to instruct. Again he may exercise his teaching office through the instrumentality of those curial congregations which he uses in the ordinary direction of ecclesiastical affairs, agencies like the Holy Office, the Biblical Commission, the Congregation of Rites, and the rest.[†] The responses and instructions of these congregations are

---

†   **Editor's Note:** The Pontifical Biblical Commission (PBC) no longer has magisterial authority since Blessed Paul VI's 1971 *motu proprio, Sedula Cura* (June 27, 1971). The PBC now serves a consultative role through its association with the Congregation for the Doctrine of the Faith. As Cardinal Joseph Ratzinger said

usually directive. Most frequently they confine themselves to the task of stating that this particular proposition which is in question can or cannot be taught safely in the schools of the Catholic Church. Naturally that infallibility which is the prerogative of the Holy Father cannot be delegated to any of these congregations.[12]

Even when the Holy Father speaks and teaches by personal letter or allocution rather than through one of the agencies provided in the curia, he only avails himself of his privilege of infallibility on those occasions when he makes full use of his apostolic power in defining a truth on faith or morals as something which must be accepted with divine faith by all Christians. Naturally he can speak and teach, even officially, in such a way as not to demand definitive acceptance of his doctrine from his subjects throughout the world. But even when he does not define and thereby use the full measure of his apostolic power, his words are of tremendous importance in showing the content of divine revelation. The theologians can and should avail themselves of the papal encyclicals and the other documents which are so efficaciously indicative of the divine revelation.

H. The Pope as a Private Theologian. His high office does not in any way prevent the Holy Father from acting in the capacity of a private theologian whenever it pleases him to do so. In acting as a private theologian, he makes no use of his apostolic power. As a result whatever writings he chooses to produce in this capacity would have only such authority as is enjoyed by and attributed to the work of any other competent worker in the field of sacred theology. It is the business of the theologian to express, clearly and unequivocally, the content of divine revelation. But in doing so he acts as a private member of the Church contributing to that work of teaching which is essential to the Church. Only

in his preface to the 1994 PBC document *The Interpretation of the Bible in the Church*: "The Pontifical Biblical Commission, in its new form after the Second Vatican Council, is not an organ of the teaching office, but rather a commission of scholars who, in their scientific and ecclesial responsibility as believing exegetes, take positions on important problems of Scriptural interpretation."

12. Cf. Joannes Gspann, *Summarium Theologiae Dogmaticae* (Paris: 1930), p. 12.

the Church herself, in her authentic magisterium, has the power to
teach Christ's message with infallible accuracy.

I. Questions Not Yet Determined by Pontifical Definition.
There are times when the teaching of the Holy See takes the form
of a declaration that some particular controversy has not as yet
been resolved. In that case the Pontiff forbids private writers to
attach any theological censure to the doctrine which they reject.
This has happened in the case of the thesis on the Immaculate Conception of our Lady. On September 4, 1483, in the Constitution
Grave Nimis, Pope Sixtus IV stated explicitly that the controversy
on this matter had not as yet been decided.[13] Since the Apostolic
See itself had not spoken, the Pontiff sharply reproved those religious preachers who had dared to tax with the note of heresy the
doctrine of those writers who did not agree with them. Later, however, Pope Alexander VII, in the Bull, *Sollicitudo Omnium Ecclesiarum* of December 8, 1661,[14] stated that the thesis which held that
our Blessed Lady had actually been conceived free from any stain
of original sin was now generally accepted throughout the Catholic Church. This doctrine was ultimately defined and the problem
thus absolutely resolved by Pope Pius IX in the Bull *Ineffabilis Deus*
of December 8, 1854.[15]

The writings of Sixtus, Alexander, and Pius form the outline
of a perfect case history in the development of a problem which
the Catholic Church first reserved the right to resolve and then at
last settled definitely. The statement to the effect that our Blessed
Mother was conceived free from any taint of original sin had first
been proposed by private theologians in the form of a theological
conclusion. They had proposed this thesis as the solution to the
problem of the meaning which must be attached to the title of our
Lady as "full of grace." They had adduced demonstrations which
showed that Mary's plenitude of divine grace was such as to include

---

13. Denzinger, 735.
14. Denzinger, 1100.
15. Denzinger, 1641.

a freedom from original sin, even in the very moment of her conception. As a matter of fact, John Duns Scotus, the greatest of all the Franciscan writers, owes his title of *Doctor Marialis* to the fact that he was one of the most brilliant and vigorous proponents of this teaching.

The acceptance of this thesis, however, was by no means universal. Before the time of Scotus some of the ablest teachers in all theological history had unequivocally denied the thesis of the Immaculate Conception. Among these professors was St. Thomas Aquinas himself.

Finally, the Church took official cognizance of the controversy. First she declared that no authentic and authoritative decision had yet been given in this matter. Then she asserted that the thesis of the Immaculate Conception had become the common doctrine within her schools, and as such had to be considered as a theological conclusion of definite standing. The last step in the process was the infallible decision given in the words of Pope Pius IX, closing the discussion forever.

As a matter of fact, even the shortest acquaintance with the literature of sacred theology is sufficient to show that there are many controverted questions in this field even in our own time. In the *Studiorum Ducem* of Pope Pius XI we have an authoritative declaration to the effect that theologians are free to choose among certain conflicting theses and accept those which they deem true. There is, of course, a definite limit set to the field of this choice. A man may hold a controversial position "on those matters upon which authors of better note are accustomed to dispute in the Catholic schools." Such matters are subject to controversy not as yet closed either by the solemn definition or judgment of the Catholic Church, or through the common consent of theologians.

Among these controverted questions there are some which the Holy See has definitely indicated that it will someday resolve. One of these is the debate about the necessity of some form of a love or benevolence for God in that act of attrition which is requisite for the remission of sins in the sacrament of Penance. Pope

Clement XII forbade the partisans of the conflicting teachings to attach the notes of theological censures to one another's doctrines, until such time as the matter had been defined or decided by the Holy See itself.[16] Likewise in the matter disputed in the famous *"Congregationes de Auxiliis"* and touched upon in the censures of Louvain and of Douai, both Pope Paul V and Pope Clement XII forbade opposing authors to tax one another with theological censures until such time as the Apostolic See should have made a decision. Pope Paul V actually announced that the decision on this matter, which he said had been awaited for a long time, would be given at some future date.[†]

V. THE ECUMENICAL COUNCIL

A. The Nature of a General Council. The second organ for the solemn judgment or magisterium of the Catholic Church is the general or ecumenical council. This council is a gathering of the bishops who, together with and subject to the Roman Pontiff, constitute the doctrinal hierarchy of the Catholic Church. In the ecumenical council this hierarchy acts as a unit. Thus the council can judge and define infallibly when it teaches the universal Church about the content of the message which was given to the world through Jesus Christ our Lord.

---

16. Denzinger, 1090 and 1097, with the notes which are attached.

† **Editor's Note:** For more on the historical, philosophical, and theological complexities involved in the *De Auxiliis* controversy surrounding grace and predestination, see Jacques-Hyacinthe Serry, O.P. ("Augustinus Leblanc"), *Historia congregationum de auxiliis divinae gratiae, sub summis pontificibus Clemente VIII et Paulo V* (Antwerp: 1709); Thomas M. Osborne, Jr., "How Sin Escapes Premotion: The Development of Thomas Aquinas's Thought by Spanish Thomists," in *Thomism and Predestination: Principles and Disputations*, ed. Steven A. Long, Roger W. Nutt, and Thomas Joseph White, O.P. (Ave Maria, FL: Sapientia Press, 2016), pp. 192–213; R.J. Matava, *Divine Causality and Human Free Choice: Domingo Báñez, Physical Premotion and the Controversy* de Auxiliis *Revisited* (Leiden: Brill, 2016); Sylvio Hermann De Franceschi, *Thomisme et théologie modern: L'école de saint Thomas à l'épreuve de la querelle de la grâce (XVIIᵉ–XVIIIᵉ siècles)* (Paris: Artège Lethielleux, 2018).

B. A List of the General Councils. There have been twenty of these general councils. We shall list them according to the time at which they were held and with the name of the Pontiff who ruled the Church during the deliberations of the assembly.

1. Nicaea, 325, St. Sylvester.
2. First Constantinople, 381, St. Damasus.
3. Ephesus, 431, St. Celestine I.
4. Chalcedon, 451, St. Leo I.
5. Second Constantinople, 553, Vigilius.
6. Third Constantinople, 680–681, St. Agatho.
7. Second Nicaea, 787, Adrian I.
8. Fourth Constantinople, 869–870, Adrian II.
9. First Lateran, 1123, Callistus II.
10. Second Lateran, 1139, Innocent II.
11. Third Lateran, 1179, Alexander III.
12. Fourth Lateran, 1215, Innocent III.
13. First Lyons, 1245, Innocent IV.
14. Second Lyons, 1274, St. Gregory X.
15. Vienne, 1311–1312, Clement V.
16. Constance, 1414–1418, Martin V.
17. Florence, 1438-1445, Eugenius IV.
18. Fifth Lateran, 1512-1517, Leo X.
19. Trent, 1545-1563, Paul III, Julius III, Pius IV.
20. [First] Vatican, 1870, Pius IX.†

C. Requisites for a General Council. In order that an assembly may fulfill the requisites for an ecumenical council, it must be called by the Holy Father, presided over by him, either personally or through his delegates, and finally, most important of all, its proceedings must be approved and ratified by the Holy See. If this last condition is lacking the acts of the council cannot be accepted as

---

† **Editor's Note:** Of course, to this list, the Church has added the twenty-first ecumenical council: Second Vatican, 1962–1965, St. John XXIII, Bl. Paul VI.

the solemn teaching and judgment of the Catholic Church. Furthermore, an ecumenical council differs from all others in that the bishops from all the parts of the Christian world are invited and enough of them do take part in the discussions and voting so that the resultant definitions may properly be termed the expression of the entire Catholic episcopate.

Not all of the twenty councils recognized within the Catholic Church as ecumenical actually possessed all of the ecumenical attributes. The First and the Second Councils of Constantinople, for example, were ecumenical neither from the point of view of their convocation nor from that of their celebration. Bishops from the western church, that is from the Roman patriarchate were neither invited to nor present at their deliberations. They were recognized as ecumenical and given the status of general councils solely through the positive will of the Roman Pontiff. They were accepted by the Holy See as authentic judgments of the universal hierarchy in the infallible Church of Jesus Christ. Furthermore, even among the acts of the twenty councils, only those decisions are valid which have been approved and promulgated by the Holy See. In the case where this approval is withheld, as it was from the twenty-eighth canon of the council of Chalcedon, the rejected teaching has no doctrinal value.

D. The Forms of Conciliar Teaching. In the doctrinal decisions of these councils, set forth under the direction and with the approval of the Holy Father, the theologian finds infallibly accurate statements about the content of divine public revelation. Sometimes that teaching is put forward in the form of a symbol or creed, as was done at the first councils of Nicaea and Constantinople. At other times it comes in the form of positive instructions, addressed to the universal Church or to groups seeking reunion with the Church. Again, and very frequently, it comes in the form of condemnations fulminated against heretical teachings. The decisions of the ecumenical council are infallible wherever the doctrine is presented as having been revealed by God and taught by our Lord and the Apostles. Again the council uses the fullness of its teaching power when it anathematizes, or cuts, off from the communion of the Church, the proponents of the teachings which it condemns.

In this way the chapters of the two constitutions, the *Dei Filius* and the *Pastor Aeternus* set forth by the [First] Vatican Council must be accepted as the infallible expression of divine public revelation. For, in the preamble to the *Dei Filius*, the constitution on the Catholic faith, Pius IX, speaking for the council which he had convened and over which he had presided, states explicitly that the council intends to "profess and declare in the sight of all, the salutary doctrine of Christ." And, in the preface to the *Pastor Aeternus* we find that the fathers intend to set forth "the doctrine on the institution, perpetuity, and nature of the sacred apostolic primacy, in which the strength and solidity of the entire Church is established, to be believed and held by all the faithful according to the ancient and constant faith of the universal Church." The canons are obviously infallible declarations, since they invoke the penalty of anathematization against those who presume to set forth the doctrines which the council reproves.

The Fathers of the Council of Trent state that the man who will not firmly and faithfully receive the doctrine on justification which they have given in their *decretum* cannot be justified. They likewise anathematize those who held the heretical teachings condemned in their canons. In the Council of Florence the famous Decrees for the Greeks, the Armenians, and the Jacobites are presented as the actual dogma of the Catholic Church which must be accepted by those who wish to enter into its communion. The Fourth Council of the Lateran set forth its teaching in two different ways. First it condemned the writings of the Abbot Joachim against Peter the Lombard. Then it set forth its own formula of faith in the very words which the Master of Sentences had utilized in forming his own theological conclusions.

E. The Members of the General Council. Although by divine right all of the bishops who are in communion with the apostolic see can enter into an ecumenical council, the law of the Catholic Church at present and for centuries past has given the privilege of membership to others not of the episcopal college. These include cardinals who are not bishops, abbots who rule as ordinaries, or who, in other words have territorial jurisdiction similar to that which bishops exercise in their own dioceses, vicars and prefects apostolic. The superiors-general of the great religious communities can also enter the council and exercise the power of voting in the assembly.

F. Particular Councils. Lesser ecclesiastical councils, such as plenary or national assemblies and provincial or diocesan synods do not, of course, enjoy the prerogative of infallibility. Some of the acts of such synods, however, constitute authentic and infallible expressions of Catholic dogma because they have been accepted and utilized as such by the Holy Father. Among those councils whose acts may be used in this way by theologians are the Sixteenth Council of Carthage, the Second Council of Orange, and the Eleventh Council of Toledo. Naturally the universal value of their teaching is to be attributed to the authority of the Roman Pontiff, rather than to the authority of the individual council as such.

Even though the pronouncements of the particular councils are not infallible, the fact that they are expressions of the legitimate teaching authority within the Church and that they are approved by the Holy See, gives them tremendous standing in the theological field. Thus the decisions of the Councils of Baltimore in our own country are matters of importance for the theologian.

VI. THE AUTHORITY OF THE FATHERS

A. Those Who Are Classed as Fathers of the Church. The Fathers of the Church were those early ecclesiastical writers who were conspicuous both for the sanctity of their lives and for the orthodoxy of their teachings. As such they are cited in the science of sacred theology as authentic witnesses of the faith and of the practice in the ancient Church. On certain points of doctrine the Church has given a special approval to the teachings of individual Fathers. Thus the Council of Ephesus accepted and utilized the anathematizations of St. Cyril of Alexandria on the matter of the hypostatic union.[17] Both Pope Hormisdas[18] and the Second Council of Orange[19] gave the weight of their authority to the writings of St. Augustine on free will and the grace of God. The former cited books of St. Augustine as expressing the revealed doctrine on this matter while the council formulated its own canons in the very terminology of the great Bishop of Hippo.

Although there is a certain similarity between them, the concept of a Father of the Church is quite distinct from that of a Doctor. The Doctor of the Church is a saint who has been approved in a special way both for the holiness of his life and for the orthodoxy of his teaching. There is no special way, on the other hand, by which an individual is designated as a Father of the Church. There are actually twenty-nine saints who are honored as Doctors of the Church.[†] Some of these, like Sts. Athanasius, Basil, Augustine, and Ambrose, are both Fathers and Doctors. Others lived after the first ages of the Church and are not designated as Fathers. Naturally, too, there are a great many Fathers of the Church who, like Sts. Clement of Rome, Ignatius of Antioch, and Irenaeus, are not listed as Doctors of the Church.

There are also a great many early ecclesiastical writers who, by reason of a lack either of manifest sanctity or of unswerving orthodoxy are not numbered among the Fathers. Among these we must range such eminent figures as Origen, Tertullian, Minucius Felix, and Lactantius. Naturally the writings of such men participate to a large extent the authority which belongs to the works of the Fathers themselves. Some who actually left the communion of the Church, like Tatian and Tertullian, wrote during their years as members of the Church. These writings enjoy a considerable

17. Denzinger, 113–24.

18. Denzinger, 3027; cf. the ruling on the authority of St. Augustine made by Pope St. Celestine I (Denzinger, 128).

19. This council was held in 529. Its canons and decrees are found in Denzinger, 174–200.

†   **Editor's Note:** There are presently thirty-six Doctors of the Church (as of the year 2018).

theological authority, not so much because of any explanations offered by the individual writers, but because they can bear witness
to the teaching and the practice of the Catholic Church at the time
they were written.

B. The Nature of Their Authority. The Fathers of the Church
can, of course, be studied and considered as private theologians.
Looked at in this way, the value of the testimony offered by each
writer is proportionate to the weight of the theological reasons
which he adduces. Thus the student of sacred theology must not
suppose that an interpretation or explanation of some passage in
Holy Scripture is necessarily valid and correct merely because someone among the Fathers has offered it. Patristic literature can be studied and evaluated by the same standards that are used to measure
the worth of later theological writings. In a given case, the reasoning
of one Father may be quite superior to that of another. Moreover,
the individual Fathers of the Church are not infallible. Erroneous
teachings or explanations are contained in the writings of various
individual Fathers. These errors were, of course, exposed as such
by the contemporary and subsequent writers of Catholic doctrine.

However, the particular and characteristic function of the
Church Fathers is their ability to speak and to teach as witnesses of
the Catholic faith during the early period of the Church's life. By
reason of their temporal propinquity to the Apostles, they were in a
particularly good position to know the content and the significance
of the apostolic message. When one Father, or a group of them,
actually stated that some doctrine had been revealed by God and
taught by Jesus Christ, this testimony has naturally a tremendous
weight and significance. But when the Fathers unanimously profess
that some doctrine is a part of the divine public revelation, then
their testimony is absolutely irrefutable. The Church knows that
the unanimous teaching of the Fathers cannot be in error on a matter of faith and morals. One Father might be mistaken. As a matter
of fact even a certain number of them might be. But, according to
the existing decrees of divine providence, it is impossible that all
the Fathers should teach falsely on the matter of divine revelation.

C. The Unanimous Consent of the Fathers and the Rule of Faith. The Council of Trent identified the unanimous teaching of the Fathers with the interpretation of the Church itself as the standard for the correct explanation of Holy Scripture.[20] Francis Sylvius' express intention, manifest in his daily protestation, to teach, write, and dictate his lectures in sacred doctrine "according to the unanimous consent of the Fathers" is typical of the attitude which governs the successful theologian. The united voice of the Fathers constitutes a real rule of faith.

In order to have the unanimous consent of the Fathers to indicate surely the divine origin of some doctrine treated in sacred theology, we need not, of course, demand an explicit declaration on the point from every writer who is listed as one of the Fathers of the Church. On almost any given question there will be a considerable number of the Fathers who have left no instructions in writing. There is such a consent when at least a moral unanimity of the Fathers who have actually dealt with this subject teach the same doctrine as having been revealed by God.

We say *morally* all of the Fathers, because the opposition of one, or even of an inconsiderable number, to the teaching which is common with the rest does not prevent the common teaching from enjoying a certain unanimity. This moral unanimity is all the more evident when a dissenting doctrine has been recognized and abandoned by all the patristic writers who came after the man who advanced it. It exists where it may prudently be said that the Fathers as a whole advance this particular teaching as something which has been given to the world by God through the preaching of Jesus Christ and of the Apostles.

D. Limits of the Patristic Period. It is important for us to realize the limits of the patristic period. It has been generally taught that St. Isidore of Seville was the last of the Fathers to teach and write in the west while St. John Damascene ended the patristic line in the oriental Church. However, there have been

20. The Council of Trent, Session IV (Denzinger, 786).

scholars who have set forth the opinion that St. Bernard of Clairvaux should be considered the last of the patristic writers. As a
matter of fact, Francis Sylvius, in the early seventeenth century,
even included Sts. Bonaventure and Thomas Aquinas in the list
of Fathers.[21]

For the purposes of sacred theology the patristic period must be
restricted at least to the times of St. Isidore and St. John Damascene.
Later writers, like St. Bernard, and *a fortiori* St. Thomas and St.
Bonaventure actually utilized the Fathers but should not be counted among them. The science of sacred theology was comparatively
well developed when they lived and wrote. They should not, in any
sense, be considered as immediate witnesses to the faith and the
customs in the early Church. Their value lay in their masterful development of sacred theology as such rather than in their testimony
about the life of the primitive Church.

E. Using the Authority of the Fathers. The practical importance of this theological place in the training of a successful theologian cannot be overstressed in our own times. It is commonplace
that a man cannot begin to qualify as a theologian until he has
gained a solid familiarity with patristic literature. The doctrine
which is expounded in the manuals and monographs of modern
theology is the same revealed doctrine which the Fathers of the
Church set forth so successfully in their own days. Actually the
intention of the theologian is to set forth the revealed deposit
according to the unanimous teaching of the Fathers. Naturally a
knowledge of what the Fathers actually taught is requisite for the
achievement of this purpose.

For example, the theologian who is studying the problem of
the efficacy of divine grace naturally strives to bring out the same
truth which St. Augustine expressed in his anti-Pelagian writings,
the documents which the Holy See itself accepted as containing
the Catholic explanation of this portion of the revealed doctrine. It
is his business, then, to know the works of St. Augustine in order

---

21. Sylvius, *Controversiarum Liber Sextus*, q. 1, a. 1.

that he may be able properly and correctly to teach their content. We know that St. Augustine's teachings are brought out accurately in every approved manual of dogmatic theology. At the same time, however, we can best realize the profundity of meaning conveyed in the modern texts when we look at their content in the perspective of St. Augustine's own writing.

Naturally the great extent of patristic literature will prevent all but the specialists in this line from knowing all parts and phases of it intimately. At the same time it is perfectly possible for the modern theologian who wishes to give his subject the scientific attention which it so obviously deserves, to acquaint himself with at least the outstanding monuments of patristic learning. Thus he can assure for his own preaching and teaching the outstanding advantage of the Fathers' own presentation of divine revelation. He can enrich his own mind through a consideration of the studied exactness by which they so successfully defended revealed truth and overthrew the heresies that threatened the people of God.

The patristic writings are eminently fitted to engender in the student of sacred theology a living appreciation of the purpose to which this science is consecrated. All of the resources of erudition and of intelligence which God had placed at their disposal were utilized toward the exact and unequivocal presentation of divine revelation. Their writings and preaching preserved the Christian people of their own times from the disaster of heresy. The works of St. Athanasius were, under God, the agencies through which the Catholic people were saved from the danger of rejecting the teaching of God while they were confronted with the errors and the power of the Arians. St. Augustine wrote in such a way that through his books untold numbers of Christians were preserved from the heresy of the Pelagians. The theologian has at his disposal the works of the Fathers themselves as well as the great books on patristic literature which offer him the results of research into the teaching of the Fathers carried on in the Catholic universities throughout the world.

VII. The Authority of the Scholastic Theologians

A. Those Who Are Scholastic Theologians. Melchior Cano wrote his treatise *De Locis Theologicis* before the custom of distinguishing positive from scholastic theology had arisen. As a result the "scholastic theologians" to whom he refers are those exponents of Catholic doctrine who have made scientific use of the resources of sacred theology. They are the men who have written during the post-patristic period as the academic and traditional exponents of Catholic teaching. Excluded from the ranks of the scholastics are, of course, heretical writers and even those orthodox religious authors who have not achieved scientific accuracy in their explanations of revealed doctrine. Those writers whose stock in trade is a lively literary style rather than exact expression of Christian doctrine have nothing to contribute toward the development of theological conclusions.

However, the type or the extent of a man's literary production have nothing to do with his qualification as a scholastic theologian. The scholastic writer may be one who has produced Latin technical works as voluminous as those of Tostatus or Suarez or merely vernacular articles in some review. He can fill his books with all the refinements of technical terminology, as did Cardinal Cajetan, or he can utilize a more popular literary style to bring out the same exactness in the presentation of Christian doctrine as Archbishop Kenrick did. It is essential for a scholastic that his writings should form a part of the traditional and scientific exposition of Catholic faith, recognized and used as such by the Church.

There is a definite reason why the scholastic theologians as such can be cited as authorities in the work of teaching revealed doctrine. By far the greater number of these theologians have been priests who at one time or another were charged with the teaching of sacred theology in some university, seminary, or religious house. As such they have acted as competent and authorized instruments of the hierarchy both in training candidates for the priesthood and instructing those priests who are preparing for theological degrees. It has been their business to know and to utilize all of the resources available for the success of theological instruction. Their studies and their professional anxiety to expound the content of divine revelation clearly and unequivocally are manifest throughout their writings. Their professional competence and the responsibilities with which they are charged give them a unique corporate authority.

B. The Nature of Their Authority. The authority of the scholastic theologians belongs primarily to these writers as a distinct class. Apart from the special approbation which the Church gives to certain individual scholastics, and which must be considered by itself, the authority of the individual theologian is directly proportionate to the value of those proofs which he adduces in support of his propositions. When a scholastic sets down a thesis, he is expected to offer evidence to show that it should be accepted as a correct explanation of our Lord's message. Other theologians who deal with the same matter must examine and evaluate the evidence which has been brought forward. If the proof is valid, the thesis stands. Should the evidence not be forthcoming, then the proposition has no legitimate place in the field of sacred theology on the authority of the previous writer.

However, when the entire body of scholastic theologians asserts that some thesis is of Catholic faith, their testimony is absolutely reliable. Because of the particular function of the scholastics, if all of them should be in error on a point of this kind, then the Catholic Church would be deceived. They are the qualified exponents of Catholic doctrine in the schools of the Church. Their unanimous testimony to the effect that a definite doctrine has been revealed by God and is to be accepted by all with the assent of divine faith mirrors the teaching of the Church itself.

This unanimity of the scholastics must be reckoned in the same way as that of the Church Fathers. The moral unanimity in the scholastic testimony to the divine origin of a certain thesis is in no way impaired if, in the course of academic history, a limited number of writers have called this thesis into question. The fact that such a denial has been reproved by an overwhelming number of theologians would constitute this thesis as one attested by the moral unanimity of the scholastics.

The testimony of the theologians is valid even for propositions which are put forward as theologically certain. When a proposition is universally received as a theological conclusion, then the contradictory to it may be qualified as a simple theological error. Should the teaching of the theologians be sufficiently clear on a point that is not received with full unanimity, the opposition to this thesis would take the form of a rash or temerarious proposition.

C. The Field of Moral Theology. Owing to the exigencies of the immediate subject matter, the authority of theologians as such plays a far more evident role in moral than in dogmatic theology. Dealing with the liceity of human acts, and necessarily taking into account the circumstances and forces which affect the morality of individual acts, an opinion in moral theology acquires a definite probability by the fact that a certain number of serious authors accept and teach it. It is generally admitted that if five or six of these serious authors can be cited in support of a proposition, then this thesis enjoys at least what is called *extrinsic probability*. In other words, it is supposed, unless the opposite can be established in any given case, that it would be impossible to gather any number of authoritative writers to assert a thesis devoid of probability. This same extrinsic probability accrues to a proposition which is put forward as an opinion in moral theology by one of the great Doctors of the Church, like St. Thomas Aquinas or St. Alphonsus.[†]

D. The Field of Dogmatic Theology. In the field of dogmatic theology the authority of scholastic theologians has its own importance. The Salmanticenses are typical theologians when they allege

---

†   **Editor's Note:** It is important to accentuate the point, however, that extrinsic probability alone remains an insufficient means by which to determine moral truth. A methodological emphasis on extrinsic probability characterized the period of moral casuistry. The 1993 papal encyclical of St. John Paul, II, *Veritatis Splendor*, called for a renewed approach to moral theology based upon an intrinsic consideration of moral objectivity. For more on these themes, see Servais

the authority of their contemporaries and their predecessors in the field of scholasticism in support of their own theses. Naturally no one cites the authority of scholastic theologians for those theses which have been defined as of faith in the solemn magisterium of the Catholic Church. It would be at least idle to quote even the greatest of the scholastics in defense of the proposition that there are three distinct Persons in the ineffable unity of the divine nature.

However, it is distinctly important to cite those writers who have taught, let us say, the doctrine of physical predetermination.[†] This thesis is not accepted by a good number of the writers in sacred theology, and as such it has not attained the full perfection of a theological conclusion, at least in the universal teaching body of the Church. It could have no such standing as it actually enjoys in the field of sacred theology if it could not be shown that innumerable theologians who were renowned at once for their accuracy of judgment and their attachment to traditional teaching had propounded this teaching as their own. The proofs alleged in favor of this thesis are in themselves convincing. But the fact that it is a traditional interpretation of Catholic doctrine, a fact that is attested in the teaching of an unbroken line of scholastics, is

Pinckaers, O.P., *The Sources of Christian Ethics*, trans. Sr. Mary Thomas Noble, O.P. (Washington, DC: The Catholic University of America Press, 1995); Romanus Cessario, O.P., *Introduction to Moral Theology*, rev. ed. (Washington, DC: The Catholic University of America Press, 2013), pp. 219–32; Romanus Cessario, O.P., "Casuistry and Revisionism: Structural Similarities in Method and Content," in "*Humanae Vitae*": *20 Anni Dopo. Atti del II Congresso Internazionale di Theologia Morale*, Vol. III (Milano: Edizioni Ares, 1990), pp. 385–409.

†   **Editor's Note:** Fenton's use of "physical predetermination" refers to the questions surrounding the efficacy of grace, predestination, and "physical premotion." For a concise summary of the fundamental themes and issues, see T.C. O'Brien, "Premotion, Physical," in *New Catholic Encyclopedia* (New York: McGraw-Hill, 1967), Vol. 13: pp. 741–43. For other considerations of the topic of physical premotion, see Thomas M. Osborne, Jr., "Thomist Premotion and Contemporary Philosophy of Religion," *Nova et Vetera*, Vol. 4, No. 3 (2006): pp. 607–32; Steven A. Long, "St. Thomas Aquinas, Divine Causality, and the Mystery of Predestination," in *Thomism and Predestination: Principles and Disputations*, ed. Steven A. Long, Roger W. Nutt, and Thomas Joseph White, O.P. (Ave Maria, FL: Sapientia Press, 2016), pp. 51–76.

itself an important element in the demonstration which is offered in support of the thesis. Naturally the writers who are quoted in support of the opposite teaching constitute an historical evidence of its probability.

E. The Use of the Scholastics' Authority. Precisely because the testimony of the scholastic theologians constitutes a resource which should be employed in deriving conclusions on the meaning of divine revelation, it is imperative that the student of sacred theology should make himself familiar with the literature in which this corporate testimony may be found. A man will never achieve any sort of competence as a theologian until he is acquainted with the theses and the demonstrations which are to be found in the outstanding modern manuals and monographs. These constitute the expression of the theological teaching in our own day. This teaching is naturally just as truly the testimony of the Catholic Church as was the doctrine of those theologians who have propounded the divine doctrine during any previous century. Taken together they express the message proposed by the Church of Jesus Christ.

At the same time a proper study of sacred theology demands the consultation of the classical works written during the sixteenth and the seventeenth centuries, the masterpieces of post-Tridentine doctrine. Such books as those of Suarez, Sylvius, Vasquez, Valentia, Bañez, John of Saint Thomas, and the College of Salamanca, to mention only a few of them, contain a fullness of theological reasoning which most of the modern manuals attempt to resume in a brief form. Furthermore, these great commentators were careful to catalog the teachings of their predecessors in such a way that the argument from the authority of the scholastic doctors is found in their works and brought out most clearly.

All of these men were commentators on St. Thomas Aquinas. Consequently the meaning of their demonstrations and the force of their testimony can be appreciated fully only when their volumes are compared with the work which they set out to explain. And, it is no exaggeration to say that the doctrine of St. Thomas can best be understood when it is looked upon in the light of Peter the Lombard's writings. The old Archbishop of Paris was the one to whom Aquinas himself habitually referred as the *Master*. The student who wishes to understand the authority of the scholastic theologians can find no way of attaining his purpose other than through a consultation of the scholastic writings themselves.

F. The Attitude of Church toward the Corps of Scholastic Theologians. A practical commentary on the authority of the scholastic theologians is to be found in the severe attitude which the Church has taken with regard to those who attempted to undermine their prestige. Furthermore, the enemies of the Catholic faith have habitually been strenuous opponents both of the conclusions and of the methods of these scholastic doctors. Michael Baius attacked a standard theological distinction as something fruitless, and St. Pius V condemned this very proposition among others taken from his writings.[22] The quietist Molinos and the heretical synod of Pistoia were remarkable for the opposition which they showed to the works of the standard and traditional exponents of Catholic doctrine.

G. The Doctors of the Church. We could not appreciate the significance of the doctrinal authority which belongs to the scholastic theologians were we to neglect those whom the Church has specially commended in naming them Doctors of the Church. From a liturgical point of view, the naming of a saint as a Doctor of the Church means that the *Credo* is recited at his Mass, that a special and distinct Mass is said in his honor, and that a specific office is assigned for his feast. Doctrinally the naming of a Doctor constitutes a declaration by the Church that this eminent servant of God was remarkable alike for the holiness of his life and the effective orthodoxy of his teaching. Naturally this effective orthodoxy is incompatible with the presence of any substantial error about faith or morals in the books which he gave to the Church. There is also a positive connotation. Not only does the Church declare that there

---

22. Denzinger, 1034; also 1061–63.

is no serious error in any of his work, but by the very fact that he is constituted as a Doctor, she commends that portion of his writings on which he may be said to have specialized and because of which he is entered upon the list of the Doctors.

Thus, for example, the naming of St. John of the Cross as a Doctor of the Church implied an ecclesiastical approval of what he had written upon the mystical life. St. Francis of Sales was commended for his spectacular success in bringing the teaching on spiritual perfection to the attention of the laity. St. Peter Canisius is a Doctor of the Church because of his manifest clarity and sureness in the all-important work of catechetics. St. Robert Bellarmine was one of the greatest controversialists ever to have labored in defense of the Catholic faith, while St. Alphonsus Liguori is the outstanding proponent of Catholic moral theology, considered primarily in its legal or casuistic aspects. St. Peter Damian wrote with matchless brilliance on the ideal of clerical holiness. St. Albert the Great succeeded admirably in explaining the relations between sacred theology and its ancillary sciences.

St. Bonaventure and St. Thomas Aquinas are Doctors who explained the entire content of sacred theology as it was taught during the Middle Ages. Both wrote commentaries on the *Four Books of Sentences* by Peter the Lombard. St. Bonaventure holds an especially high position in the history of mystical theology.

F. The Authority of St. Thomas Aquinas. However, the authentic declarations and commands of the Catholic Church with reference to St. Thomas Aquinas give him a place apart among the theologians.[†] The Code of Canon Law, in its part concerning ecclesiastical seminaries, commands that "professors treat the studies of rational philosophy and of theology, and the teaching of the students in these branches of knowledge, entirely according to the reason, the doctrine, and the principles of St. Thomas Aquinas"

[†]   **Editor's Note:** For an excellent study of the Church's perennial esteem for St. Thomas Aquinas, see Santiago Ramírez, O.P., "The Authority of St. Thomas Aquinas," *The Thomist*, Vol. 15, No. 1 (1952): pp. 1–109.

and that they "hold these inviolate."[23] The encyclical of the late Pope Pius XI, the *Studiorum Ducem*, confirms this precept and thus renews the approbations and the commands of the Roman Pontiffs since the days of Pope John XXII. However, in this same encyclical, Pope Pius XI makes it quite clear that neither the precept of the Code nor the teaching of the *Studiorum Ducem* forbid the adoption, on controverted questions, of theses which have been held by other competent theologians against the doctrine of the Common and Angelic Doctor of the schools.

Taking the two declarations together, the intention of the Church as manifest in the pronouncement of the Holy Father is quite evident. While the Church does not wish absolutely to forbid the holding of theses which are not in accord with the teaching of St. Thomas, she insists that the candidates for the priesthood being educated in her seminaries should learn their theology from the Angelic Doctor. For, if professors of sacred theology actually treat their science according to the order or the method of St. Thomas, utilizing his theses or conclusions and observing the principles out of which he derived his own doctrine, and thus instruct the students who are confided to their care, then the process of seminary education must be profoundly and essentially Thomistic. This is exactly what the Catholic Church wishes the clerical education to be.[†]

Should the man who has been educated according to the teaching of St. Thomas later choose to hold some theses not in accord with traditional Thomistic doctrine, he is perfectly free to do so, provided, of course, that the theses have been taught heretofore by reputable theologians. However, the exceptional approval given to the writings of the Angelic Doctor makes it quite evident that the Church considers his teaching as singularly free from error and equivocation. She regards it as the most scientific and efficacious process for propounding the truths of divine revelation. The

---

23. The Code of Canon Law, Canon 1366, §2.

†   **Editor's Note:** The Second Vatican Council reiterated this point. See Vatican II, Decree on Priestly Training, *Optatam totius*, no. 16.

scientific principles upon which his system is constructed, the characteristic conclusions which he upheld, and the very order according to which he arranged the content of sacred theology stand in the eyes of the Catholic Church as particularly apt for bringing the student to realize exactly the content of that message which God gave to the world through Jesus Christ our Lord.

As a result, the manual or article in sacred theology utilizing the doctrine of St. Thomas may be considered to stand on a higher scientific plane, all other things being equal, than one which propounds a teaching not in harmony with his. The Thomistic work exploits resources of authentically approved accuracy calculated to aid in the construction of that theological concept which the Church wishes her students to possess. As such it is objectively preferable to those books which set forth opposing theories. In approving the teaching of St. Thomas, the Church naturally does not mean to imply that each individual thesis set forth by him must be accepted as true. In one definite case, the thesis on the Immaculate Conception of the Virgin Mother of God, St. Thomas was clearly in error. However, this teaching in no way militates against the rest of his doctrine. Neither the Angelic Doctor himself nor the great corps of his followers ever attempted to bring out this denial of the Immaculate Conception as a central part of his theology. Historically that which was and is the characteristic teaching of St. Thomas, recognized and proposed as such in the great universities and in the houses of studies of his own order, is the doctrine approved by the Catholic Church.

I. The Authority of St. Alphonsus Liguori. In the field of moral theology the Church has given special approval to the writings of St. Alphonsus Liguori. This unique approbation has been stated in a negative manner, by the declaration that the Church has never found anything worthy of censure in his writings. In this way St. Alphonsus has been pointed out as a worthy guide in a field that offers more than ordinary measure of difficulty. The province of moral theology has to do with the education of those who are to administer the sacrament of Penance, and thus to care for and direct the souls of Christians. In such a field the official testimony that the doctrine of St. Alphonsus is trustworthy and acceptable is of immense value to the theologian.

J. The Authority of the Canonists. Melchior Cano rightly attached the authority of teachers in canon law to that of the scholastic theologians. The law is an ordinance of reason promulgated for the common good, by the one who has charge of a community. The law of the Church, then, looks to that good which is the possession of God in the beatific vision by those who, through their union with the Church, obtain the gift of eternal salvation. Its purpose is the glory of God, to be procured in the fullness of Christ in the sanctification and salvation of those for whom Christ shed His blood. Canon law is formulated by the Holy Father as the Vicar of Christ on earth, and by the ecumenical council which is subject to and in communion with him. It is thus the work of the hierarchy responsible for the direction and the instruction of the people of God.

At present the canon law of the western or Latin Church is codified in the 2414 canons which have been in force since Pentecost, 1918.[†] Among these canons we find several dogmatic pronouncements. These naturally enjoy tremendous authority, even though it is quite certain that Pope Benedict XV never intended that these declarations of the Code should be received as definitions.

But the very law of the Church is an expression of that directive force which orders Christians toward the attainment of their final end. The men who have been charged with the function of teaching that law are able authoritatively and competently to show how the precepts and the counsels of our Lord are made manifest in the society which He founded. Thus their teachings are indicative of the actual content and meaning of the message which God gave to the human race through Jesus Christ. The teacher of canon law is able to indicate the actual direction given by the living and infallible Church.

[†]   **Editor's Note:** St. John Paul II later promulgated a 1983 edition of the Code of Canon Law.

With the authority of the theologians, the list of resources proper to the science of sacred theology ends. The seven theological places with which we have dealt are those which will be of service only in the task of ascertaining the meaning of revealed doctrine. The subsequent places are those which are of service in accomplishing the work of other branches of discipline. However, these are utilized, each in its own way, in effecting the purpose of sacred theology.

* * *

Chapter VII

The Equipment of Sacred Theology: Part III

VIII. HUMAN REASON

A. Limits of Competence of the Human Reason in the Field of Theology. The competence of *human reason* in the work of sacred theology has been clearly marked out in the teaching of the [First] Vatican Council.[†] First of all both in the Council and in many other pronouncements the Catholic Church has insisted that human reason is utterly incapable of learning, by any natural process whatever, those truths which are designated as the revealed mysteries.[1] These truths are outside the natural field of competence of the human intellect, and for that matter of any created mind, actual or possible. They are truths which have reference to the intimate life of God, to God as He is known by and in Himself rather than merely as the necessary First Cause of creatures. These mysteries are intrinsically or essentially supernatural. As such they would never be known by any creature unless God had chosen to communicate them by a process which is at once distinct from and superior to the way in which the creature would naturally acquire his knowledge. Thus not only are these truths of faith themselves intrinsically supernatural, but they have also been brought to man in a supernatural way. Not only would these mysteries have been entirely unknown had they not been revealed to man, but even after they have been communicated by God and accepted by man with the certain and intrinsically supernatural assent of divine faith "they remain covered with the veil of faith and hidden in a cloud, as long as we are pilgrims from the Lord in this life for we walk in faith and not in light."[2] The clear vision and understanding of the Object with which the divine message is concerned is, of course, reserved for another life. The very felicity of heaven consists essentially in the clear apprehension of that same truth which we believe in divine faith.

B. The Direction of Human Reason in Theology. Human reason, then, can never hope to attain, in this life, a clear vision or understanding of the Thing which it considers in the science of sacred theology in the same way that it can obtain evidence of those objects which are studied in merely human disciplines. All of the mind's activity in the course of sacred theology must be ordered toward a distinct end, the work of grasping and understanding the *message* which contains these mysteries, and appreciating that message in all the objectivity of its meaning. Even though the Object described in them remains hidden, the sense of the formulas in which that divine message is conveyed is perfectly clear. The theologian can utilize his reason in order to grasp that meaning, in order to realize what God teaches men in the message which He has communicated to mankind through Jesus Christ. The divine public revelation stands as a definite message. It is the business of the theologian to exploit the resources of human intellectual activity in order that he may know the definite significance of the teaching which God has given to us about the Object we are to see in the ineffable clarity of heaven.[†]

---

†   **Editor's Note:** See also St. John Paul II's 1998 papal encyclical *Fides et Ratio* ("On the Relationship Between Faith and Reason").

1.   The [First] Vatican Council, the Constitution *Dei Filius*, Chap. 1, on faith and reason and the corresponding canon (Denzinger, 1795 and 1816).

2.   Ibid. (Denzinger, 1796).

†   **Editor's Note:** For consideration of themes Fenton discusses in these sections, see Reginald Garrigou-Lagrange, O.P., *The Sense of Mystery: Clarity and Obscurity*

The mode of this activity has been pointed out by the [First] Vatican Council. "When reason, enlightened by faith, seeks from God seriously, piously, and soberly some understanding of the mysteries, it obtains this most precious guerdon, both by way of analogy with the things it knows naturally and through the connection of the mysteries among themselves and with the ultimate end of man."[3] This is the process by which the theological process, properly so called, is educed. It is a complex operation in which all of the force of human reasoning is meant to be employed.

We have already seen that the theological conclusion is formed through the use of analogy and comparison. However, in order to appreciate this function of reason in the development of theological teaching, we must realize the special work it performs in studying the preambles of faith, fundamental theology, and the apology of dogma. The characteristically theological conclusion is drawn after a process of comparison with the rule of faith. His operation presupposes a definite rational procedure. Logically one must realize the existence of God before he can take anything on His authority. The truths of the natural order relative to the existence and the attributes of God are known as the preambles of faith.

C. Proof of the Existence of God.[†] The force of human reason is obviously sufficient to recognize the One True God, our Creator and Lord, as the principle and the end of all things. According to the explicit teaching of the Catholic Church, the existence of God becomes evident from a consideration of the created universe itself. The Church speaks quite explicitly and employs technical terms to bring out the clarity and force of her message. She tells us in the Anti-Modernist Oath that the human mind

in the Intellectual Life, trans. Matthew K. Minerd (Steubenville, OH: Emmaus Academic, 2017).

3. Denzinger, 1796.

† **Editor's Note:** For a listing of some recent resources which examine the proofs for God's existence, see the editorial note above on p. 35.

can actually *demonstrate* the existence of God through the visible works of creation, as a cause is demonstrated from its effect.[4]

God, then, has actually revealed to us that His *existence* can be demonstrated. To deny this is to reject a statement which we are meant to accept with the assent of Christian faith. However, the human mind is perfectly capable of carrying out the demonstration by the use of its own native forces. When the demonstration is completed, the man who has made it sees the statement "God exists" as something evidently and necessarily true.

Obviously, as St Thomas has pointed out, it is impossible at one time to have faith and evident knowledge of the same truth. It is of the very essence of our faith that the object of that faith be something not seen in the light of natural evidence. For if the object is seen, then it is impossible to say that the intellect assents to the truth of the judgment concerning it precisely on the word of someone who tells us about it. Consequently, once a man has actually made a demonstration of God's existence, he no longer accepts this truth precisely on divine faith. The person who has neither made nor learned the demonstration can, of course, accept this statement and assent to it because of the authority of God who has revealed it. A person must know and admit the fact of God's existence before he can accept any of the doctrine which constitutes Catholic dogma. Furthermore, according to this same teaching of the Vatican Council, the proof of God's existence actually terminates in man's acknowledgment that there is One True God who is the Creator and Lord of all things. Then according to this authentic declaration of the Catholic Church the human mind is competent to prove by its own natural forces the existence of at least some of the *divine attributes*. Thus by the very fact that he has a human intellect, man can see that the existence of things which are moved, caused, contingent, partially perfect, and ordered to a purpose in this world necessarily indicates the existence of a First Cause who is not subject to motion or causality, who is absolutely

---

4.   Denzinger, 2145.

necessary, who is at once the fullness or perfection, of being and the Supreme Intelligence which orders all things distinct from Itself to the attainment of their ultimate good. This One, who is Subsistent Being itself, is shown to be simple, all perfect, immutable, the Lord and Creator of all things.

D. The Formation of Theological Concepts. This activity of human reason has necessarily a tremendous part to play in the essential work of sacred theology. It results not only in a proof of the existence of God, as that term is properly understood, but in the formation of that *basic concept of God* which is used throughout the course of the science. In showing God as the evidently existing First Cause, human reason offers to sacred theology a concept of God which is perfectly correct even though it can never adequately bring out the full wealth of perfection which is the Living God. This concept of God as the First Cause is capable of being elaborated by the information which the Creator has given us about Himself in the course of public revelation.

What is revealed is, of course, a body of truth. It is axiomatic that the truth is contained and expressed in the second act of the mind, the judgment, rather than in the first which is the simple apprehension. As a matter of fact the content of divine revelation is conveyed to mankind in a certain body of propositions. The terms which enter into those propositions signify ideas which can be formed naturally by the human mind. Thus, for example, when we say that there are three Persons in God, we express one of the intrinsically supernatural truths which it has pleased God to communicate to the human race. But we express this mystery in a sentence composed of terms well within the natural competence of the human intellect. For it is quite obvious that man can naturally know the meaning of the terms "to be" and "three" and "persons." Likewise man can know what is meant by the term "God."

When a man has used his reason in the work of sacred theology for demonstrating the existence of God, he is well aware that the term means basically that self-subsistent Being whose existence is made manifest from the activity and the reality of visible mundane creatures. Should he fail to accept this basic meaning, and presume to think of God merely as some intangible reality who possesses human characteristics and powers in a much more perfect way than man himself possesses them, then he has fallen into the ever present trap of anthropomorphism, and he has made it impossible for himself accurately to accept and expound the revealed teachings about God our Creator. But, on the other hand, if he utilizes this accurate and correct notion of God which is elaborated through that process in which God's existence is demonstrated, man can grasp the objective and traditional meaning of those intrinsically supernatural truths which came into the world in the teaching, of Jesus Christ our Lord.

Thus human reason is competent to ascertain by its own natural power the truths which constitute the preamble to divine faith. In this work, through the proper demonstration of God's existence, and through the process of pointing out those attributes or perfections which, according to the mode of our human knowledge and predication, characterize the divine nature, human reason makes one of its great contributions to the essential work of sacred theology.

E. The Work of Comparison. Again human reason, with all its power of comparison and inference, has a theological function to fulfill in comparing any doctrine with the proper and immediate rule of faith which is the doctrine given to the Catholic Church by the Apostles, publicly accepted and set forth within the Church as a teaching which all must accept under penalty of exclusion from the unity of Christ's mystical body. This living apostolic teaching is, as we have seen, distinctly evident. The theologian can and should be able to use his reason in such a way as to judge the acceptability of any teaching in the light of this standard. He can examine a thesis or an opinion in order to see if that statement is in open and flagrant contradiction to the rule of faith. If this is the case, he finds the proposition is heretical. Should this proposition, on the other hand, contain inferences or implications which stand in opposition to the rule of faith, then the proposition as it exists is at least erroneous. In such judgments, however, human reason acts with the full enlightenment of divine faith.

F. The Judgment of Credibility. Another function of human reason in the work of sacred theology is found in the judgment of credibility with reference to Catholic dogma. It is a cardinal principle of Catholic apologetics, stressed by the [First] Vatican Council,[5] and again still more explicitly in the oath against the Modernists,[6] that human reason is naturally able to see that Catholic dogma is rationally credible. This dogma is the doctrine contained in Holy Scripture and in Tradition, and set forth by the Catholic Church, either in her solemn judgment or in her ordinary and universal teaching office as having been revealed by God and as a teaching which all must accept on the authority of God who has revealed it. When we say that it is *credible* we mean that it can be received with the assent of divine faith rationally and prudently. The basis of this judgment of credibility is the fact that, first, no contradiction is involved in the claim that Christian dogma is revealed, and secondly, that this doctrine carries with it manifest or naturally evident indication of its divine origin.

Human reason is competent to ascertain the possibility of revelation by its own natural powers. In order to perform this task a man must first see exactly what the Catholic Church means by saying that the teaching which she is commissioned to present to the world is actually *revealed* by God. Once it has been seen that a divinely revealed doctrine is actually a communication which God has addressed to man in speaking to him and enlightening him on some matter which man did not know previously, the mind can see clearly and naturally that this orthodox concept of divine revelation involves no self-contradiction, and at the same time is evidently compatible with the manifest natural knowledge about God and man.

A man recognizes naturally an indication of the divine origin of the Catholic message through a consideration of the criteria of revelation. Among these criteria, miracles and prophecies are of primary

5.   Denzinger, 1790 and 1794.
6.   Denzinger, 2145.

importance. Human reason can easily demonstrate the possibility and the significance of miracles by its own natural powers. So far as the possibility is concerned it is fully within the natural competence of the human mind to realize that the Creator of the world is in no way subject to the physical laws which govern the created universe. As a matter of fact these laws depend essentially upon the One who has made the world. Thus it is evidently possible for the Creator to perform within the created universe acts which are visibly beyond the natural power of any creature, actual or possible, and manifestly the work of that One who is the absolute Master of the world. Such works are evidently performed by God freely, and at the same time intelligently. God knows all of the circumstances which surround the performance of the miracle. So if a miracle or a series of miracles should occur in answer to the petition of a man who cites these effects as indications of the divine origin of the doctrine he proposes, then it is evident that God freely sanctions that claim.

Human reason is naturally competent to ascertain, moreover, that such miracles, and those prophecies which are miracles in the intellectual order, actually substantiate the claim made by Jesus Christ our Lord, that the doctrine which He preached to the world is really divine revelation. As a result, human reason can see that Christian revelation is credible that the person who accepts it with the assent of divine faith acts prudently and well. And this investigation of the criteria of revelation, of which human reason is capable and which it contributes to the integral work of sacred theology can consider, not merely the physical miracles wrought by our Lord, but the Church herself as a miracle, and all of the other indications that Christianity's claim is valid. This evidence can be seen by any person who is willing to examine the facts.

G. The Apology of Dogma. Finally there is another way in which human reason contributes to the work of sacred theology. The mind of man is naturally able to recognize the invalidity of any objection urged against Catholic dogma.[7] Reason will tell us,

---

7.   Denzinger, 1797.

of course, that not every shout raised against the Church, her practices, and teachings deserves the name and the dignity of an objection. Actually an objection is a process of reasoning, the conclusion of which contradicts the teaching it opposes. Consequently, should the doctrine against which objection is made be true, the objection is necessarily false. Its imperfection can proceed from one of two sources: either the process of reasoning itself is incorrect, or at least one of the propositions upon which the objection rests is erroneous.

It is actually of faith that no one is or ever will be able to show that any statement included in the fabric of divine revelation is false. Furthermore, any objection urged upon natural grounds can be shown to be false by the native powers of the human mind. In any such case the theologian can reason in such a way as to show with evident certitude either that the reasoning process which enters into the objection is faulty, or that one of the statements involved in the objection in such a way that the force of the conclusion depends upon it is erroneous. Naturally this error can be either the misstatement of a reality within the natural order or a faulty presentation of that revealed doctrine which is the subject of attack.

One cannot turn a page of the standard theological literature without finding examples of human reason's place in the work of sacred theology. It is the glory of sacred theology that in her service the human mind has demonstrated its most perfect powers and accomplishments. In her pages we find an analysis of concepts and of statements clearer and more rigorous than that which distinguishes the work of any other human study. The theologians of the Catholic Church have ever realized that the doctrine they are commissioned to examine and to propound is that which has its origin in the ineffable beauty of the Triune God. It was preached on earth by Jesus Christ the Son of God, and brought to the children of men by the witnesses who were His Apostles.

The theologians have employed every device of which the human mind is capable to expound that doctrine clearly and unequivocally. They have labored with success to repel the attacks raised against it by false brethren within the Church and by its enemies from without. In scholastic times they have built up masterpieces of intelligence like the *Summa Theologica* of St. Thomas Aquinas in which that doctrine has been set forth. They have answered the objections against sacred doctrine with all the solid brilliance of a St. Robert Bellarmine or a Francis Sylvius. In and through these works the best that human reason has to offer is and will be devoted to the work of sacred theology.

IX. The Authority of the Philosophers

A. Competent Philosophers. The authority of the philosophers contributes to the work of sacred theology quite differently from human reason itself, and it is never used as a substitute for the work of reason. Philosophy, of course, is a name which applies to the highest scientific knowledge within the purely natural competence of the human being. It is the knowledge of all things in function of their ultimate causes, in so far as these can be known by the natural power of the human mind. The philosopher is the man who considers this subject professionally. Those philosophers have authority who have actually instructed their fellow men on the ultimate and basic explanation of the universe in such a way that their teaching has been widely accepted. Or from a practical point of view they are the men whose works and teachings must be considered in any objective and scientific history of philosophy.

Not all of those philosophers who have been important enough to have influenced the history and the literature of this subject actually can be used in sacred theology. Those who have been proponents of the perennial philosophy, that systematic teaching which was set forth by Aristotle in the ancient world, by St. Thomas Aquinas in the Middle Ages and by the innumerable Catholic writers in our own modern times, can be of service to philosophy. Although there have been and still are important divergences in the doctrine of these men, as a group they recognize the basic problems of reality, agree on fundamental principles, and utilize the traditional wisdom of humanity in setting forth their own conclusions. Those writers and teachers whose tenets could not be classified within the limits of the perennial philosophy, although they may have been brilliant and learned, could not make the same contribution to the work of sacred theology.

B. The Definition of Terms. Naturally the easiest way to understand the function of the authority of the philosophers in the work of sacred theology is actually to examine the content of theological literature for the use of this "*place.*" First of all, of course, the authority of the philosophers is used in the line of definitions. The medieval theologians, in describing the characteristics of their own subject, spoke of it as a science. They had recourse to the philosophy of Aristotle for the definition of a science, and St. Thomas with his school was able to show that the Aristotelian concept of a science was verified in that discipline which we call sacred theology. Likewise, then, they discussed the practical and the speculative characteristics of sacred theology, they utilized the terms practical and speculative as they had been employed and defined by the corps of philosophers who had preceded them.

In exactly the same way theologians examined the traditional meaning of the words *person, nature,* and *supposit* when these terms were first employed in propositions expressing the content of divine public revelation. As a matter of fact these terms were not used in the divinely inspired pages of Holy Scripture. Our Lord Himself had not employed them in teaching His message to His Apostles, and these divinely appointed witnesses had not utilized them for the expression of their doctrine.

However, the authentic proponents of Christian doctrine found these terms to be admirably suited for the expression of Christ's message in such a way as to preclude any possibility of error and equivocation among those who had been exposed to the heresy of Arius. The term "person" was fitted to designate the Father, the Son, and the Holy Spirit. The term "nature" or

"essence" was fitted to signify that in which the Father and the
Son and the Holy Spirit subsist, that which is not distinct from
any one of them while each of the three Persons is really distinct
from the two others.[†]

In adopting these terms and in explaining their use, the corps
of Catholic theologians naturally had recourse to the writings of
traditional philosophers. Since the theological term is meant by its
very nature to give unequivocal expression to the divine message,
it is imperative that it should convey that meaning which the great
majority of cultured men have always seen in it. It would have
been no advantage whatever for the Nicene fathers to have utilized
the term "consubstantial" unless the majority of men recognized
a common meaning for "substance" and "substantial." That common meaning is contained and explained in the writings of philosophers. So it is that the philosophers can and should be cited
as authorities on the use of the terms to be employed in sacred
theology.

C. The Limits to Authority of the Philosophers. But, while
the authority of the philosophers can be alleged for the meaning of
terms which are used in theology, naturally their consent has nothing to do with the actual proposition of divine mysteries. The mystery as such is a truth about the intimate life of God, a truth which
is over and above the natural competence of any creature, actual or
possible. Since it can be made known to man only by the process of
divine revelation, and since it can be accepted with certitude only
with the assent of theological faith, it is evident that the philosopher who, as such, is interested in what is objectively and naturally
evident about the ultimate explanation of the world in which he
lives, can never teach the content of these mysteries. He can only
deal with those matters in which the theologian, according to the
teaching of the [First] Vatican Council, can find analogies to aid
him in his clear and unequivocal proposition of the revealed truth.

---

†   **Editor's Note:** See Gilles Emery, O.P., *The Trinitarian Theology of St. Thomas
Aquinas* (Oxford: Oxford University Press, 2007).

D. The Preambles of Faith.[†] Naturally the authority of the philosopher has a considerable part to play in elucidating the preambles of faith. It is revealed by God that man can demonstrate the existence of his Creator in so far as the movement and the being of created reality are such as to show a necessary dependence upon an actually existing First Cause. As a matter of fact philosophers like Plato and Aristotle long ago demonstrated God's existence, using the very proofs or arguments which the great Doctors of the Catholic Church have developed and incorporated into the fabric of sacred theology. The theologian can and should allege these proofs at least as valid evidence that the existence of God can be demonstrated by those who have not accepted the content of divine public revelation.

On this point, however, we must be very careful to avoid a misconception which would vitiate the use of this theological place. The authority of the philosopher, with reference to the proof of God's existence or in any other section of sacred theology, in no way replaces the work of human reason. We do not accept the proofs for the existence of God merely on the word or on the authority of those philosophers who have successfully made such a demonstration. A man has completed the proof for the existence of God which belongs to sacred theology only when it has become perfectly evident to him that a contingent and caused being could not be or act except in so far as it is kept in existence and in activity by One who is Pure Act.[††] A proof accepted merely on the word of another is at best an exercise of memory.

The authority of the philosopher has been used, and properly used, to show what the philosopher actually taught about that Being whose existence is known by way of demonstration. Thus it was perfectly legitimate for Francis Sylvius to insist in his treatise,

---

[†]   **Editor's Note:** For a contemporary consideration of the preambles of faith, see Ralph McInerny, *Praeambula Fidei: Thomism and the God of the Philosophers* (Washington, DC: The Catholic University of America Press, 2006).

[††] **Editor's Note:** See Serge-Thomas Bonino, O.P., *Dieu, « Celui qui est » (De Deo ut uno)* (Paris: Parole et Silence, 2016), pp. 51–227.

De Motione Motoris, that the Aristotelian philosophers had found that their concept of that Being whose existence is shown by the being and the movement of creatures is a concept of One who moves those creatures in such a way that every fiber and aspect of the movement, in so far as it is real and good, can really be attributed to Him as a First Cause and to the creature in so far as it is the secondary cause.[8] In citing the Christian disciples of Aristotle, as well as the great philosopher himself, the Douai master shows clearly that the proofs of the existence of God which they offer are such as to demonstrate that God concurs with His creatures not only in producing effects but also in acting upon the secondary cause itself, attributing to that secondary cause every spark of reality which belongs to its activity. Sylvius cites St. Thomas, not only as a theologian but in his capacity as a philosopher, and with him a host of writers who have contributed materially to the enrichment of Catholic philosophy. And long before him the master whom he loved and followed had consecrated the authority of Aristotle in calling him the Philosopher, and had utilized the good in the teachings of the Mohammedan Averroes so well as to recognize him as the Commentator *per excellentiam*.[9]

X. THE AUTHORITY OF THE HISTORIAN

A. The Direction of This Authority. This last among the theological places is an important instrument for the proper presentation of theological truth. Sacred theology utilizes the authority of historians and the force of human history particularly in the work of Christian apologetics. When she sets out to establish the

---

8.   Sylvius, *De Motione Primi Motoris, Pars Secunda*. This work is among those included in the edition of the *Opuscula* published by Father Norbert D'Elbecque, O.P., at Antwerp in 1698. Cf. also the article about this opusculum by Fenton in the *New Scholasticism* for June 1939.

9.   St. Thomas and his fellow scholastics naturally used the authority of the philosophers also to disprove assertions that the Christian teaching contradicted propositions which are evident in the light of natural reason.

rational credibility of Catholic dogma, she is faced with the task of showing that the teaching which Jesus Christ our Lord set forth as divinely revealed actually was certified by miracles and prophecies. The basic documents which tell of the miracles and prophecies of our Lord, and of His life and teachings, are the books of the New Testament, particularly the four Gospels. Obviously in showing the rational credibility of Catholic dogma it would be useless to appeal to the Gospels as inspired books. The inspired character of Holy Scripture is, after all, the object of the very faith the rational credibility of which we are attempting to manifest.

Consequently the authority of history is utilized to manifest in the Gospels and in the other books of the New Testament the factual, historical accuracy which engenders the proof of credibility. The theologian makes use of the studies of St. Irenaeus, Clement, Origen, Eusebius, and St. Jerome, among others to show that the four Gospels are historically reliable. The judgment of credibility which results from these historical proofs is perfectly certain, from an objective point of view. However, the certitude which accrues to it is entitatively inferior to the certitude of faith itself. The certitude of the judgment of credibility depends upon evidence adduced by the human reason. The certitude of divine faith depends upon the strength and clarity of the divine intelligence.

The authority of historians and of those modern archeologists who have contributed so much to the advance of historical science, is used extensively throughout fundamental dogmatic theology. In teaching the thesis on the Church, we rely upon the authority of the historians and the archeologists to show that St. Peter lived in Rome and died there as the bishop of that city. The writings of historians are used to show how the ancient councils were summoned, and how they acted under the direction of the supreme pontiff. And again history is used to show exactly what the condemned teachings of the early heretics were. It must not be forgotten that one of the condemned propositions from the *Augustinus* of Jansenius is historical in its form. In teaching that the Semi-Pelagians had taught the same doctrine as that set forward by some theologians of his own time, Jansenius fell into the evil of heresy by a misuse of history.

B. Use of the Authority of the Historians. All of this equipment, surpassing the resources of any other study which men can pursue, is available and actually should be used in order to set forth the teaching of Jesus Christ in all the force and purity of its meaning. The theologian manifests his sincere love of our Lord in laboring incessantly so that through his efforts, and by his mastery of the content and the procedure of his chosen science, the people of God may receive the salvific supernatural doctrine which they need, free of adulteration or ambiguity. In utilizing this matchless equipment for the purpose of sacred theology the theologian, by the grace of God, finds realized in himself that ideal which St. Thomas Aquinas, the prince of the theologians, expressed in his inaugural discourse as a Master of Sacred Theology in the old University of Paris. He becomes a channel through which the life-giving waters of divine grace flow down to the people to bring them the serenity they need in this life and eternal happiness in the next.

* * *

Chapter VIII

The Scientific Character of Sacred Theology

A. Theology a True Science. During the years, the main body of Thomistic theologians have been adamant in their assertion that sacred theology is a real science. They sponsored this proposition, not out of mere loyalty to the terminology of their favorite author, but as a basic truth about the nature of theology itself. The concept of scientific knowledge which they applied to sacred theology was that of St. Thomas himself, and basically that which had long ago been put forward by Aristotle in his *Posterior Analytics*. According to St. Thomas that knowledge is scientific which receives a certain assent in so far as it is drawn from certain definite principles.[1] The object of scientific knowledge is that doctrine which is seen as manifestly true, not by reason of its own evidence, but in the light of other certain propositions from which it is inferred.

The basic Aristotelian doctrine on the nature of a science is brought out in this paragraph. "We suppose ourselves to possess unqualified scientific knowledge of a thing, as opposed to knowing it in the accidental way in which the sophist knows, when we think that we know the cause on which the fact depends, as the cause of the fact and of no other, and further that the fact could not be other than it is."[2] He adds that "the proper object of unqualified scientific knowledge is something which cannot be other than what it is" and that we know this object "by demonstration." This demonstration is "a syllogism productive of scientific knowledge, a syllogism, that is, the grasp of which is *eo ipso* such knowledge." Certain conditions must be fulfilled in the premises from which this scientific knowledge is drawn. Such premises must be true, primary, immediate, better known than and prior to the conclusion, which is further related to them as effect to cause. Such is the rigorous Aristotelian notion of science which is found verified in that discipline which we know as sacred theology.[†]

St. Thomas and the great commentators predicated the term "science," of sacred theology because the "sacred doctrine" which they taught could be understood and treated properly only when it was recognized as a science. Furthermore, an examination of theological literature will show very clearly that a good many denials that sacred theology is a science in the strict Aristotelian sense of the term are really motivated by failure to appreciate the full perfection of the study itself. If we look at the actually existing accomplishments of sacred theology we can see that it fulfills the requisites for a true and perfect science.

We must not lose sight of the fact that the thing, in function of which sacred theology is said to be a science, is the theological

---

1.   In *ST* II-II, q. 4, a. 1, and again in the *Quaestiones Disputatae*, "*De Veritate*," q. 14, a. 2, distinguishes the intellectual acts of science from those of opinion, conjecture, suspicion, faith, and understanding.

2.   Aristotle gave his doctrine on the nature of scientific knowledge in the second chapter of the first book of his *Analytica Posteriora*. We have used the translation by G.R.G. Mure, M.A., in the first volume of the Oxford edition (Oxford: 1928). The Commentary of Sylvester Maurus, S.J., published in the Latin edition of the works of Aristotle under the direction of Cardinal Ehrle, S.J., at Paris in 1885, will be helpful for the understanding of this question.

†   **Editor's Note:** For more on the nature of Aristotelian "science" and its theological appropriation, see these two texts from James A. Weisheipl, O.P.: *Aristotelian Methodology: A Commentary on the* Posterior Analytics *of Aristotle* (River Forest, IL: Pontifical Institute of Philosophy/Dominican House of Studies, 1958); "The Meaning of *Sacra Doctrina* in *Summa Theologiae* I, q. 1," *The Thomist*, Vol. 38, No. 1 (1974): pp. 49–80.

conclusion or thesis, properly so called. This thesis is the response
to a theological problem, the resolution of a difficulty about the
meaning inherent in divine revelation. The truth of this resolution is
established by a real process of reasoning, through which it is shown
that the true theological conclusion actually must be considered as
a necessary expression of the perpetual and public teaching within
the Catholic Church. The contradiction to the proper thesis can be
shown to involve a denial of or an error in the faith itself.

B. The Demonstrative Proof in Sacred Theology.[†] In this way
it is obvious that the theologian knows "the cause upon which the
fact depends, as the cause of the fact and of no other." We are in-
vestigating within the order of sacred theology, we must remember,
and the *thing* about which we are concerned is the meaning of a
revealed doctrine rather than some naturally evident object. If we
are to consider the One about whom the science of sacred theology
is organized, then it is obvious that we could never find anything
which could be considered as a cause in His regard. But there definitely is a cause or reason why this resolution or this theological
thesis is objectively acceptable. That reason is the *rule of faith*, easily
ascertainable by the theologian or by anyone else. The theologian
puts forward his thesis as a certain or real theological conclusion because this resolution is demanded by the teaching of Jesus Christ our
Lord as that teaching has been guarded and set forth in the infallible
magisterium of the Catholic Church. And thus the divine revelation
which we accept on faith is the cause of the theological conclusion.

It is the cause of this fact or conclusion and of no other. Any
resolution opposed to a proper theological conclusion would be
incompatible with our faith. The divine revelation which is manifest in the magisterium of the Catholic Church, then, demands
this particular resolution to a problem raised about its meaning.
Thus the conclusion could not be other than what it is. Thus far

---

[†]   **Editor's Note:** See William A. Wallace, O.P., *The Role of Demonstration in Moral
Theology: A Study of Methodology in St. Thomas Aquinas* (Washington, DC: The
Thomist Press, 1962).

the basic Aristotelian definition of a science is manifestly verified in sacred theology.

The conclusion is known by a demonstrative syllogism, if it is to be considered as scientific in the sense expressed by the great Stagyrite. This demonstrative syllogism is one the very grasp or understanding of which constitutes scientific, knowledge. It is a real illative act, in which the mind shows an inference and sees the conclusion precisely as something inferred. Now, obviously there is no real inference, no passing from one truth to another required in composing a statement set down as a theological conclusion with precisely the same formula as it has been defined by the infallible authority of the Catholic Church. Thus the thesis that the true and historical Christ immediately and directly founded His Church while He dwelt among us is a statement contained in the Oath against Modernists. A man could not make a syllogism of which the statement of the oath would be a premise and the thesis would be a conclusion. But he would very definitely be compelled to go through an actual and proper process of reasoning in order to show that this thesis alone is expressive of the divinely revealed truth contained in Holy Scripture and in Tradition, and expressed by the Church and by her teachers throughout the course of history. He would have to demonstrate that a denial of this thesis would be incompatible with scriptural and patristic teaching.

Father Schultes spoke of the improper process of reasoning, that is, the one in which there is no real *transitus* from one truth to another, as alone capable of engendering a thesis which could be defined as of faith.[3] Actually, of course, the existing theses manifest in the literature of sacred theology show far more than an improper demonstration. The theological conclusion is meant to be established by proving that it is the resolution demanded, not only by the express definition of the Sovereign Pontiff or the Ecumenical Council, but by the divinely revealed doctrine as it is contained in Holy Scripture and in Tradition. In all of this complex process

---

3.   Schultes, O.P., *Introductio in Historiam Dogmatum*, p. 197.

of showing that the sources of revelation and the declarations of the Catholic Church render a denial of the theological conclusion impossible, there is certainly a true process of reasoning. A glance at a text of sacred theology, the Salmanticenses for example, will show that there is something more than improper reasoning used in establishing a theological conclusion.

C. Premises in the Theological Demonstration. The premise in this complex process which is the actual theological proof fulfills all the requisites for Aristotelian science. The doctrines which God has revealed to the world through Jesus Christ our Lord are perfectly *true*. They are primary and indemonstrable truths for this science. That which we accept with the assent of divine faith is seen immediately and intuitively by God in that act of supreme intelligence which is not distinct from His own essence. It is seen as true intuitively by those who, according to the decrees of God's mercy, enjoy the eternal felicity of the beatific vision. There is no ulterior truth in the light of which the content of public revelation must be known and accepted because that revelation conveys knowledge about the intimate life of God our Creator. As a result these truths of faith, in the light of which we show that the theological conclusion is actually a correct and unequivocal statement of the meaning of revealed doctrine, are in themselves primary and indemonstrable.

They are *better known* than the conclusions which are based upon them, since the certitude of faith is indubitably superior to that of theology. Furthermore, the doctrines of faith and the pronouncement of those doctrines in the living magisterium of the Catholic Church are certainly *prior to* the theological conclusions as they enter into the study of sacred theology. They are the *causes* of the conclusions, since the theological conclusion is advanced as an explanation demanded by and in the very content of Catholic teaching on the content of divine revelation.

In this way, sacred theology as it has actually been taught and expressed in the traditional Catholic literature by men who have been recognized as its authentic and competent proponents, is a science in the strict sense of the term. The fact that the dogmas which serve as

principles in this study are accepted on the authority of God who has
revealed them, rather than seen intuitively as true by the theologians
does not prevent theology from proceeding as a science. However, we
can say that this science exists in a less perfect condition as long as
its principles are received on faith rather than known in the light of
the beatific vision. For the habit of theology will not be destroyed by
death. It will exist in a perfect state in the glory of heaven.

 D. Theology a Subalternate Science. Sacred theology is qualified by St. Thomas Aquinas and by those writers who constitute
the Thomistic school as a *subalternate* science.[4] The term itself is
not particularly important. St. Thomas himself did not use it in
the article in which he establishes and demonstrates the scientific
character of sacred theology. But the idea conveyed in the term is
absolutely essential for any proper understanding of the science. A
science is said to be subalternate when it proceeds from principles
which are known in the light of a higher science.[†] The principles
which sacred theology utilizes in establishing its conclusions are the
dogmas of faith. These propositions, as intrinsically supernatural,
are seen to be true in the light of God's knowledge and in that
beatific vision by which the saints in heaven enjoy an ineffable and
eternal happiness in the possession of a truth and reality which they
could never hope to obtain by their own unaided natural activity.
The knowledge of God is properly called science, in the accepted

---

4. *ST* I, q. 1, a. 2.

† **Editor's Note:** For more on subalternation, see Reginald Garrigou-Lagrange,
O.P., *The One God: A Commentary on the First Part of St. Thomas' Theological
Summa*, trans. Dom Bede Rose, O.S.B. (St. Louis, MO: B. Herder Book Co.,
1943), pp. 43–56; Cajetan's commentary on *ST* I, q. 1, a. 2; and John of St.
Thomas, *The Material Logic of John of St. Thomas*, trans. Yves Simon, John Glan-
ville, and G. Donald Hollenhorst (Chicago: University of Chicago Press, 1955),
pp. 510–24; Bernard Mullahy, C.S.C., "Subalternation and Mathematical
Physics," *Laval théologique et philosophique*, Vol. 2, No. 2 (1946): pp. 89–107.
Examples of recent considerations of this important topic include: M.V. Dougherty, "On the Alleged Subalternate Character of *Sacra Doctrina* in Aquinas,"
Proceedings of the American Catholic Philosophical Association, Vol. 77 (2004): pp.
101–10; Guy Mansini, O.S.B., "Are the Principles of *sacra doctrina per se nota*?",
The Thomist Vol. 74, No. 3 (2010): pp. 407–35.

terminology of the theologians, not because it is progressive and
discursive, but because it recognizes the nexus of causality in the
realm of truth. The knowledge which the blessed in heaven possess
is a formal and physical participation of this divine knowledge,
and, as a result, it too, must be considered as a science.

The propositions or teachings which theology uses to establish
its own conclusions are thus seen as true in the light of a higher
science. They are supernatural truths, and the body of truth which
they constitute, that which we know as the deposit of faith is itself
distinctively and intrinsically supernatural. The theological conclusion is shown to be true in the light of this supernatural doctrine
and, moreover, it is shown to be a manifestly objective statement
of the real meaning contained in the supernatural deposit of faith.
From this point of view all authors agree that sacred theology is
fundamentally supernatural. The truth which it sets out to expound and to elucidate and in the light of which its conclusions
are shown to be true is a message about that very reality in the
sight of which the angels and saints in heaven find their eternal and
ineffable beatitude. In this way theology is necessary for the people
of God, not merely as some extrinsic means for attaining eternal
happiness, but as that science which teaches about the very reality
in which alone men can hope to find their eternal joy.

**E. Theology Fundamentally a Supernatural Discipline and
Formally Natural in Character.**[5] But while sacred theology is *fundamentally supernatural*, by reason of its mode of procedure it is
formally natural. The process of proof by which it sets forth and

---

5.   Cf. Ioannes a Sancto Thoma, *Cursus Theologicus. In Quaestionem Primam
      Primam Partis*, disp. 2, a. 8. Many authors, as Molina, Zumel, and Conten-
      son spoke of sacred theology simply as a supernatural science. However, these
      men considered it as specified by its *obiectum formale quod* rather than by the
      obiectum formale quo. There was also a tendency among the older scholastics
      to distinguish between a theological conclusion which was deduced from two
      premises, both of which are received with the assent of divine faith and one
      which is derived from one premise of faith and another known as true in the
      light of natural reason. Such a distinction, however, is irrelevant in the light of
      modern studies on the theological method.

establishes its conclusions is quite in accordance with the natural method by which a man ascertains any other kind of scientific truth. Thus sacred theology is distinct from the gifts of the Holy Spirit. In these gifts of the Holy Spirit man is rendered docile to that divine movement under which he performs salutary acts in a way at once distinct from and superior to the way in which he ordinarily acts in accordance with the exigencies and the powers of his own nature.[†] The prayerful act of contemplation which a man performs under the influence of the gift of wisdom is just as much his own act as any other which he has ever elicited. But it is performed in a different way. In the natural manner of acting in the intellectual order as in the study of sacred theology, man arrives at his full knowledge progressively, in the sense that the ultimate act depends for its perfection on those which have gone before. The science of sacred theology is something acquired, and required by study and application at least equal to that required for the attainment of any other kind of scientific knowledge. Those acts which are supernatural in the manner in which they are performed are not acquired at all. A man cannot be said to study for an act of contemplation. The enlightenment which God granted, for example, to St. Catherine of Siena was in no way dependent upon any previous study on her part. But the theological knowledge of a Vasquez or a Sylvius was very definitely acquired. It was the result of years engaged in reading and research. God could give this knowledge to a man who had not prepared for it, but in the existing designs of His providence He does not concede it in this way. Theology is formally natural in the sense that it will not be obtained and possessed except by those men who are willing to study and labor to acquire it.[††]

[†]   **Editor's Note:** For a profound and classic consideration of the Gifts of the Holy Spirit, see John of St. Thomas, *The Gifts of the Holy Spirit*, trans. Dominic Hughes, O.P. (Tacoma, WA: Cluny Media, 2016).

[††]   **Editor's Note:** For a moving reflection on the "spirituality" of sacred study, see Reginald Garrigou-Lagrange, O.P., *The One God: A Commentary on the First Part of St. Thomas' Theological Summa*, trans. Dom Bede Rose, O.S.B. (St. Louis, MO: B. Herder Book Co., 1943), pp. 31–37.

F. The Possessor of Sacred Theology. Because sacred theology is fundamentally supernatural, it can be possessed only by those men who believe what God has taught us through Jesus Christ our Lord and proposed to us in the infallible magisterium of the Catholic Church. The content of divine revelation is intrinsically supernatural. It can be seen as true by a creature only in the essentially supernatural act of the beatific vision. In this world, where men are meant to prepare themselves for that eternal joy, it can be accepted with certainty only with the assent of divine faith. For, when evidence is lacking, the only kind of assent which a person who had not made an act of faith could possibly give would be one based either on his own choice or on the authority of some human being. But neither the whim of one man nor the authority of any other creature could ever engender an objectively certain assent in this matter.

It is characteristic of Christian faith that a man who denies or doubts one article or dogma actually loses the gift of faith itself. The motive of faith, the light in which all of the revealed teachings are accepted, is the authority of God revealing. Should a man choose to reject that authority on one article, he destroys the force of this motive in influencing any further assent on his part. The man who rejects the teaching of God on the infallibility of the Roman Pontiff, or on the Immaculate Conception has cast out doctrines which are just as truly revealed by God as are the dogmas of the Trinity and the Incarnation. If he should choose to accept the doctrines of the Trinity and the Incarnation, he could not do so because he receives the authority of God. Thus a heretic, an apostate, or an infidel cannot have the *habitus* of sacred theology because he could never be able to propound its theses as certain scientific conclusions. And, for that matter, an enemy of the Church as such cannot possess that science which Peter the Lombard so well declared that he took up out of a "zeal for the house of God."[6] Theology demands the faith, and the love of the faith and of the

---

6.   The prologue to the *First Book of Sentences*.

Church which is charged with the duty of propounding it, that
which Francis Sylvius called the "love of the brotherhood."[7]

**G. The Classification of Sacred Theology in Terms of a
Speculative and Practical Science.** As a true science which is fundamentally supernatural sacred theology falls strictly within the
category, neither of speculative nor of practical disciplines.[8] The
speculative science is one which is worthwhile for its own sake, one
which is not ordered to human activity distinct from itself as an
end. The practical science, on the other hand, is essentially directed
toward the performance of certain acts.[†] Naturally all human science which is purely natural must fall within one or the other of
these two categories. All of man's intellectual activity is either for
the sake of some end distinct from itself or such as to constitute
its own end or purpose. The individual who studies a speculative
science like metaphysics may do so with the purpose of teaching
it, but the science itself remains speculative. On the other hand,
an individual may study a practical science, as ethics for example,
merely for the sake of information, but the science as such is ordered toward the performance of proper human activity.

The science which God possesses is naturally not classified with
reference to man's action. It is entirely outside of and above both
the category of the speculative and that of the practical. As a result sacred theology, which is a formal and physical participation
of God's own knowledge, is essentially outside that classification
because it is not subject to the division on which the classification
is based. Strictly speaking, then, sacred theology can be designated
neither as a speculative nor as a practical science.

In so far as we can predicate these terms of sacred theology,
however, it is evident that this science must be regarded as more

---

7.   *Liber Tertius Controversiarum*, q. 1, a. 2.

8.   *ST* I, q. 1, a. 4.

†   **Editor's Note:** For a contemporary articulation of the distinction and relation-
ship between the speculative and the practical, see Steven A. Long, "Speculative
Foundations of Moral Theology and the Causality of Grace," *Studies in Christian
Ethics*, Vol. 23, No. 4 (2010): pp. 397–414.

speculative than practical. Theology possesses within itself the full measure of perfection of both classes of science. It is eminently speculative in so far as its formal subject is that Reality in the vision and possession of which men hope to find the only ultimate and eternal happiness available to them. As that science which declares and demonstrates the objective meaning of divine revelation, sacred theology is a kind of knowledge which is definitely and primarily worthwhile for its own sake. But it is also eminently practical since it tells of God who is our ultimate End, and of the ways by which we can attain the eternal beatitude God wills us to possess.

According to the teaching of John Duns Scotus, theology is essentially a practical branch of knowledge.[9] Keen logician that he was, the subtle Doctor did not dispute the actual content of St. Thomas' teaching. His objection and his thesis are based on his use of the word *practical*. He insisted that any doctrine which has some orientation toward human activity should properly be considered and designated as practical. He was perfectly correct in his contention that the sacred doctrine was meant to guide men in their progress toward eternal happiness rather than merely to delight them with its sweetness and profundity in this world. He was so enthusiastic in his concept of theology as a dynamic discipline, a source of spiritual life and activity within a man, that he preferred to adopt a terminology which does not express the equally important fact that sacred theology involves a knowledge of that Being in whom alone we are to find our eternal happiness. His terminology does not succeed in stressing that central truth to the effect that sacred theology looks at its object, not as this can be seen in the natural light of any created mind, but as it appears in the light of the divine intelligence. And, since sacred theology actually is a partaking of the divine knowledge, it deals principally and primarily with the intimate life of God rather than with those human acts by which we attain to God.

---

9.   Ioannes Duns Scotus, O.F.M., *Commentaria Oxoniensia, In Prologo*, qq. 4 and 5, a. 5. The edition used is that of Quaracchi, directed by Father Marianus Fernandez Garcia, O.F.M., 1912.

H. Theology as Wisdom.[†] The traditional teachers of sacred theology are unanimous in referring to it as "wisdom."[10] When they designated the science in this way they were pointing out tremendously important characteristics which a study of its literature brings out very clearly. Basically, wisdom is the most valuable and perfect type of knowledge. As a result the ancients were accustomed to speak of a certain restricted kind of wisdom in every department of intellectual activity. The knowledge of the architect is *wisdom* with reference to the art or skill of the stonemason or the carpenter. These latter work so as to dispose the materials in accordance with the architect's directions in such a way that these materials may be used in the construction of the building over which the architect is in charge. Thus his knowledge or plan directs the skill of the workers, and conversely the workers' art is subject to his provision.

There is a wisdom in the order of human activity, that which we know as prudence. Every other practical intellectual resource with which man is equipped is meant to contribute to the end of prudence, for the prudent man is one who judges with practical correctness on each individual moral act with which he is faced. There is likewise a wisdom in the speculative line, the ultimate human wisdom in the natural order. This is the first philosophy, that scientific discipline which we know as metaphysics. This is above all other branches of knowledge which lie within the purely natural competence of man, because it deals with what is absolutely the ultimate cause or explanation of reality. Every science deals with some kind of cause. Otherwise it could not be a science. But metaphysics explains reality in function of that One who is the First Mover and the Last End of the Universe. Any branch of learning which deals specifically with some cause which is itself subject to God, is by that reason inferior to metaphysics in the natural order.

[†]   **Editor's Note:** For a further consideration of theology and wisdom, see Kieran Conley, O.S.B., *A Theology of Wisdom: A Study in St. Thomas* (Dubuque, IA: The Priory Press, 1963).

10.   *ST* I, q. 1, a. 6.

However, sacred theology teaches about God from a much more perfect and lofty point than does metaphysics. This latter science knows about God only in so far as He is a cause, that is to say only in so far as His existence and nature can be known from an examination of that created reality which He moves and holds in being.† Sacred theology knows of God as He knows Himself. It considers Him in His intimate life. Hence sacred theology is a higher type of wisdom than even metaphysics. While it is inferior to the gift of wisdom, because of the fact that this latter operates in a supernatural manner in offering a knowledge of God, sacred theology remains the supreme science available to man.

I. The Dignity of Sacred Theology. This science, as we have already seen, surpasses all others in the firmness of that certitude which it engenders, and thus stands supreme among the speculative sciences which man is capable of acquiring. It directs man to an end which is absolutely ultimate and thus it takes precedence over all of the practical disciplines within the competence of man.[11]

In the hierarchy of practical sciences it is only natural that the discipline which leads and directs man to the achievement of his goal surpasses all of the others. A practical science exists for the sake of operation distinct from itself and this operation in its turn is finalized and specified by the object to which it is ordered. The science which is directed to a subordinate end is naturally subject to the one which has reference to a higher purpose. For example, the science of military operation as such definitely takes precedence over the art of handling the mechanized equipment for modern warfare. The only reason why the mechanized equipment is used at all is to attain victory and the victory is won by the army as a whole. The art of shipbuilding is subject to the science of navigation since

---

†   **Editor's Note:** The most comprehensive consideration of the relationship between the science of metaphysics and the existence God, in the light of contemporary philosophical controversies, remains Thomas C. O'Brien, O.P., *Metaphysics and the Existence of God*, ed. Cajetan Cuddy, O.P. (Tacoma, WA: Cluny Media, 2017).

11.   *ST* I, q. 1, a. 5.

the purpose of the shipbuilder is to produce a vessel which can be used fitly for transportation on water.

In the order of purposes, the end to which sacred theology leads is supreme and ultimate. The other practical sciences contribute to the attainment of ends which are themselves used for the possession of that ultimate Good in which alone man is to find the eternal beatitude he desires. Sacred theology is so intimately connected with the attainment of this ultimate end that in the corporate life of humanity this good will not be obtained without the sacred doctrine.

J. Influence on Other Sciences. By reason of its character as wisdom and as the supreme science within the attainment of man, sacred theology can and must judge about the principles and the conclusions put forward in other branches of learning.[12] Thus sacred theology occupies with respect to other forms of intellectual activity a place analogous but not entirely similar to that held by metaphysics. If a man wishes to establish the basic principles set forth in any lower science, eventually he must resolve his inquiry into questions about the first principles of being, the principles of causality, of sufficient reason, and of contradiction. All scientific knowledge is valid in function of these principles, and it is the province of metaphysics, and of this science alone to deal with them. Thus metaphysics performs a general and *positive* function in setting forth those truths which are implicit in every scientific demonstration or explanation.

It is not within the scope of sacred theology positively to set forth principles which enter into the fabric of the purely natural sciences. Its sapiential judgment has a purely negative influence. It is the business of sacred theology to examine the teaching set forth in the name of these purely natural sciences and to point out and correct any statement in opposition to revealed truth. Naturally this function of sacred theology must be considered very carefully in order that its scientific purpose may be achieved. Considerable

---

12. *ST* I, q. I, a. 6, the responses to the second and the third objections.

harm has been done to the prestige of sacred theology in misinter-preting its influence on other human sciences, and in claiming a control over the body of human theology which the science itself rejects. Furthermore, even in dealing with the proper negative in-fluence exercised by sacred theology as a science upon other hu-man studies, care must be taken to see that the statement to which exception is made actually is opposed to the content of Catholic faith. For this reason only the professionally competent theologian is qualified, as a rule, to express this critical judgment of theology on the findings of the other sciences.

By reason of the divinely instituted order among the sciences, purely natural disciplines can exercise no similar judgment about the content of sacred theology. Thus it lies perfectly within the competence of the theologian to declare and to prove that this statement, set forth in the name and with the apparatus of an in-ferior science, is incorrect. When that statement contradicts the revealed teaching which God has given to the world through Jesus Christ our Lord, then it is false, and it is within the power of sacred theology to say so. God is the Author of all truth within the natu-ral order as well as within the domain of supernatural revelation. He cannot contradict Himself. And since divine revelation is set forth, not as a dead letter but as a living doctrine in the infallible magisterium of the Catholic Church, the theologian can know the meaning of that revelation, and know it with perfect certainty. In the light of this revelation he is competent to recognize both the fact that this teaching has been contradicted, and the erroneous character of the statement which involves the contradiction.

Thus sacred theology is able to say with perfect certitude that a statement denying the fact of creation, and put forward under the heading of biology or of geology is utterly false. In the formation of this judgment sacred theology makes use only of those resourc-es which constitute its essential equipment. It has no need of the apparatus which is proper to the physical sciences themselves. The statement which is criticized by sacred theology is evidently false in so far as it contradicts the manifest content of divine revelation.

It would be absolutely incorrect to assert that sacred theology has or claims the power to deny scientific facts. There never has been, and there never will be a truth enunciated by any inferior science which contradicts the actual content of sacred theology. The statement contradictory to the principles of theology and set forth in the name of another science is either a groundless hypothesis or a crass misinterpretation of a fact. Even though the lower science in itself is not competent to grasp the reason why sacred theology objects to this particular teaching, the very fact that it can prevent serious error at least in those fields which have some relation to revealed doctrine makes this negative influence of sacred theology beneficial to the sciences over which it is exercised.

As wisdom, it is the business of sacred theology to recognize and point out the actually existing hierarchy of values in the created universe. The man who possesses this science knows the only ultimate and eternal end in which man is meant to find his full happiness. Furthermore, in the light of that divine revelation which sacred theology sets out to expound and explain, the theologian is able to ascertain exactly how the creatures of this world are meant to contribute toward the attainment of that end. To put the matter concretely, the theologian realizes that there are some possessions, like habitual grace and the theological virtues without which a man will not attain his eternal salvation. He knows well that all natural or temporal goods are such that, used properly, they can contribute toward the attainment of man's supernatural end. Used improperly they retard a man's progress toward God or turn him away entirely from his Creator. In the light of sacred theology, the supreme scientific wisdom available to man, he can recognize the order which God has placed in the universe, and see the proper disposition of those agencies by which he is meant to attain life everlasting and the temporal well-being which he seeks in this world.

* * *

Chapter IX

Opinions, Systems, and Schools

A. The Existence of Theological Opinions. We cannot actually begin to appreciate the scientific character of sacred theology until we realize the place and function of theological opinions within the discipline itself. The properly scientific conclusion that in function of which sacred theology is characterized as a true science, is perfectly certain. As a matter of fact, the true theological conclusion is endowed with a certitude higher than that possessed by the theses of any purely natural discipline. Nevertheless, the discipline of sacred theology, as it actually exists today and as it has been since it was first brought into scientific order, includes theses which are put forward merely as opinions. These are set forth in such a way that the theologian allows for the possibility that the opposing theses are true.

In one of the best modern manuals, that of Franz Diekamp, a good number of these opinions are found. In the matter *De Deo Uno* the author proposes the thesis "God does not know things distinct from Himself, either existent or possible, immediately in themselves" as the "more common teaching."[1] As a teaching which is merely "more common" it is not absolutely certain. It is contradicted in theses of Scotists, Molinists, and Nominalists, some of

193

which are actually taught in the schools, and which are not condemned by the Church. Thus Diekamp recognizes the possibility that the meaning of divine revelation may be that God really knows creatures, actual or possible, immediately in themselves.

Again as a Thomist he teaches that the medium of the divine knowledge of those free acts which are conditioned futures or futuribles is the eternal conditioned divine decree itself.[2] Here he attaches no theological note and brings out clearly and scientifically the opposite or Molinistic opinion. The Molinistic opinion is ably and publicly defended in the Catholic schools, and until the Church has made some definitive decision, neither Diekamp's teaching nor its opposite can be condemned. Neither may lay claim to the full measure of scientific theological certitude. Neither may be classed as a theological conclusion in the strict sense of the term, because the denial of a strict and perfect theological conclusion constitutes an error and may be designated as such. Diekamp's teaching in this case, like that of any other Thomistic theologian, is aimed at showing that his thesis is actually true, and that objections launched against it fail to manifest any real weakness or improbability. Thus it is an opinion in the strict sense of the word, a statement to which the mind assents as motivated by real reasons, which, however, are not in themselves sufficient to destroy the possibility of the contradictory being true.

B. The "*Sententia Fere Communis*." The "*sententia fere communis*" is a true and certain theological conclusion in itself, although it is not manifestly the doctrine of all qualified exponents of the sacred discipline. An example of such a thesis in the theology of Diekamp is his declaration to the effect that "God exercises vindictive justice most freely so that He can forgive a penitent sinner

---

1.   Diekamp, *Theologiae Dogmaticae Manuale*, Vol. I, p. 211.

2.   *Ibid.*, p. 217. The Thomists hold that, since every fiber and aspect of reality in the creature is something produced by God as a First Cause, the only way in which God could know the free activity of the creature is in that eternal plan by which He has arranged for the production of this activity. The Molinists, on the other hand, teach that these free acts of men are knowable by God in themselves.

without inflicting any punishment whatsoever upon him." As this thesis stands, according to the great Munster theologian, it is perfectly certain, yet it cannot actually be said to constitute the common doctrine of Catholic writers. According to the Bull *Sollicitudo Omnium Ecclesiarum* of Pope Alexander VII, the thesis that our Blessed Lady was in the first instant of her conception, preserved from the stain of original sin had gained so many adherents that, at the end of the year 1661 he could say that "now almost all Catholics accept it."[3] It was a declaration that at this time the thesis of the Immaculate Conception was *sententia fere communis.* The common teaching is, of course, a proper theological conclusion which, by reason of the authority of a moral unanimity of scholastic theologians, can be received as true Catholic doctrine. It would be at least rash to deny it.

C. The More Probable Opinion. However, when Diekamp set forth the thesis that "those who are not predestined to glory are negatively reprobated before their demerits are foreseen" as *more probable,*[4] he is establishing a real theological opinion but merely qualifies it by stating that the reasons for holding this opinion are definitely and manifestly stronger than those which militate against it. In dogmatic theology these stronger reasons are almost exclusively intrinsic. A proposition is said to be more probable in so far as logically demonstrated that the actual proofs offered, in support of the opposite contention have not the demonstrative value of those which support the thesis in question. In moral theology, by reason of the multiplicity of details attendant upon the classification of human acts, and by reason also of the fact that the moralist's teaching is frequently in itself an authority for placing this particular act in this definite category, the number of competent supporters of a given thesis can give it an extrinsic probability. If six or seven authoritative moral theologians teach that some act is

---

3. Diekamp, *Theologiae Dogmaticae Manuale*, p. 248; the teaching of Pope Alexander VII is found in Denzinger, 1100.

4. Diekamp, *Theologiae Dogmaticae Manuale*, p. 282.

licit or illicit, the thesis is extrinsically probable by reason of that very support. If the greater number of moralists support a thesis, it is constituted as extrinsically more probable than its opposite. However, in moral as in dogma the ultimate appeal must be to the scientific reasons alleged in defense of a thesis.[†]

D. Theological Opinions and Development of Theology and Dogma. A theological opinion exists where there is either an actual controversy or at least the possibility of such a discussion. It is set forth as the resolution to a real theological problem, a question about the meaning or significance of some part of divinely revealed doctrine. Or we can say that it is a question about the implications of some Catholic dogma, always recalling that such an implication has reference to the dogma's intrinsic meaning. The theological opinion is the first response to some theological problems, that is, to those which may freely be discussed in the Catholic schools. As time goes on the great body of theologians can recognize more fully the truth of that resolution which had first been taught tentatively, in the form of a theological opinion. They can teach it as more probable, then afterward as they progress corporately in their science, they can put it forward as certain. The time can come when the conclusion becomes the common teaching of theologians and is defined as of faith.

An examination of the history of sacred theology and of the history of dogma, which by the way are quite distinct fields of research, will show us very quickly that not all dogmatic definitions have originated in this way. The teaching of Athanasius against Arius was never a mere theological opinion. The heresiarch stated that the Word of God had been made or produced, and had had a beginning. "There was a time when He was not." It was the business of the competent theologians of that time to recognize and denounce the teaching of Arius for what it was, a manifest and violent contradiction of Christ's doctrine. But the positive use of the term "consubstantial" to denote the subsistence of the three

---

[†]   **Editor's Note:** See the editorial note above on pp. 151–52.

divine Persons in One and the same nature or substance was quite
another matter. The Fathers could and did show that the use of
this term obviated all of the errors which had sprung up about the
Blessed Trinity. The term itself was most probably condemned in
the writings of Paul of Samosata, in so far as it contributed to the
expression of one of the errors propounded by this heretic. Men
had to be persuaded that this term, then, could be used properly in
teaching revealed truth in all of its purity and perfection.

We must not forget that the teaching Church herself differentiates between the theological conclusion in the strict sense of the
term, and the mere theological opinion. The individual Thomist,
and the Thomistic school as a whole can be properly sure that their
theses constitute a correct statement of Catholic teaching. But only
the teaching Church which is entrusted with the care and expression of that revealed word is competent authentically and infallibly
to declare that correctness. As long as she allows these Thomistic
theses to be opposed in her schools, the Thomists cannot claim for
them the full measure of theological certitude.

The theological opinion is very definitely a factor in the development of dogma as well as in that of sacred theology. The Vatican
Council has used the words of St. Vincent of Lérins to declare as
a matter of faith that the understanding of one man as well as that
of the Church as a whole, can progress and grow in its grasp of the
revealed truth, and that this growth always takes place in one and
the same sense and meaning.[5] There can be no question, of course,
of new doctrines, of propositions which the ancient Church did
not recognize as revealed, but which the same Church in later years
accepted as having been communicated by God. Neither can there
be question of some statement which God added to the deposit of
faith after the death of the last Apostle. As a matter of fact there
has been no addition whatever to the content of public revelation
since the death of St. John the Evangelist. The Church is and has

---

5.   The end of chapter four in the Constitution [of the First Vatican Council] *Dei
     Filius* (Denzinger, 1800).

been since her inception perfectly infallible in her teaching of the revealed truth. Since she first came into being she has taught the entire doctrine which God gave to the world through Jesus Christ our Lord without error.

Then the definite progress in dogma and in sacred theology has come in the process of resolving problems and questions in such a way that the true and objective meaning which was contained in the divine teaching is set forth continually in answer to attacks against Catholic doctrine, and for the enlightenment of the piety of the faithful throughout the ages. The theological opinion is set forth as the teaching of a limited number of theologians explaining the meaning of divine revelation with reference to a particular problem.

E. The Thesis on the Immaculate Conception. In the time of St. Thomas Aquinas the thesis of the Immaculate Conception had the status of a theological opinion.[†] As a matter of fact the most prominent schoolmen refused to accept it. As time went on a satisfactory theological explanation was given by John Duns Scotus, and this thesis was generally considered as certain. Finally it was defined by the Holy Father as having been revealed by God to be believed of all men. The Church had always believed that our Blessed Lady was "full of grace." The teachers of Catholic doctrine had recognized in her a singular freedom from every trace of sin. The question of the expression of this very truth with reference to the conception of our Lady[††] was raised, and the work of the

---

[†]   **Editor's Note:** For more on Aquinas's understanding of the issues surrounding the Immaculate Conception, see Thomas U. Mullaney, O.P., "Mary Immaculate in the Writings of St. Thomas," *The Thomist*, Vol. 17, No. 4 (1954): pp. 433–68. For a brief consideration of this topic with regard to major figures in the Thomist tradition, see Romanus Cessario, O.P., "Mary in the Thomist Commentatorial Tradition," in *Sapienza e libertà. Studi in Onore del Prof. Lluís Clavell*, ed. Miguel Pérez de Laborda (Rome: EDUSC, 2012), pp. 81–88. Also of interest is Thomas M. Izbicki's essay "The Immaculate Conception and Ecclesiastical Politics from the Council of Basel to the Council of Trent: The Dominicans and their Foes," *Archiv für Reformationsgeschichte*, Vol. 96, No. 1 (2005): pp. 145–70.

[††]   **Editor's Note:** In the original text, Fenton says "with reference to the conception of our Lord…" This appears to be a mere typographical error, and thus we have changed it to "our Lady."

theologians was to answer this query by giving the true and exact meaning of the revealed deposit. The opinion first offered and the definition ultimately given are definitely intrinsic to this fabric of public revelation. And the opinion is meant to resolve itself ultimately into a true theological conclusion.

F. Schools and Systems as Expressions of Theological Opinion. Theological systems and schools can only be understood in function of these opinions. Because of the strong organic unity of sacred theology, one real theological opinion set forth by an author will naturally have its repercussions throughout the fabric of his teaching. For example, St. Thomas taught that essence and existence were identified in God and really distinct in all creatures. He brought this teaching into his question on the divine simplicity. It was his contention that all created things were known by God, not in themselves, but in the eternal decrees by which they are brought into existence. These teachings obviously influenced his doctrine on the divine intelligence and will, and his theses on providence, predestination, and creation. Thus we can speak of the Thomistic system.

Those theologians who use St. Thomas as a teacher and who propound his system constitute the Thomistic school. Obviously not every individual who puts forward a personal explanation or opinion could be said to have produced a system, or much less founded a school. Only those opinions which have influence through the fabric of sacred theology as a whole can be said to engender systems. And only those systems which have been taught and expounded by serious and approved theologians in the Catholic universities and houses of study can be said to be defended by a school.

When a man takes up the study of theology in our own day, he is struck at once with the existence and the importance of schools and systems. The most important systems in sacred theology are actually taught by well-defined and powerful schools, in such a way that the bulk of scholastic theological literature is the product of one or another of these bodies. The most important schools, those which have a practical monopoly in the field of present-day theology are the Thomistic, the Molinistic, and the Scotistic.

G. Thomistic School. The Thomistic school propounds the system of St. Thomas Aquinas. Its distinctive theses include, of course, the real identity of essence and existence in God and their real distinction in all creatures, and the causality of God requisite not only for the production of any effect by a creature but even for the activity of that secondary cause. The Thomists teach that the actual efficacious grace which God gives to men has its efficacy prior to any consent or cooperation on the part of the man to whom it is given; that it is efficacious from within, by reason of its own essence. Thus, according to their common teaching, God by this efficacious actual grace really predetermined the activity produced under the influence of the grace to such an extent that every scintilla of reality and goodness in the act is from God and from the creature. However, according to their doctrine the act and the perfection come truly from God as from a primary cause, and truly from the creature, but as from a secondary cause. In this way the very determination of the creature comes from God. God's influence is prior to the movement of the creature with a priority of nature rather than of time. It is in this sense that the Thomist teaches that God *pre*moves and *pre*determines all created forces, even the human will in its free activity.

The Thomists teach that liberty or the freedom of the will consists in the active indetermination of that faculty with regard to any particular good, seen as conducive to but not absolutely necessary for or identified with the good as such.[†] They are insistent upon the fact that the will is not free with regard to its adequate object, the good as such in this world, and God who is Subsistent Goodness as seen in the light of the beatific vision. It is their contention that no particular good, and not even God as He is known in this world,

---

[†]   **Editor's Note:** For a more extensive Thomistic consideration of human freedom vis-à-vis the divine premotion, see Steven A. Long, "Providence, Freedom, and Natural Law," *Nova et Vetera*, Vol. 4, No. 3 (2006): pp. 557–606.

can actually necessitate and determine the act of the human will. And, since the will really acts and operates with regard to one determinate object, the determination or the direction to this particular object must come from the will itself. But, according to Thomistic teaching the will acts and determines itself precisely in its capacity as a creature. Consequently the will acts and determines itself in so far as it is moved and determined by God, with that motion and determination which is always prior with the priority of nature rather than of time.

This systematic teaching is manifest not only in the treatise on divine grace, but also in that part of sacred theology which deals with God's government of His creatures. The Thomistic school teaches unequivocally that God really operates in every activity of every creature, since He is the source of every fiber and aspect of good found in the created universe. The Thomistic proofs of God's existence, particularly the first two among them, are really an application of this same truth. Every motion manifest in this world is an indication of God's existence because upon examination it becomes evident that no creature could move except in so far as here and now it is moved by God. And the causality of creatures would be impossible were it not for the fact that this same activity is from the creature and from One who is Subsistent Being Itself.

H. Scotism and Thomism. Thomism shares the Catholic schools of sacred theology with two systems and schools which are opposed to it in very different ways. The Scotists are those theologians who base their teaching upon that of John Duns Scotus, the Subtle Doctor of the Catholic schools. Scotus, like St. Thomas the Common Doctor, expounded the entire content of sacred doctrine. And as St. Thomas set forth characteristic and systematic opinions throughout the course of sacred theology, the system of Scotus embraces every part of theology. These masters differed in their basic description of sacred theology. For St. Thomas it is a science in the strict sense of the term, in itself outside of and above the classification of speculative and practical as embracing the perfections of both categories to an eminent degree, but more truly speculative

than practical. For Scotus it lacks something of the full essence of
a science, and it is primarily practical. Their concepts of the nature and function of sacred theology were practically identical, but
they differed sharply in the definitions of those terms which they
applied to this discipline. Both were consummate logicians. As a
result both use terms consistently throughout their works. Thus
where there is a question of terminology involved, the conclusion
of one cannot scientifically be compared with that of the other unless their respective definitions are taken into consideration.

Sometimes, however, they differ on conclusions in a way that
is quite independent of any mere terminology. Thus, for instance,
St. Thomas and his school teach that, according to the actually
existing decrees of divine providence, the Son of God would not
have become incarnate were it not for the sin of Adam. Scotus,
on the other hand, insists that, even if Adam had not sinned the
Incarnation would have taken place because God would not be
perfectly glorified in the universe without the Word made flesh.

An approximate comparison between the two schools, but one
which has definitely been overstressed, can be made by stating that
St. Thomas is intellectualistic while Scotus is voluntaristic. Properly
understood this comparison means simply that the Common Doctor
of the Catholic schools is prone to explain the divinely revealed truth
in function of the divine intelligence. For him the divine intelligence
is the cause of the universe. The decree or command by which the
created universe came into being and is conserved in existence is in
itself formally an intellectual act. He does not deny the causality of
the divine will, but, according to his doctrine the intellect has a definite priority over the will. Scotus and his school see the causal divine
decrees as formally belonging to God's will.

I. The System of Molina. The opposition of Molinism to
Thomism is of quite a different sort.[†] Molinism is the system which

---

[†]   **Editor's Note:** For a consideration of the foundational differences between
Aquinas and Molina, see Romanus Cessario, O.P., "Molina and Aquinas," in *A
Companion to Luis de Molina*, ed. Matthias Kaufmann and Alexander Aichele
(Leiden: Brill, 2014), pp. 291–323.

was advanced by Luis de Molina, a great theologian of the late sixteenth century. Although Molina was a competent moralist, his teaching on this portion of sacred theology has little to do with the system or with the school bearing his name. He set forth an explanation which in his opinion would obviate difficulties inherent in earlier theological teaching on the place of free will in the working of divine grace. Molinism, then, is basically a theological teaching which aims to expound Catholic teaching on free will, and to explain the operation of divine grace in such a way as not to conflict with the central and obvious fact of human liberty. It centers in this particular treatise of sacred theology, and if it has its repercussions elsewhere, these are only applications of the essential doctrine on grace and free will.

Molinism, as Molina taught it, was very aptly summed up in the *Concordia* itself in four principles.[6] The first and fundamental principle is that manner in which God concurs with the work of his creatures. His influence is, according to Molina, exercised in regard to natural acts of free will by way of a general concursus, and in regard to supernatural acts by way of special aids. This first and fundamental principle in the teaching of Molina involves his own definition of liberty. A man is said to be free in the strictest sense of the term, to have liberty of the will when, "having posited all things requisite for acting, he can act or not act, or can so perform one act that he is also able to perform its opposite."[7] The "general" concursus of which he speaks does not touch the secondary cause itself, as if this secondary cause were to act when it had received a prior motion from God, but it touches or effects the action or the effect of the secondary cause immediately with this created cause itself.[8] According to this thesis, then, Molina declares

6. Ludovicus Molina, S.J., *Concordia Liberi Arbitrii Cum Gratiae Donis, Divina praescientia, Procidentia Praedestinatione et Reprobatione.* The pagination to which we refer is that of the commonly used Paris edition of 1876. The four principles basic to his system are proposed by Molina on pp. 548–49 of this edition.

7. Ibid., p. 10.

8. Ibid., p. 153.

that God concurs immediately with the immediacy of a supposit
with secondary causes for the production of their operations and
effects. This happens in such a way that the secondary cause immediately elicits its own operation, and through this operation it
produces a term or an effect. God, then, by His general concursus immediately brings about that operation with the secondary
cause, and through that same operation or action He produces the
terminus or effect.

This vitally important and fundamental tenet of Molina is set
forth precisely as a denial of the famous thesis which St. Thomas
Aquinas enunciated in the *Summa Theologica*, in the first part,
question 105, article 5.[9] It was the contention of the Common
Doctor that God actually operates by way of efficient causality in
all of His creatures in that He moves them to act by applying their
forms and powers to the actual operation, and again in so far as He
is the Creator of their powers and still conserves them in existence.
Molina admitted, of course, the dependence of all created forms
upon the conserving power of God, while the central and fundamental principle of his own system is a denial that God actually
moves the secondary cause to its act. It was his contention that the
effective concursus of God affected the operation and the effect,
but not the created force by which these effects were produced.

The second of the four principles in the light of which Molina
intended to clear up the difficulties inherent in the older theological explanation of the relations of effective grace and man's free
will has to do with the gift of final perseverance. It is his teaching
that two factors are requisite for this gift of final perseverance. One
of these conditions or factors must come from God, who decides
to confer those helps with which He foresees that the adult will
freely persevere. The other condition is on the part of the free will
of the adult. It is a condition without which God's intention to
confer these definite aids would not be an effective will to grant
the gift of final perseverance. It consists in the adult's free future

9.   Ibid., p. 152.

and persevering cooperation with these graces. This perseverance is within the power of the adult.

The third, and by far the best known, of the four principles is the famous thesis on the "*scientia media*." According to Molina there is a kind of divine knowledge which is *between* the free science of God and that which is merely natural. The free science to which Molina alludes is that which the theologians of our day designate more commonly under the term *science of vision*. It is the knowledge which God possesses of His creatures, those things which exist, have existed, or will exist in the created universe. Their existence, of course, depends upon Him. He brings them into being and conserves them freely. The "merely natural" knowledge is that of *simple intelligence*, by which God understands His own essence and the infinite multiplicity of ways in which this essence may be imitated in creatures. The *scientia media* of Molina was a kind of knowledge distinct from both of these. It was that knowledge by which God is said to understand, antecedently to any free act of His own will, what any intellectual creature would do freely in any possible set of circumstances if God were actually to place him in these circumstances. It was Molina's contention that this principle showed that the liberty of a created free will could stand with God's perfect knowledge of the future.

The fourth principle of Molina's explanation is that God's action in establishing the actual order of things in the created universe, an order in which he concedes to some and not to others those aids with which he sees that they would cooperate freely so as to attain eternal life, was in no way caused or influenced either by those who are to be saved or by those who are to be lost forever. In this way he teaches the absolute gratuitousness of predestination, and completes one of the most ingenious theories which has ever been formed by the mind of man.[10]

Molina himself was under no illusions about the novelty of his own system. He had never seen this theory of his for explaining the

---

10.   Ibid., p. 550.

concord of free will with divine predestination taught by any previous theological writer. He had no doubt that St. Augustine and
the other Fathers would have approved his teachings in their entirety had this teaching been known to them. Had his system always
been taught and explained, Molina thought that the Pelagian heresy might never have arisen, the Lutherans might never have dared
so impudently to deny the liberty of our will, contending that this
liberty was incompatible with divine grace, prescience, and predestination. Moreover, his system might have prevented many of the
faithful from being disturbed by the opinion of St. Augustine and
from joining the Pelagians. In the light of his teaching, if it had
been offered at the time, the last of the Pelagians in Gaul, those
who are mentioned in the epistles of Hilary and Prosper, might
have been divorced from their heresy.[11] The regrettable fact was
that this system had not been offered, and that all of these disasters
took place as a result. The amazing brilliance of the writer, his scru-
pulous honesty and clarity all serve to explain very well how Luis
de Molina has had his school in the Catholic universities for three
hundred years.

   J. Some Modern Concepts of Molinism. Before we begin to
compare Molinism and Thomism in their relations to present-day
theology, it would be well for us to realize that many of those who
deny some of the four principles of Molina still venture to invoke
his name upon their teaching. For example, one of the most important modern theologians, Father Boyer, in his *Tractatus de Gratia Divina* mentions a "system of congruous vocation"[12] as one of
the Catholic theological systems offered to explain the efficacy of
divine grace. This system of "congruous vocation" is the one which
Father Boyer himself adopts. He speaks of it as Molinistic and declares that there are many ways within Molinism itself of explaining the divine concursus in which efficacious grace consists. In his
latest edition he teaches, although less insistently than before, that

<hr>

11. Ibid., p. 548.
12. Carolus Boyer, S.J., *Tractatus de Gratia* (Rome, 1938), pp. 304–23.

this concursus of God is prior to the act of the creature, that it is the cause of the creature's application to its operation, and that it is thus in the creature a true "*praemotio physica*." This premotion is, of course, in the teaching of Father Boyer, a motion to a determinate act, although he rejects insistently the designation of physical predetermination.

Father Boyer's explanation is ingenious and intensely interesting. At the same time, however, we must realize that there is little scientific historical reason to speak of it strictly as "Molinistic." Molina did not attempt to explain the efficacy of grace formally in function of the divine concursus at all. According to his clearly expressed teaching a grace or supernatural favor is efficacious, and is given as efficacious grace, in so far as God foresees with infallible accuracy that the adult will actually and freely cooperate with this grace and use it in the direction of salutary activity. Moreover, the general concursus of God, as defined and explained by Molina was not in any sense a moving of the creature. This secondary cause, according to the *Concordia* does not act as first moved by the Creator. In short, the explanation offered by Father Boyer denies the fundamental principle on which the real system of Molina rests.

Still this recent work is quite indicative of a modern attitude toward the system and its founder. Today there is a tendency to designate any explanation of efficacious grace which admits the *scientia media* in any form whatsoever, and which denies physical premotion as Molinism. Under this broad and somewhat negative heading there are naturally many individual systems and schools. However, the teaching of Molina himself is logical and clear, and quite incompatible with many opinions which have since been offered in the name of his system. And, for the theologian, the *Concordia* is and will remain the authentic source for the study of Molinism.

K. Benefits Derived from Theological Controversy. Naturally a considerable benefit accrues to the teaching Church through the existence of these systems and schools, and from the discussions which are engendered in their contact. We can form an excellent idea of that benefit by comparing a good treatise which appeared before the controversy occasioned by the rise of Molinism, as for example the *De Libero Arbitrio* of Richard Smith with a representative work on the same subject after the controversy had taken form, a work like the treatise *De Gratia* of the Salmanticenses. There is an explicitness, a technical perfection in the later works which but for the Molinistic discussions, never would have appeared. The genius of Molina seized upon the very fundamentals of the traditional Thomistic teaching, and the Thomistic writers took advantage of the controversy to develop their system to its full perfection. A great work like the *De Motione Primi Motoris* of Sylvius owes its very perfection to the fact that the Douai Master was able to stress and explain the very points which had been criticized by the brilliant Spaniard.

L. Abuse of the Theological School. But, like every other beneficial agency, the theological system can very easily be abused. There is always a strong temptation for the members of a school to close ranks, and to act as members of a high school debating team rather than as men privileged to work toward the clear and unequivocal exposition of divine public revelation. That temptation has overcome far too many of those who have written or taught in the matter of the Thomistic-Molinistic controversy. Certain writers of both schools were reproved by Pope Clement XII for childishly attaching notes of heresy to systems opposed to their own.[13] Even in our own time there have been Thomists who have attempted to find in Molinism a resemblance to almost every kind of intellectual vagary which has ever distressed the children of men. And there have been Molinists who through an otherwise laudable loyalty to their own system, have tried to assert that Molina only put forward the true teaching of St. Thomas, while the Thomistic school followed a theological invention of Dominigo Bañez. Writing of this loose and unscientific variety does good neither to the system it is supposed to support nor to the great science of sacred theology.

---

13. A note to Denzinger, 1097.

The theological opinion, as we have already seen, is orientated toward the scientific conclusion, the theological thesis properly so called. And the man who studies and teaches one system is meant to labor toward the certain possession of theological truth. The science of sacred theology is such that labor in its regard is, as Peter the Lombard put it, taken up out of zeal for the house of God which is the Church of Jesus Christ our Lord. The loyalty we owe to God and to his Church in the study and the exposition of sacred theology certainly takes precedence over the loyalty we owe to any of these splendid servants of God who have formulated theological systems and founded theological schools. And in setting forth any system with more obstinacy than enlightenment, we do small service to the memory of the great theologian who organized that system.

The man who attempts to discuss these systems must necessarily make himself familiar with the classical works of the schools themselves. Actually no one is competent to pronounce on the comparative merits of Thomism and Molinism unless he knows the texts of St. Thomas and Molina quite well. And the man who utilizes these words in the spirit of the masters will necessarily seek for that true and unequivocal expression of the revealed truth which the masters themselves labored to attain. St. Thomas and Molina, Suarez and Sylvius, were all perfectly conversant with the technical literature of scholastic theology. They were scrupulously honest and rigidly scientific in their evaluation of that literature. They never allowed themselves to be animated by what best may be described as partisan motives. Using their labors and working in the spirit which dominated them, today's theologians can advance the cause of their science.

* * *

Chapter X

Unity and Pedagogical Division
in Sacred Theology

A. The Nature of Theological Unity. Since it has one function, one formal subject of attribution, and one motive in the light of which its conclusions are acceptable, the science of sacred theology has an organic unity unsurpassed among branches of human knowledge. It pursues one purpose, the clear and unequivocal statement of that teaching which God gave to the world through Jesus Christ our Lord. It has one formal object which is attained, or one formal subject of attribution; namely, God in His intimate life.[1] All the conclusions of sacred theology are actually meant to bring us a more perfect knowledge of God as He knows Himself, and as He has told us about Himself in the content of Christian revelation. But the ultimate and perfect basis for that unity which sacred theology possesses is the oneness of its light or motive, the formal reason under which alone all of its content is scientifically proper, the light of virtual revelation.

B. The Connection of Theological Theses. This formal unity of sacred theology is an affair of tremendous moment for the study of the science. The result of this unity is that each conclusion has its repercussions through the entire content of sacred theology. Consequently the study of sacred theology has always progressed, not only by way of analysis, the detailed examination of each thesis which enters into the fabric of the science, but also along the way of synthesis, the view of these conclusions in their proper order and background. Thus it is impossible to gain any adequate knowledge of one thesis in sacred theology apart from a realization of its relation to all the rest of theological teaching. When the Abbé Anger wrote one of the most brilliant modern treatises on the Church as the Mystical Body of Christ, he was compelled to point out the ramifications of this teaching in every other portion of sacred doctrine.[2] When De la Taille and Vonier[3] wrote their monographs on the essence of the Eucharistic sacrifice, they were compelled to recall the doctrine on the sacraments in general, the teaching on faith, and the treatise on the end of man.

The reason for this is quite clear. Every true theological conclusion is shown to be acceptable scientifically in so far as it is shown to be the actual sense or meaning of the divine public revelation. A perfect theological conclusion is such that the denial of it would involve rejection of a definite portion of revealed doctrine, or at least regrettable confusion in the exposition of that teaching. Even the theological opinion which actually belongs to sacred theology sets itself forward as an explanation of the meaning of divine revelation.

C. Practical Consequences of Theological Unity. So far as the individual student is concerned, this high unity of sacred theology is a matter of intense practical importance. It means first of all, that the beginner cannot hope to have a concept of those sections in sacred theology which he studies first which will compare with the knowledge he will gain by studying this same matter after he has been through the course in this science. For example, the young man who studies the treatise on the Blessed Trinity, and who is struck with the glorious truth set forth in the section on the divine

---

1.   Cf. *ST* I, q. 1, a. 3.

2.   Abbé Joseph Anger, *La Doctrine du Corps Mystique de Jesus-Christ*, 4th ed. (Paris: 1924).

3.   Mauritius de la Taille, S.J., *Mysterium Fidei*, 3rd ed. (Paris: 1931), and Dom Anscar Vonier, O.S.B., *The Key to the Doctrine of the Eucharist* (London: 1925).

missions will find that this teaching is seen in its full meaning only when he has finished the treatise on divine grace, and learned to know the nature of habitual grace itself. Those who consider the necessity of the Church for salvation will see the orthodox and scientific conclusion on this matter in their proper meaning when they examine them in the light of the Tridentine teaching on the preparation for the justification of an adult.

For all practical purposes, then, the student cannot consider the various treatises of sacred theology as hermetically sealed off one from the other. He cannot begin to appreciate one except in so far as he looks at it in the light of the others. In many ways the early part of the nineteenth century constituted a "Dark Age" in the history of sacred theology, and some appreciation of the reason why this is so may be gained from Cardinal Newman's account of his experiences with continental theologians immediately after his conversion. These men, professors of sacred theology, informed the distinguished neophyte that it was not then the fashion to utilize the integrated teachings of St. Thomas and the great scholastics, but that it was the custom to treat each section of sacred theology independently and separately.

Because it is the science in which the content of divine public revelation is taught and expounded, the unity and profundity of sacred theology are unsurpassed in the realm of human study. The message which is the divine public revelation is perfectly consistent within itself. If it is impossible that God should put forward any statement in the content of divine revelation which would be at variance with some truth which could be observed naturally, it is all the more necessary and true that the various statements which constitute the divine message are perfectly in accord, one with the other. And, as a matter of fact, both the dogmatic formula and the theological conclusion are expressions of truth which God has brought out with incomparable richness and profundity in the inspired books of Holy Scripture, and which are set forth with magnificent clarity on the pages of the Fathers. The one process of proof in sacred theology manifests a practical and scientific unity.

D. Courses in Sacred Theology. The unity of sacred theology is organic because the science itself is complex or composite. The perfect oneness of the science shines out in all of the academic or pedagogical complexity in which it is presented. In the actually existing theological literature, and in the organization of theological teaching in the seminaries and universities empowered to grant pontifical degrees in this science, the matter of sacred theology is divided into several distinct courses. In its instruction for carrying out properly the commands of the Apostolic Constitution *Deus Scientiarum Dominus*, the Congregation for Seminaries and Universities prescribes three sets of courses to be taught by the University Faculty of Sacred Theology.[4] The first set, the principal courses or disciplines, includes six headings:

1. Fundamental Theology.
2. Dogmatic Theology.
3. Moral Theology.
4. Holy Scripture (Introduction and Exegesis).
5. Ecclesiastical History, Patrology, and Christian Archeology.
6. Canon Law.

The second group, the auxiliary disciples or courses, contains four subjects:

1. Hebrew, Biblical Greek.
2. A systematic and historical treatment of the liturgy
3. Ascetical theology.
4. Theological questions pertaining to the Eastern Church.

---

4.   The Apostolic Constitution *Deus Scientiarum Dominus*, issued on May 24, 1931 and the set of rules promulgated by the Sacred Congregation of Seminaries and Universities on June 12 of that same year both have reference to the training of men who are being prepared for degrees in the science of sacred theology. All of the principal and auxiliary disciplines and a good many of those who are listed as electives are actually taught in every seminary which prepares men for the priesthood. All of these courses cooperate toward enabling the student to acquire the *habitus* of sacred theology.

The third group which comprises special courses given to candidates for theological degrees is not prescribed in the same way as are the contents of the first two groups. The Congregation puts this list forward as a suggestion, rather than as a definitive and obligatory set of instructions. The individual faculties are permitted and even encouraged to divide these courses, to add others and otherwise to deal with the matter in accordance with the needs of their students and the specialties of their instructors. The tentative list set forth by the Congregation includes the following subjects:

1. Sacred History of the Old and New Testaments.
2. Biblical Theology of the Old and New Testaments.
3. Selected Questions on Inspiration and Hermeneutics, especially about their relation to fundamental and dogmatic theology.
4. Exegesis of the most important texts of the New and Old Testaments.
5. Theological Doctrine of some Fathers or Doctors of the Church.
6. Selected Questions from Patrology.
7. Interpretation of selected texts from the Fathers or St. Thomas Aquinas.
8. Selected Questions from speculative dogmatic theology.
9. Selected Questions from speculative moral theology.
10. More recent problems in Apologetics.
11. Mariology.
12. Pastoral Theology.
13. Mystical Theology.
14. Liturgical Theology.
15. Selected Questions from Christian Archeology.
16. Sacred Eloquence.
17. Catechetics.
18. Pedagogy.
19. Ecclesiastical Historiography.
20. History of religion.

21. History of dogmas.
22. History of the councils.
23. History of theology and especially of the scholastic method.
24. History and Sources of Moral Theology.
25. History and Sources of Canon Law.
26. History of the liturgy.
27. History of the Missions.
28. Missiology.
29. Sacred Art.
30. Those ancient languages useful for theological studies.

E. Positive and Scholastic Theology. In the above list we find included practically every kind of course which is given in the Catholic schools of sacred theology today. The science itself is perfectly and pre-eminently one, but the importance and profundity of the subject matter, together with the tremendous development of the science during the nineteen centuries of its history render it imperative that it should be brought to the student in a departmentalized form. According to the ordinary pedagogical classification of these departments or courses, the fundamental distinction is that of positive from scholastic theology. The positive branch of sacred theology concentrates upon the sources or the apparatus of which the science makes use in drawing and developing its own theses. The second, and the essentially important branch, scholastic theology, is directly concerned with the unequivocal and objective explanation of divine revelation.

We must not allow ourselves to imagine that the scholastic theologian, or the treatise in scholastic theology does not use the sources and authorities on which theological conclusions are based. Some modern manuals take great pains to insist that their method is "positive as well as scholastic." These are ordinary manuals of scholastic theology for the most part. If the writer makes no use whatever of the authoritative sources, his work will not be theology at all. Actually that book or course is classified as scholastic in which the content of the revealed doctrine itself is exposed in the drawing of proper theological conclusions. The properly positive treatise or lecture is that in which the sources themselves are explained and arranged. We may consider general positive theology, and then the particular studies which are listed under that heading.

F. General Positive Theology. Petavius and Thomassinus are regarded as the founders of positive theology as such, or the general study of sacred theology under the positive method. Petavius intended to expound all the sections of sacred theology in his *Theologica Dogmata*. However, his theology is meant to be "not that polemic and subtle discipline which, almost alone, had occupied the schools, and which consequently has been properly designated as scholastic, but another more elegant and fruitful."[5] This positive theology was directed to give the place which had previously been accorded to dialectical disputations to the study and the exploitation of the proper resources of sacred theology. As a matter of fact Petavius justly remarked that many of the ordinary theological books of his time offered faulty and sometimes even misleading citations from the Fathers.

To remedy what he saw to be a serious imperfection in the theological literature of his time, he set forth the central thesis of theology and then gave the scientifically exact and complete citations of those patristic works in which the same thesis had been upheld. He succeeded admirably in showing that the real theological conclusion is established as such when it has been shown to be the expression of that doctrine which has been taught in and by the Catholic Church from its very inception. He used his immense erudition and linguistic ability to show the objective and traditional meaning of the Fathers and the Councils, and in so doing he brought out one of the most valuable works at the disposal of the modern theologian.

Petavius and Thomassinus used all of the proper resources of sacred theology, and thus their works may be classed as

---

5. Dionysius Petavius, S.J., *Opus de Theologicis Dogmatibus* (Bar-le-Duc, France: 1864), Vol. 1, p. 1.

general positive theology. However, the literature of sacred theology abounds in works of strictly positive orientation, in which attention is focused upon these resources considered individually. Thus there are biblical studies, those on the Fathers, on the Symbols, on the Councils, and on the liturgy. Furthermore, we can consider as distinct studies in positive theology those on the history of dogma and of theology, and that Christian archeology which throws such valuable light upon the faith and the practice of the infant Church.

G. Biblical Studies. Biblical studies include the introduction and exegesis. Introduction to Sacred Scripture, or *Sacred Hermeneutics* as the study is frequently designated, is one of the most complex and important portions of sacred theology. It opens with a study on the canon of scripture and on the meaning of the term inspiration. The canon is the official list of those books which are accepted by the Catholic Church as works which have God Himself as their author. It is the first business of Sacred Hermeneutics to study the formation and the definition of the canon both for the Old and for the New Testament, as well as the story of the promulgation of that canon by the Catholic Church. The same branch of sacred theology considers the meaning of inspiration, both with respect to the book of which God is the Author, and to the human writer whom God used as a free and complete instrument in the writing of a canonical book.

The Introduction to Sacred Scripture then proceeds with a consideration of the individual books which compose the Old and the New Testaments. The student is taught the internal and external evidence about the time when this book was written, its human author, the language in which it was written, and the integrity of the text which has come down to us. There must also be a scientific consideration of any important objections which have been raised against the acceptability of any book. There follows a treatise on the literary classification of the canonical books, and on the rules and kinds of Hebrew poetry. The same study must also include a discussion of the various versions or translations of Holy Scripture, and especially of the history and authority of that Latin version which we know as the Vulgate.

In Hermeneutics we must also study the historical and religious background of the Holy Scripture. The historical study includes a history of the chosen people up to the time of our Lord, and the elements of ancient history of the peoples who lived around Palestine and Egypt. This involves a serious study of biblical archeology. It must be accompanied by an explanation of the various ancient Oriental religions, to the practice or existence of which allusion is made in the inspired books. The introduction to the New Testament must include a scientific life of our Lord, as well as a history of the Catholic Church during the first century. Naturally, such historical work demands a treatment of the political, ethnic, and economic geography of the Holy Land during biblical times, and an explanation of such weights and measures among the Hebrews and their neighbors as are mentioned in the sacred writings. The introduction to Holy Scripture terminates with the principles of exegesis. The student is shown how the real text of Holy Scripture is and must be interpreted in accordance with the teaching of the Catholic Church as manifest in the unanimous consent of the Fathers. This includes a discussion of the various types of meaning which the Holy Scripture is capable of expressing.

That to which Hermeneutics properly constitutes an introduction is *exegesis*, the actual explanation and interpretation of the inspired writings. This exegesis can take the form of a verse for verse commentary, or an explanation of the dogmatic content of some book or group of books. The commentary is the outstanding work of scriptural scholarship. The author, utilizing all the resources of his erudition, sets forth each verse of Holy Scripture, shows its authenticity and then, in the light of traditional Catholic teaching, sets forth the meaning which God attached to this portion of Holy Writ, and which the Church as such has always found in it.

Using such commentaries, and sometimes including them in their texts, many authors bring out the dogmatic content contained in the Scripture as a whole, in one or the other Testament, in an individual book or group of books, or in some passages which contain our Lord's instructions. Thus there can be an explanation of the parables in which our Lord brought out the teaching on the kingdom of God, as well as theologies of the New Testament and of St. Paul.

H. Patristic Theology. In the field of positive theology we must also allocate the study of the Fathers and the other early ecclesiastical writers. The study of this literature as a whole is known as *Patrology*. In this course the student learns the identity of those early writers whose works are indicative of the belief within the early Church, the books they actually wrote, and the time these books were produced. The student of Patrology must know the topics on which the various Fathers wrote, and must be familiar with the text of at least the most important works. He is taught the best editions of these texts, and the light which they throw upon the history of Catholic dogma. Naturally, the field of Patrology is such that works of specialization are rendered altogether necessary. We must have individual studies on the teachings of each Father, as a whole, or with particular reference to those parts of sacred theology which he exposed most fully. From Patrology the theologian is expected to draw that appreciation of the patristic expression of Catholic thought without which he will be unable to draw and appreciate scientific conclusions.

I. Symbolic and Conciliar Studies. *Symbolic* is that portion of positive theology which considers the Catholic acts of faith or creeds, with reference to the individual errors and heresies excluded by them. *Conciliar theology* takes up the study of the ecclesiastical councils, both ecumenical and particular. In order properly to exploit these tremendously important resources of Catholic teaching, the theologian must know what councils have actually been held, how they have been assembled and sanctioned, and what they have pronounced. For this reason the theologian must be familiar with the history of ecclesiastical councils. Because of their relation to the true councils, he must also be aware of those ecclesiastical gatherings which never had the approval of the Church, councils like that of Rimini in which false doctrine was proposed. The fact that such councils put forward heretical teaching makes it easier for the student to appreciate the true faith of the Catholic Church as it was expressed and contradicted in early times. This portion of positive theology concludes with a study of the content and the history of the liturgy, in so far as this is expressive of Catholic dogma.

J. History of Dogma. The most important part of all this positive theology is that course in which the results of the others are expressed and arranged, the subject which we know as the *History of Dogma*. The dogmas are those assertions which are contained in Holy Scripture and in tradition and proclaimed by the Church either in her solemn judgment or in her ordinary and universal magisterium, as having been revealed by God to be accepted by all with the assent of divine faith. As a result, the history of dogma is an entirely different thing from the history of revelation. This latter would pertain primarily to the field of Scripture study. It would mark out the various stages at which God added to the store of divine public revelation which he confided first to the Israelite authorities and then to the Catholic Church. These additions were substantial. At definite times in the history of the true religion God gave to his people some truth which hitherto they had not known. It was a new statement which was not implied in the previously existing revealed deposit in such a way that the believer could actually deduce it from that doctrine which he had hitherto held on the authority of God. Such additions to the revealed deposit ceased definitively with the death of the last Apostle.

Consequently the history of dogma marks the various stages in which precisely the same doctrine has been set forth infallibly and authoritatively by the Catholic Church. But, although it is always the same teaching, with exactly the same sense and meaning, it has been proclaimed more and more explicitly as the years have gone by. As heresies have arisen, with danger that misinterpretation of the Church's dogmatic teaching would result in a loss of faith, or as the Christian life and devotion of Catholics have demanded, the Church has set forth her divine teaching in such a way that danger of equivocation of malinterpretation has been removed. It is the business of the history of dogma to examine these dogmatic declarations and to point out the process and the direction of this progressively more explicit Catholic teaching.

K. History of Theology. Closely allied to History of Dogma, yet really distinct from it, is the *History of Sacred Theology*. In this latter course we look for the actual progress of the science, rather than that of the dogmatic teaching of the Church itself. The history of sacred theology sets forth the various writers and schools that have contributed to the science, and shows how those contributions were made. This is one of the least developed sections in all of positive theology. Although the history of theology in ancient and medieval times has been written quite well, little serious work has been done in the direction of an adequate and scientific expression of the history of sacred theology since the Council of Trent.

L. Fundamental Theology. *Scholastic* theology is either fundamental or special. Fundamental theology considers those conclusions which have to do with the body of divine revelation as a whole, while special theology considers the individual doctrines which go to compose the message which God has given to the world through Jesus Christ our Lord. *Fundamental* theology naturally begins with the explanation of the nature, purpose, competence, and division of sacred theology itself. This reflective study of the science itself is called the *Methodology of Sacred Theology*.

The second part of fundamental theology is the science of *Apologetics*.[†] Any extensive acquaintance with modern literature in this field shows that there is no section of sacred doctrine more widely discussed and more freely treated than this. The questions are not so much about the truth of the conclusions offered in apologetics. As a matter of fact, in few portions of sacred doctrine is there such strong backing for individual theses as in apologetics. The question in apologetics seems to refer to the order and competence

---

[†]   **Editor's Note:** See Avery Cardinal Dulles, S.J., *A History of Apologetics* (San Francisco: Ignatius Press, 2005).

of the science. There are authors who set forth their apologetics in the form of treatises on the true religion. Others make it revolve around and lead to the conclusion that belonging to the Catholic Church is a requisite for eternal salvation, and that men are morally obligated to enroll themselves as members of the Church. Still others, in accordance with the masterful methodology of Father Gardeil, consider apologetics as that study which demonstrates the rational credibility of Catholic dogma as divine revelation. This last view is in accordance with the teaching of the Church and with the actual defense of the Catholic faith through the centuries.

Ultimately apologetics is set forth as the rational defense of Catholic truth. Its purpose is to show that it is prudent and reasonable to assent to this teaching. Since the essential content of Catholic dogma is intrinsically supernatural and as such beyond the natural competence of any created intelligence, the apologist cannot demonstrate the truth of this teaching. He could never, for instance, show that the statement that there are three Persons in God is evidently true in the same way that the mathematician can actually demonstrate the truth of the proposition that the sum of all the angles within a triangle is equal to two right angles. Consequently the only procedure by which the apologist can demonstrate, even to the man who has not the faith, that it is not unreasonable to accept Catholic dogma as divinely revealed, is to demonstrate clearly that this dogma carries with it definite evidence that it really is what it claims to be, a message which God has given to the world to be believed by all men. To this end the apologist first shows that there is no contradiction involved in that concept of divine revelation which the Catholic Church predicated of its own dogma. Then it shows the existence and the value of true criteria of revelation, notably miracles and prophecies. Finally it demonstrates that Catholic dogma as it is actually presented to mankind is shown to be a true divine message in the light of these criteria.

Apologetics differs sharply from an *apology of dogma*. This latter belongs to the realm of special, rather than of fundamental theology. It consists in the defense of some individual dogma or group of dogmas. In the apology of dogma the defender can demonstrate that this individual teaching, for example that of the real presence of our Lord Jesus Christ under the appearances of bread and wine in the Sacred Eucharist, is actually contained in the two authentic sources of divine revelation. He can demonstrate to anyone that no contradiction is involved in the true Catholic doctrine, and, furthermore, he can show that any objection brought to bear against the true meaning of divine revelation actually fails to achieve its objective.

The apologetics to which we refer is, of course, the traditional science which is habitually presented as an integrating factor in the organization of sacred theology. There are certain branches of study, or to be more exact, certain theories about Catholic dogma which present themselves as the "new apologetics." In general these constitute attempts to show the acceptability of Catholicism independently of miracles and prophecies, the outstanding and primary motives of credibility. Those which attempt to show that miracles and prophecies have no demonstrative value contradict authentic doctrine. Others which merely attempt to supplement the effects of miracles and prophecies are acceptable, but have no place in the fabric of sacred theology as distinct studies. As a matter of fact the traditional apologetics takes full cognizance of other motives of credibility. Such approaches to apologetical methods as the "immanentism" of Maurice Blondel and the "experimental method" of Henri Morice are classified as "new apologetics."

The course of fundamental theology concludes with *the treatise on the Catholic Church*. Naturally not all of the revealed doctrine pertinent to the activity and the prerogatives of the Church is included in this treatise, since the entire content of sacramental theology has to do with the Church's life and organization. But the teaching on the Church as the divinely constituted and infallible exponent of divine public revelation must hold a place apart in the organization of sacred theology. Under this heading the student of fundamental theology must consider the Catholic Church as the authorized proponent and mistress of all revealed teaching.

The treatise on the Catholic Church first of all considers this organization in function of its four causes. The efficient cause is God Himself, since the Church was immediately and directly instituted by the true and historical Jesus Christ while He dwelt upon this earth. The final cause is the glory of God to be accomplished in the fullness of Christ through the salvation of souls. The material cause is the membership of the Catholic Church, embracing only or all of those baptized persons who have not been brought away from the unity of the Church through heresy, schism, or the full measure of excommunication. The formal cause, that by which the members are bound to one another under Christ their Head and Leader, is the Blessed Trinity, and by appropriation, God the Holy Spirit. Under His guidance the Church functions as a monarchical and hierarchical society. It teaches, governs, and sanctifies. The treatise on the Church which is integrated into fundamental theology does not deal extensively with the sanctifying mission of the Church, since this treatment is within the proper province of sacramental theology, of moral, and of ascetics.[†] But it does teach of the Church's infallibility, of the matter in the teaching of which the Church exercises her prerogative of infallibility, and of those within the Church who are competent to speak infallibly in setting forth divinely revealed truth.

The Catholic Church itself is the Mystical Body of Christ, and that portion of the treatise on the Church which is devoted to explaining how that Church is actually joined to Jesus Christ our Lord constitutes the theology of the Mystical Body. The treatise concludes with an investigation into the necessity of the Catholic Church and the relations which exist between the Church and the state.

M. Special Dogmatic Theology. Special theology is either dogmatic or moral. Sometimes there is a course in *sacramental*

---

†   **Editor's Note:** For a recent study of the Church in light of the teachings of the Second Vatican Council, see Benoît-Dominique de La Soujeole, O.P., *Introduction to the Mystery of the Church*, trans. Michael J. Miller (Washington, DC: The Catholic University of America Press, 2014).

theology in which all of the content of divine revelation which has to do with the seven sacraments is expounded. Quite as frequently, however, this teaching on the sacraments is divided between moral and dogmatic, according to the exigencies of the individual theses. Most of the currently used textbooks divide the matter on the sacraments in this way.

Special dogmatic theology takes in all of those treatises which are included in the first and the third parts of St. Thomas Aquinas' *Summa Theologica* and in addition the part on divine grace, which St. Thomas himself incorporated into the *Prima Secundae*. Thus it takes in the treatises on the One God, on the Blessed Trinity, on creation and the divine government, on original sin, on divine grace, the incarnation, the redemption and the last things. It is in this part of sacred theology that the great systematic controversies are discussed.[6]

N. Moral Theology. Moral theology is that portion of scholastics which admits of the greatest number of pedagogical subdivisions. The principles and the main conclusions of all those branches of moral which today are taught as separate courses are contained in the second part of the *Summa Theologica*. The most important and the fundamental part of this content is presented today in that course which is designated simply as *moral theology*. Under this heading the theologian considers human acts, conscience which is the practical judgment about the matter with which a person is immediately concerned, laws, the sins, and the virtues in general. After this general consideration, the theologian considers the individual precepts of the moral order. Sometimes the division of these commandments is made according to the Decalogue and the

---

6. Special dogmatic theology, as distinct from sacramental, is divided by Katschthaler into four parts. The first of these is theology strictly so called, embracing the treatises on the unity and the trinity of God as well as that on God the Creator. The second is Christology, which includes all of the doctrine about the Incarnation and the Redemption. The third is Charitology which takes in the section on original sin and on divine grace. The fourth and last is Eschatology, the teaching on the final lot of man. Cf. Joannes Katschthaler, *Theologia Dogmatica Catholica Specialis* (Regensburg: 1877), Vol. 1, introductio, pp. xii–xiii.

chief precepts of the Catholic Church. At other times they are considered with reference to the virtues, to the activity of which they are ordered.[†] Then moral theology considers the particular duties which follow from the acceptance of certain states in life, with special stress being placed upon the duties of clerics and religious. The last, and the most extensive portion of moral treats of the liceity of acts which are connected with the sacraments. Two of the sacraments, penance and matrimony, demand long and profound treatment in this branch of theology.

Moral theology deals with the liceity and the illicit character of human acts. Because of its very nature the use of examples or cases constitutes an excellent pedagogical means for learning and explaining this discipline. For this reason the subject itself is sometimes known as *casuistic* moral. The term must never be used in a pejorative sense, since that teaching which is set forth in the traditional moral textbooks has often been approved by the Church herself. There is always unfortunately a tendency among those who have never taken the trouble to master the field of moral theology to find fault with it because it "does not offer a high enough ideal." As a matter of fact the moralist fulfills one of the most important functions in the explanation of Catholic teaching. Were he to confuse the counsels and the commandments he would be guilty of making a fatal misstatement of that teaching which God revealed to men through Jesus Christ. It is his immediate business to point out what God has taught us as demanded by that life of grace which He has conceded to us in this world. In order to teach this properly, he must point out those acts which are not in accord

---

†   **Editor's Note:** The pedagogical structure of moral theology Fenton relates here reflects the casuistical methodology still in effect during the early twentieth century. The significance of St. John Paul II's 1993 papal encyclical *Veritatis Splendor* is difficult to overestimate. The following two books serve as key resources for anyone interested in the methodology of moral theology before and after *Veritatis Splendor*: Servais Pinckaers, O.P., *The Sources of Christian Ethics*, trans. Sr. Mary Thomas Noble, O.P. (Washington, DC: The Catholic University of America Press, 1995); Romanus Cessario, O.P., *Introduction to Moral Theology*, rev. ed. (Washington, DC: The Catholic University of America Press, 2013).

with the life of grace, and those which are so opposed to that life as to be incompatible with it.

The principal subject of controversy in the realm of moral theology is the nature of that reflex principle which a man uses in order to take away the speculative doubt which might stand in the way of his action. A man who has no objective means for knowing whether the action proposed to him here and now is licit or not must obviously have recourse to such a principle. There have been those who have held the principle that only in those cases where the act seems more probably licit, the man can act. Others hold that a man acts properly if it is equally probable, or even solidly probable that the act is licit. The proponents of the first system are called probabiliorists. Those who teach the second one are called aequiprobabilists, and the third is exposed by probabilists. There are also those who hold that the importance of the act must be the ultimate norm. If the act is such that illicit operation would be more serious, then a stronger probability is required for its performance.[†]

O. Spiritual Theology. When we consider the human acts, not merely with reference to their liceity, but precisely in so far as they are directed toward the perfection which God asks of Christians, then we study them in that portion of sacred doctrine known as *spiritual* theology. In this course we look at the nature and the necessity of Christian perfection itself, and then at the manner in which God brings the soul to it. *Ascetical theology* tells about that portion of the soul's advance toward God in which the prayerful activity of that soul is conducted in the manner which is natural to man. *Mystical theology*, on the other hand, tells of that stage in the advance of the soul in which it acts in a manner at once distinct from and superior to the natural way in which man operates for

---

[†]   **Editor's Note:** For more on the speculative foundations of the casuistic systems, and their practical implications, see Romanus Cessario, O.P., "Casuistry and Revisionism: Structural Similarities in Method and Content," in "*Humanae Vitae*": *20 Anni Dopo. Atti del II Congresso Internazionale di Theologia Morale*, Vol. III (Milano: Edizioni Ares, 1990): pp. 385–409.

the attainment of an end. Both of these disciplines treat of activity which is essentially and intrinsically supernatural. The prayerful activity of the ascetic has the same supernatural orientation as that of the mystic. The same supernatural organism of habitual grace, the virtues, and the gifts of the Holy Spirit acts as a principle of operation in each case. But the activity of the mystic, that which is performed according to the manner of the gifts is supernatural in manner or mode as well as in essence. The mystic is said to be *passive* in so far as he is moved by God in this supernatural manner.

The outstanding controversy in this field has to do with the methodology of the science itself. Father Poulain is considered the leading authority in holding that mystical theology has no immediate contact with the field of ascetics.[7] According to this theory, mysticism has to do with those phenomena which are properly classified as *gratiae gratis datae*. These are outside the normal course by which God wills that the soul should grow to its ultimate perfection in this life. As a result the supporters of this theory maintain that the entire progress of the soul to perfection is made according to the laws which govern the activity which man performs in a natural way.

The other theory, which is taught in the greater number of courses on spiritual theology, is that of which Father Garrigou-Lagrange was the outstanding proponent in our times.[8] According to this teaching, the normal progress of the soul to the highest stages of perfection brings the soul into a position in which the demands of prayerful activity are beyond the capacities of the natural mode of human operation. In this way God *normally* guides men to and in the highest stages of spiritual perfection by bringing them to act in the supernatural manner. Thus mystical theology constitutes, not a study of certain phenomena which may accompany

7.   The theory of Father Poulain, S.J., is set forth in his classical *Des Graces d'Oraison*, 5th ed. (Paris: 1906). The work has been translated into English.

8.   Cf. Reginald Garrigou-Lagrange, O.P., *Perfection Chrétienne et Contemplation* (Saint Maximin, Var, France: 1923), 2 Vols. There is an excellent English translation of this book.

the life of grace, but the consideration of those activities which are normally performed by those men whom God has deigned to lead to the summit of the spiritual life.

P. Pastoral Theology and Missiology. The next special subject attached to moral theology is *pastoral*. In pastoral we consider the special duties of the priest toward the flock which is committed to his care. The subject is of great practical importance, although the principles which it elucidates are put forward as conclusions in dogma and in moral.

Finally there is *missiology*, the study of the Catholic missions. This branch of sacred theology attaches itself to fundamentals, since it expounds the necessity of revelation and of the Catholic Church with particular reference to the people among whom the Church is being established by the missionaries. It is attached to pastoral theology since it explains the duties of the missionaries toward those to whom they bring the word of God and the means by which the work of these missionaries can be made most effective.

＊ ＊ ＊

Chapter XI

The Development of Sacred Theology:
The Patristic Period

The present-day literary expression of sacred theology, in manuals like those of Diekamp, Connell, and Hugon, in monographs and encyclopedias, is the product of nearly two millennia of development. And so clearly does this literature bear within itself the marks of that development that no man can approximate a scientific evaluation of sacred theology until he is at least cognizant of the main stages in its history. More clearly than any other discipline, sacred theology speaks with the voices of those who have labored on it in the past. The terms which are commonplaces in the modern manual were selected and polished by the theological study of other times. The rigorously correct conclusions are products of the most painstaking examination and discussion in third-century Alexandria, in thirteenth-century Paris, and in seventeenth-century Douai.

A. Theological Reasoning Found in Holy Scripture. Actually, of course, theological reasoning is as old as Christian doctrine itself. Our Blessed Lord reasoned to show His attackers that He did not drive out devils by the power of Beelzebub himself. He showed them that while He overcame the powers of darkness in single combat, the dominion of Satan was still exercised over men.

If He had been of the house of Satan, then, of course, that house could not endure. The fact that it actually held dominion indicated clearly that He was outside of it.[1]

St. Paul put down a denial of the general resurrection with a perfect theological proof. "Now if Christ be preached that He arose again from the dead, how do some among you say that there is no resurrection of the dead? But if there be no resurrection of the dead, then Christ is not risen again. And if Christ be not risen again, then is our preaching vain, and your faith also is vain."[2] The Apostle of the Gentiles showed clearly that the denial of one article of faith involved the denial of another, and ultimately the destruction of the faith itself. It was his way of proving that this doctrine actually expressed the teaching of Jesus Christ our Lord.

B. The Apostolic Fathers. The literature of sacred theology boasts of documents which come from the end of the first century and from the early years of the second. Classified as apostolic fathers are St. Clement of Rome (98), St. Ignatius of Antioch (107), and St, Polycarp (155). Closely associated with them are the ecclesiastical writers, Hermas (c. 140), Papias (c. 150), and the authors of the Didache (c. 90), the so-called Epistle of Barnabas (c. 130) and the letter to Diognetus (c. 150). The most important of these writings are letters addressed to individual communities or persons, to overcome some particular difficulty. They explain the content and the meaning of Christian doctrine, but naturally without resort to any scientific terminology. The teaching of Papias and Hermas was not entirely reliable. But the letters of Sts. Clement, Ignatius, and Polycarp indicate very clearly the belief and teaching in the primitive Church.

C. The Apologists. From the middle of the second century, the apologetical literature of sacred theology began to develop rapidly. We know of the writings of Aristides (c. 138), a converted Athenian philosopher. The brilliant "Letter to Diognetus," a jewel

---

1.   Matthew 12:24–30.

2.   1 Corinthians 15:12–21.

of ancient Christian writing, is also a work which defends the faith. So, too, were the books of St. Justin Martyr (c. 165) the most important among the ancient apologists, of Theophilus of Antioch (181), Athenagoras (193), and Tatian (c. 180). These men wrote in Greek, while Tertullian (c. 222) and Marcus Minucius Felix (c. 185) founded Latin theological literature with their defenses of the Catholic faith against the attacks of the pagans. St. Justin and Tertullian wrote to show that the persecutions which raged against the primitive Church were entirely unjustified. Minucius Felix composed a preparation or introduction to the faith. Writing in dialogue form, this brilliant spokesman of Catholicism responded to the arguments of the pagan and finally led his adversary to seek the truth which Jesus Christ preached to men.

D. St. Irenaeus. St. Irenaeus (202), bishop of Lyons, wrote against the heretics, and in particular against the various sects of Gnostics who troubled the Church of his time. In the course of his writing he set forth the content of Catholic faith as a whole. His pitiless investigation of Gnosticism and his excellent exposition of the Catholic rule of faith have won for him the designation of the first scientific theologian within the Catholic Church.

E. Clement of Alexandria. At the same time his contemporary, Clement of Alexandria (202), was producing the first of those literary works which were to be the glory of the catechetical school of the Egyptian metropolis, the first organized and permanent school of sacred theology of which we know. Using the terminology and sometimes even the mentality of the neo-Platonic philosophers of Alexandria, Clement's literary works set forth the apologetic arguments for the conversion of a pagan, and then gave the neophyte direction for attaining to the summit of Christian perfection.

F. Origen and His School. Origen (230), his great pupil and successor, was by all means the most prolific writer in the history of sacred theology. Apart from his tremendous scriptural work in which he developed the allegorical exegesis which had already appeared in the so-called Epistle of Barnabas and his magnificent accomplishments for Catholic apologetics in the work *Against Celsus*,

Origen's most important contribution to theological literature was the famous volume, *On the Principles*. This was a third-century *Summa Theologica*, a complete and ordered exposition of Catholic doctrine. Like the works of St. Irenaeus and Clement of Alexandria, his books were by no means free from error. Moreover, the order of the treatise *On the Principles* suffers greatly by comparison with the later books of the same motivation, works like the *Orthodox Faith* of St. John Damascene, the *Four Books of Sentences* of Peter the Lombard, and the *Summa Theologica* of St. Thomas Aquinas. But we can gain some idea of Origen's genius, and his tremendous influence upon the development of sacred theology when we realize that over five hundred years were to pass before another man set to work on a plan as extensive and scientifically ambitious as that which motivated the production of *On the Principles*.

This volume is divided into four books. The first deals with the three divine Persons and with created spirits, the second with the material world and with man. The third book treats of the foundations of the Christian world, and the fourth of the inspiration and meaning of Sacred Scripture. This division was improved upon by writers who lived centuries after the time of Origen, but the master plan of *On the Principles* constituted the material out of which the scientifically perfect theological syntheses of later times were elaborated. Furthermore, Origen's treatise *On Prayer*, in which he discusses the nature of prayer as petition and then explains it in function of the *Pater Noster*, constitutes one of the great contributions to the literature of spiritual theology. Tertullian had written previously on prayer, and St. Cyprian of Carthage, his great admirer imitated this Latin work. But neither achieved the scientific perfection attained by the great professor of Alexandria.

It was the glory of Origen to have been the first among the Catholic theologians to have founded a school. So overpowering was his genius, that not only his pupils, like St. Gregory the Wonder-Worker and Firmilian of Caesarea, and his successors in the schools of Alexandria, like St. Dionysius, St. Athanasius, and Didymus the Blind, followed his teachings, but actually his literary work was considered as a sort of public property from which any man might borrow freely. Until the end of the fourth century there is hardly an ecclesiastical writer of importance who has not incorporated some of Origen's theses in his own writings. At the end of the fourth century there arose three writers who were destined forever to break the monopoly which Origen's teachings enjoyed in the schools of Christendom. St. Epiphanius, St. Jerome, and Theophilus of Alexandria attacked the writings of Origen with pitiless insistence. They pointed out the many flaws in his writings on the Blessed Trinity, his doctrine on the successive trials which all men were supposed to undergo, even after death, so that ultimately all men would attain to the eternal happiness of heaven, and finally his admitted abuse of the allegorical interpretation of Holy Scripture.

As time went on the *ex professo* defenders of Origen came to be those who held the errors which Origen had taught, rather than those who utilized the tremendous theological resources which he had made available to Catholic scholars. It was to this type of "Origenism," the acceptance of all the writings and opinions of the master without regard to the opposition between some of these and Catholic truth, that men like Sts. Methodius, Epiphanius, and Jerome objected. It was this same "Origenism" which stressed and exaggerated the errors of the great Alexandrian and added some new ones on its own account, which Pope Vigilius condemned in 543 and which the Second Council of Constantinople, the fifth ecumenical council, proscribed ten years later.[3] These condemnations ended what might be called a definite Origenistic school. However, they did not prevent future theologians from taking advantage of the splendid scientific production of Origen himself and they were never intended to do so.

G. Tertullian and St. Cyprian. While Origen was building up the first scientific synthesis of theology in the east, the great Tertullian (c. 222) was starting the traditional Latin theological literature.

---

3.   Denzinger, 203–11 and 223.

Although it is quite probable that the *Octavius* of Minucius Felix antedates the *Apologeticus*, one of the earliest and most important of Tertullian's theological works and one which shows a sharp similarity to the *Octavius*, the turbulent genius of the great African enriched the library of sacred theology with writings on many phases of Christian doctrine not touched upon by Minucius. Tertullian's is the glory of having first made Latin a definite theological language, and of having left his followers a rich scientific terminology.

From 197 until about 206 Tertullian wrote as an orthodox Catholic theologian. From the latter time until about 212 he leaned toward the heresy of the Montanists which he embraced at the end of that period. His last writings were produced while he was separated from the Church of God. Yet this most tragic figure in the history of sacred theology definitely left later writers in his debt. Ironically enough this brilliant and harsh genius made some of his most useful contributions when he attacked the Catholic position after having abandoned it. His statement of the very doctrine he was opposing has been of immeasurable value to historians writing on the history of Catholic teaching, particularly on the sacrament of Penance.

St. Cyprian of Carthage (258) made magnificent use of the orthodox writings of Tertullian. His principal contribution to the literature of sacred theology was his teaching on the unity of the Catholic Church. Despite some confusion and misstatement, St. Cyprian is the first great master in the matter of ecclesiology.

H. The Writings Against Arianism. The second and most brilliant period of patristic theological writing began in the fourth century with the campaign against Arianism. The greatest leader in this theological warfare was St. Athanasius (373). Associated with him were some of the most powerful and brilliant writers who have ever written on sacred theology. In the east there were the three great Cappadocians, St. Basil the Great (379), St. Gregory Nazianzen (399) called the Theologian, and St. Gregory of Nyssa (395), the brother of St. Basil. These men, together with St. Cyril of Jerusalem (386), the great master of catechetics, explained the revealed teaching of the Blessed Trinity in such a way as to destroy the principles upon which Arius had constructed his heresy. The Cappadocians were most interested in showing that the revealed doctrine, as contained in Holy Scripture and in tradition required the use of the term "consubstantial" which entered into the Nicene Creed. They showed that the denial of this term involved an admission of heretical teaching. Sts. Athanasius and Basil through their writings on the monastic life contributed much to the foundation of spiritual theology.

In the Latin west, the campaign against the Arians was carried on by St. Hilary (366) and St. Ambrose (397). The latter aided greatly in the development of moral theology as well. St. Jerome (419) wrote brilliantly on dogmatic, moral, and spiritual topics but made by far his most important contribution in the field of Holy Scripture. To him we owe the Latin version of Holy Scripture, the Vulgate, recognized as the official Catholic text for use in preaching the word of God. His Latin commentaries, and the Greek explanations of St. John Chrysostom (407) are invaluable for Scripture study. St. John Chrysostom was the greatest product of the Antiochian school of Christian science and his commentaries have contributed a great deal to the development of sacred theology. The Alexandrian school produced its last great figure in St. Cyril of Alexandria (494), the leading figure in the Council of Ephesus and the arch foe of Nestorianism. It was the privilege of St. Cyril to have vindicated for our Lady her title of "Mother of God."

I. St. Augustine and His Influence. By far the most important figure in patristic theology was St. Augustine, Bishop of Hippo (430). His writings have dominated Latin theology to an extent which has never been equaled. He wrote on the mystery of the Blessed Trinity, and, in giving the death stroke to Arian errors, he gave to sacred theology his masterful analogies of the revealed doctrine with the created "trinities" of the spiritual order. In his books *On the City of God*, he offered an invaluable explanation of history in the light of Catholic apologetics. He showed that the Catholic faith was beneficial to society and to the state, and exposed the hideous fallacies of those who claimed that the acceptance of this faith had sealed the doom of the Roman Empire. Furthermore, his scriptural commentaries express the content of Catholic tradition with matchless scientific accuracy.

Like most of the other Fathers, St. Augustine's most important teaching was set forth against the heretics of his times. He examined the problems raised by the objections of the heretics, and then proceeded to demonstrate the true and traditional resolution of these problems. He gave particular attention to the extirpation of three heresies, all of which threatened the Christians of his native Africa as Arianism and Nestorianism had never done. These three heresies were Manicheanism, Donatism, and Pelagianism.

Against the first of these three heresies St. Augustine wrote profound treatises on the nature and the influence of the good, for its adherents had been deluded into imagining that there were two independent supreme principles, the one good and the other evil. It was the work of the great Bishop of Hippo to show clearly that according to the revealed doctrine which the Manicheans claimed to accept, there is only one God, and that all the things, spiritual and material, which He has created are good in so far as they proceed from Him. Against the Donatists, who erred about the Church and the sacrament of Baptism, he wrote to demonstrate the unity of the Church, the fact that it includes sinners as well as those in the state of grace, and the absolute efficacy of that Baptism which a man cannot receive more than once.

The greatest work of St. Augustine, however, was done against the Pelagian heresy. The positive teachings of the Pelagians shifted as each previous position was battered down by the logic of the Bishop of Hippo. But they denied the absolute necessity of divine grace for the attainment of eternal salvation, for faith, and for the beginning of good works. St. Augustine brought all the force of his unrivaled scriptural erudition, and all the power of one of the keenest minds ever possessed by a human being to bear against this error. He showed that the process of salvation in every one of its aspects depends upon that help which God freely gives to man over and above the exigencies of man's nature. The terminology he used to describe grace in its various functions is still employed in the literature and the lecture halls of sacred theology.

His anti-Pelagian writings made St. Augustine the great doctor of the supernatural order. He distinguished more clearly and explicitly than any writer before him between what is due to human nature and what is a free gift of God. To the attainment of his end he brought out the theology of original sin and its effects, describing the weakness of human nature which is consequent upon the fall of Adam. On the other hand, he had to bring out the first great theological treatment of predestination, since he had to show that the attainment of eternal glory on the part of any man was consequent upon the free gift of God to this man. Here, too, he taught the relation of man's free will to divine grace and predestination. In this field of grace and the supernatural, and the related tracts on original sin and on providence and predestination, St. Augustine is the approved exponent of Catholic teaching.

Pope St. Hormisdas declared in 520 that what the Catholic Church teaches on grace and free will is to be found in the various books of St. Augustine, and especially those to Hilary and Prosper. The Second Council of Orange (529), confirmed by Pope Boniface II and directed against the Semi-Pelagians, used the very words and sentences of the great Doctor in condemning heretical tenets on original sin, grace, and predestination. In his intensely personal writing against Pelagius and his followers the great Bishop of Hippo had spoken for the Catholic Church.

On the matter of grace and free will, then, it would not be entirely true to say that St. Augustine founded a school. The theological school is, after all, the proponent of a teaching which is freely discussed in the Catholic Church. Those who opposed the teaching of St. Augustine as set forth by the master himself or by his great disciples, St. Prosper of Aquitaine (c.226), St. Fulgentius (533), and St. Cesarius of Arles (543), found their teaching condemned.[4] Thus the Augustinian tradition in sacred theology was

---

4.   Denzinger, 3027 and 174–200.

far greater than that of any school, properly so called. When, over seven hundred years after the death of St. Augustine, the young and nourishing universities of Europe demanded a textbook for sacred theology, they found one in the *Four Books of Sentences* by Peter the Lombard. The *Sentences* were accepted precisely in so far as they expressed the living Latin theological tradition in the twelfth century. That tradition was Augustinian. The *Sentences*, although distinctly a personal work, are pieced together with excerpts from the Fathers. And there is more of St. Augustine in them than of all the others together. They use the authority, the statements, and the terminology of St. Augustine for every portion of sacred theology.

As a result the literature of western theology which was developed in the universities dominated by Peter the Lombard was itself pre-eminently Augustinian. Commentaries like those of St. Thomas and John Duns Scotus used the authority of St. Augustine as advantageously as had Peter the Lombard, although St. Thomas availed himself of other patristic sources quite freely. Later when the northern universities of Louvain and Douai were setting forth their great theological treatises, they made special use of St. Augustine. Sylvius and his followers, like Randour and Van Coverden, claimed to be Thomists and Augustinians. Later still, writers like Noris and Berti set forth an Augustinian solution as one of the Catholic systems for the problem of efficacious grace. This Augustinian solution placed the efficacy of grace in a moral rather than in a physical motion. In other words, it claimed for divine efficacious grace an operation along the line of final rather than of efficient causality.

J. Misuse of St. Augustine's Teaching. However, the authority of St. Augustine has been abused at certain periods in the history of sacred theology. Michael Baius of Louvain claimed the patronage of the Bishop of Hippo for his teaching which was condemned repeatedly by the Sovereign Pontiffs and disavowed by the important theologians in the northern universities. The book which set off the disastrous heresy of Jansenism was the *Augustinus* by Cornelius Jansenius, an attempted solution of the problem of grace and free will with respect to original sin in the light of St. Augustine's writings. Subsequent writers in the Jansenistic school claimed that the teaching of Jansenius and their own books constituted simply a restatement of St. Augustine's doctrine.

The competent Augustinian scholars of their own times as well as those who have come after them recognized very clearly that the Jansenistic teaching was a travesty on that of St. Augustine. When Libertus Fromondus and Sinnichius reproached the great Sylvius for having abandoned the teaching of St. Augustine when he condemned the book of Cornelius Jansenius, the old Douai master retorted dryly that they did not refer to the same "Augustine" as the one he venerated, for they sponsored an Augustine of Flanders while he followed an Augustine of Hippo. As a matter of fact the heretics used citations from the great African Doctor to draw conclusions utterly at variance with his actual teachings.

In spite of the fact that St. Augustine threw light upon practically every department of sacred theology, he never set forth the entire content of science in didactic order. All of his writings, numerous though they were, were intended as answers to definite questions and as resolutions of definite heresies. It remained for Peter the Lombard to synthesize the Augustinian theology, using the principles enunciated by the saint himself.

K. Fifth-Century Fathers. Cassian (435), Faustus of Riez (c. 490), and St. Vincent of Lérins (c. 450) were among those who refused to accept St. Augustine's teaching on grace in its entirety. Cassian, despite his Semi-Pelagianism, laid the foundation for the literature of spiritual theology in the west with his reports and explanations on the teaching of the oriental monks. St. Vincent of Lérins wrote so effectively on the development of dogma and of sacred theology that the [First] Vatican Council incorporated his very statements into the Constitution *Dei Filius*. Faustus of Riez exercised a tremendous influence upon later theology, although the content of his work on grace is of little value. In working to overcome false teaching on the matter of predestination he came to oppose the doctrine of St. Augustine himself. Any attempt to use his teaching on grace and free will in later times was reproved by the standard theologians.

Theodoret of Cyr (c. 458) and the pseudo-Dionysius (c. 500) contributed a great deal to the development of sacred theology. The former, the last great representative of the Antiochian school, left sacred theology a valuable explanation of Holy Scripture and historical works. Due to his unfortunate friendship with the heretic Nestorius, whom he defended against St. Cyril of Alexandria, his memory has suffered greatly. He was one of those included in the condemnation of the three chapters by the Second Council of Constantinople in 553.[5] Later he corrected the justly suspect views he had expressed at the time of his controversy with St. Cyril.

Around the end of the fifth century there appeared in the east some books written in the name of that Dionysius who had been converted after hearing the sermon of St. Paul in the Areopagus of Athens. To this day no man knows the author of these works. Centering about the approach of the human soul to God, these books stressed the necessity of analogy for knowing God in this world, the order among the spiritual creatures made by God, and the various stages of purification by which God leads the soul to that contemplation which is normally characteristic of the highest degrees of sanctity in this world. On these points this teaching was eagerly sought out and used by the great medieval theologians. St. Thomas Aquinas has left us invaluable commentaries on the pseudo-Dionysius and has utilized this doctrine in the *Summa Theologica* itself.

In the west St. Leo the Great (461) was responsible for the great triumph of orthodoxy over the monophysite heresy at the Council of Chalcedon (451). His letters made him the great doctor of the Incarnation in the matter of the hypostatic union. The same doctrine, as well as that of the Holy See as a rule of faith, was taught by St. Peter Chrysologus (450). Nearly a century later St. Leontius of Byzantium (c. 531) was to summarize that same doctrine for the

---

5.   Denzinger, 213–228.

east. St. Gregory the Great (604) made the outstanding contribution to moral theology in patristic times. Boethius (524) used the equipment of philosophy to explain the revealed doctrine. He did not utilize Holy Scripture as extensively as did the other patristic writers, but preferred to analyze the concepts which entered into sacred theology. Cassiodorus (570) described the benefits accruing to mankind through the study of sacred theology. St. Isidore of Seville (636) is ordinarily reckoned as the last of the Latin Fathers. A genius of encyclopedic erudition, he summarized the theological learning of his times and left the way open for the development of medieval writing.

L. St. John Damascene. The last of the great Greek Fathers was St. John Damascene (c. 753). Although his outstanding polemic achievement was the defeat of the Iconoclast heresy, he contributed more to the development of sacred theology through his organization of the science than through any treatment of a particular section. His masterwork is the *Source of Knowledge*. In the first section of this work he listed and explained the definitions of the terms used in sacred theology. He made valuable capital of the definitions and the conclusions of Aristotle. In the second portion he sets off one hundred and three distinct erroneous doctrines, contradictory to Christian revelation, which had made their appearance between the first years of the Church and the middle of the eighth century. But it is the third section, the work *On the Orthodox Faith* which really has earned for St. John Damascene the high place he holds in the history of sacred theology. Arranged as a sort of commentary on the Nicene Creed, the work offers a complete outline of Christian revelation. It is divided into four books, as the volume *On the Principles* by Origen had been before it.

In the first book St. John Damascene treats of the unity and the trinity in God. The second treats of the works of God. The third deals with the Incarnation, and the fourth with those mysteries and doctrines which are mentioned at the end of the Nicene Creed. It ends with a treatise on the last things. Among other teachings, the famous double definition of prayer given in the third book *On the*

Orthodox Faith became a theological commonplace. St. Thomas Aquinas incorporated this definition into his *Summa Theologica* and made all his teaching on prayer depend upon it. It is evident that the division of St. John Damascene influenced that of Peter the Lombard, and through him the organization of all the theology of the west.

* * *

Chapter XII

The Development of Sacred Theology: The Medieval Period

The medieval or part-patristic theologians fall naturally into three classes. There are the early scholastics and the pre-scholastics, those who served as the channels by which patristic thought came to the great theologians and the universities of the Middle Ages. The second group embraces the great masters who taught during the golden age of the University of Paris. The third includes those who followed the great scholastics, either continuing their tradition or going off into those nominalistic theories which had a great deal to do with the origin of Protestantism.

A. The Pre-Scholastics. The first group of theologians played a great part in the development of the great scholastics' doctrine. The writings of St. Thomas Aquinas contain a tremendous number of citations from these earlier medieval writers. In his *Catena Aurea* as well as in the other writings he cites men like Paschasius Radbertus and St. Bede on the same level and to the same effect as the patristic authors themselves. Modern investigation into the sources of Peter the Lombard shows that in his *Commentaries* as well as in the *Four Books of Sentences* he makes liberal use of earlier scholastics, sometimes incorporating considerable portions of their works into his own.

St. Bede the Venerable (735) is one of the first and the most important among these pre-scholastic writers. His chief contribution to the development of sacred theology is made in his explanation of Holy Scripture. Alcuin (804) was the principal figure in the schools of Charlemagne, and as such prepared the way for the great universities which developed out of the Carolingian schools. His authority was greatly appreciated by St. Thomas, although, like that of most of the writers of this period, his scientific method was quite primitive. Rabanus Maurus (856), the disciple of Alcuin, carried on his master's work of encouraging theological studies in his native Germany. His teachings were widely quoted by subsequent theologians.

Several controversies on sacred doctrine aided the development of sacred theology in the ninth century. Aeneas of Paris (870) and the monk Ratramnus (c. 865) wrote against the schismatic Photius of Constantinople. Alcuin had to attack and destroy a kind of ninth-century Nestorianism in Spain, put forward by Elipand of Toledo (809) and Felix Urgel (818), as did Agobard of Lyons (840).

The monk Gotteschalc (869) taught an heretical doctrine on predestination, holding that the predestination of the saints to eternal happiness was entirely similar to that of the evil to eternal death. Like Jansenism in later years, the doctrine of Gotteschalc was an abuse of St. Augustine's teachings. Hincmar of Rheims (882) took a leading part in the attack on Gotteschalc, who was finally condemned by several synods. In this controversy Hincmar was joined by Rabanus and St. Remy of Lyons (875). At the suggestion of Hincmar the erudite and brilliant John Scotus Erigena (c. 880) entered into the controversy. However, his literary contribution was even more unfortunate than those writings which Hincmar had opposed. He in his turn was censured by Prudentius of Troyes (861) and Florus of Lyons (c. 860), both competent theologians. Scotus Erigena possessed one of the most remarkable minds of his day, as attested by his ingenious but erratic treatise *De Divisione Naturae*. However, he was not sufficiently concerned with traditional Catholic doctrine to be an important figure in the history of sacred theology. His rash hypotheses actually endangered the cause of speculative theology during the ninth century.

The most important among the ninth-century controversies was that on the Blessed Eucharist. Paschasius Radbertus (c. 865) and Ratramnus both wrote *De Corpore et Sanguine Domini*. Radbertus insisted upon the identity of the historical and the Eucharistic body of our Lord in the sacrament, while Ratramnus and Rabanus Maurus stressed the symbolism of the sacrament without denying the real presence.[†]

In the same century Jonas of Orleans (842) brought the west a treatise against that Iconoclasm which had overrun the Byzantine Empire during the previous century. Amalarius of Metz (c. 850) gave the medieval world its textbook in liturgical theology. Walifrid Strabo (849) and Haymo of Halberstadt (853) wrote exegetical works and supported Paschasius Radbertus in his controversy on the Blessed Eucharist. This pre-scholastic medieval period ended with the writings of Ratherius of Verona (974), Gerbert of Aurillac, who became Pope Sylvester II (1003), Fulbert of Chartres (1028), founder of the great school of that city, Hugh of Langres (1051), Guitmund of Aversa (1095), St. Peter Damian (1072), the great proponent of ecclesiastical sanctity who is listed among the Doctors of the Church, and Lanfranc (1089), the master of St. Anselm. The heretical teaching on the Eucharist set forth by Berengarius of Tours (1088) occasioned an elaborate scientific treatment of this sacrament at the end of this period.

The pre-scholastics performed a notable service in taking the Christian doctrine, as it is contained in Holy Scripture and in tradition, and expressing that doctrine in the language and for the minds of the new western peoples. They accomplished their mission for the most part in writing the simplest sort of didactic

---

[†]   **Editor's Note:** For more on the Eucharistic debates, see James T. O'Connor, *The Hidden Manna: A Theology of the Eucharist*, 2nd ed. (San Francisco: Ignatius Press, 2005); Lawrence Feingold, *The Eucharist: Mystery of Presence, Sacrifice, and Communion* (Steubenville, OH: Emmaus Academic, 2018).

treatises, or in monographs destined to crush a dangerous and crude misconception of Christian teaching. Their work suffers in comparison with that of the great writers who followed them, but these latter, with better and more complete literary equipment, actually carried on the work to which the earlier theologians had devoted themselves. The great scholastics counted the works of their predecessors as valuable resources, and they used them freely in the construction of those splendid literary monuments which are the glory of the medieval universities.

Work on the earlier scholastic writers is far from complete. In recent years the investigations of men like Grabmann, Longpré, and Landgraf have made the writings of the less widely known among the earlier scholastics available to the general public for the first time. Only in the light of these earlier works can we understand the historic background of the scholastic masterpieces, the writings of St. Thomas Aquinas.

B. St. Anselm. Generally counted as the first among these early scholastics is St. Anselm of Canterbury (1109). While he did not attempt to organize sacred doctrine as a whole, St. Anselm treated various portions of sacred theology with a profundity and scientific maturity which had never been achieved by his predecessors since the days of the great Fathers. He wrote on the motive of the Incarnation, on grace and free will, on the Blessed Trinity, and on the proofs for the existence of God. It is in this last field that his influence has been felt most in sacred theology. After having written the masterpiece he called the *Monologion* in which the traditional proofs of God's existence were set forth, he decided to attempt an easier and simpler demonstration. This, as expounded in the *Proslogion* was what we know today as the ontological proof for the existence of God. His first premise was that God is conceived as One who is superior to all others, One greater than whom nothing could exist. Then he reasoned that such a being must possess existence for, if it were nonexistent it would certainly be surpassed by a being which actually possessed it. Consequently according to this reasoning God must exist.

The monk Guanilo of Marmoutiers was keen enough to recognize the fallacy in this reasoning as soon as it had appeared. He saw that it involved a totally illegitimate *transitus* from the ideal to the real order. The being greater than whom nothing could be conceived must possess existence, as it exists in the mind, but there is no guarantee in this argument that such a being exists in the order of reality. The great St. Thomas Aquinas did little more than repeat the criticism of Guanilo, merely adding that it is not at all certain that the idea of God as depicted by St. Anselm is the basic concept which men universally possess.

C. Other Twelfth-Century Writers. St. Anselm's disciple, Anselm of Laon (1117), was spectacularly successful as a teacher in his own time. He is the author of the earliest organized compendium of sacred theology which we know to have been written during the Middle Ages, the *Sententiae*. Gilbert of Poitiers (1154) and John of Salisbury (1180) are the two best-known products of the school of Chartres, a very important center of theological and literary activity during the twelfth century. John of Salisbury's influence was literary rather than strictly theological. Gilbert was condemned by the Council of Rheims in 1148 for teaching false doctrine. Other representatives of the Chartres school, such as Bernard of Chartres (1129), Thierry of Chartres (1155), and William of Conches (1145), were prone to misstate Catholic teaching. Bernard of Tours (c. 1155) inaugurated the pantheistic teaching which was to do much harm in the universities in later years.

D. Abelard. By far the most important center of studies at this time was in Paris, and the theological life of this city was dominated in the early years of the twelfth century by two men, William of Champeaux (1122) and Peter Abelard (1142). William's personal writings are of much more interest to the history of philosophy than to that of sacred theology, for the individual work with which his name and reputation are most intimately associated is the defense of realism against the nominalism of Roscellin and the criticism of Abelard. Theology thinks of him chiefly as the founder of the great school of St. Victor which was destined to give so many brilliant theologians to the service of the Church.

The brilliant, turbulent, and tragic Peter Abelard influenced the literature and the teaching of sacred theology as few men have ever done. His rash dialectics and his evident anxiety to shock and impress all with whom he came in contact led him to definite mis-interpretations of sacred doctrine. St. Bernard of Clairvaux (1153) was too robust and keen a defender of the faith to allow these errors to go unchallenged. Consequently Abelard found himself condemned by the Council of Sens, and the condemnation was confirmed by Rome.

The work which troubled many of Abelard's contemporaries, but which contributed a great deal to the advancement of sacred theology was known as *Sic et Non*. In this work he took one hundred and fifty important questions in theology, and then listed opinions of the Fathers for and against each resolution. It was a bold venture. Some of his contemporaries accused him of showing contempt for patristic teaching in trying to demonstrate that the Fathers actually contradicted one another. Actually Abelard's method was faulty. But he merely opened these questions for discussion, so that out of this conflict of explanations the true theological conclusion might be found in each case. To Abelard, and to those who have profited by the scholastic method which he initiated, the clash of opinions has been a means to an end, the certain apprehension of truth. Abelard saw in the conflicting statements of patristic writers a fact which admitted of and demanded explanation. Merely to point out con-tradictory teachings was to do comparatively little for the advance of sacred theology. But in his own writings and especially through the works of the men he trained, Abelard showed very clearly that he did not regard the indication of conflicting statements as the ultimate end of his studies. The movement he began was to bear fruit in the works of Peter the Lombard and his other students, and through them to form the method of Latin theology. The first of the medieval canonists, Gratian (1155?), applied this same method to canon law and thus aided in the development of moral theology.

Abelard wrote summaries of the entire content of sacred theology. More important than these, however, are the *Summae* and the *Books of Sentences* left by his pupils and successors. There was no work in scholastic theology properly so called which did not feel his influence. As a matter of fact the very method which Abelard gave to the Church would very certainly have been discredited because of the naïve cocksureness of its author had it not been for the excellent works in which his own pupils utilized his procedure for the proper end of sacred theology.

E. St. Bernard and the Victorines. The name of Abelard is inseparably joined in the history of sacred theology with that of his great opponent, St. Bernard of Clairvaux, whom we honor as a Doctor of the Catholic Church. The most influential man of his time, and one of the most forceful characters ever to have served the Church, the literary influence of St. Bernard was brought to bear principally upon the field of spiritual theology. His writings had the happy effect of bringing the mystical teaching into close contact with moral and dogma. His intensely personal love for our Lord's humanity, and the stress he placed upon devotion to our Lady proved to be dominating factors in forming the corporate spirituality of the Middle Ages. Less influential, but still tremendously important were the spiritual and theological writings of the School of St. Victor, founded by St. Bernard's friend, William of Champeaux. Hugh of St. Victor (1141) and Richard of St. Victor (1173) are the chief representatives of this school.

F. Peter the Lombard. By far the most important of the twelfth-century theologians for his influence on the history of sacred theology was Peter the Lombard (1160).[†] As Cayre remarks, the Lombard exhibited neither the profundity of St. Anselm, the subtlety of Abelard, nor the originality of Hugh of St. Victor.

---

†   **Editor's Note:** For an extensive collection of essays on those who commented on Abelard's *Sentences*, see G.R. Evans, ed., *Mediaeval Commentaries on the Sentences of Peter Lombard: Current Research*, vol. 1 (Leiden, Brill: 2002); Philip W. Rosemann, ed., *Mediaeval Commentaries on the Sentences of Peter Lombard*, vols. 2–3 (Leiden, Brill: 2009/2015).

Nevertheless, this man was destined to supply the world with the most spectacularly successful theological textbook in history. Despite certain incidental errors, the *Four Books of Sentences* constitute a work which was definitely and appreciably traditional. The terminology of the Fathers, and in particular that of St. Augustine which dominates the volume, formed a welcome relief after the somewhat confused verbiage of contemporary dialecticians. The University of Paris used the *Four Books of Sentences* as a basic text in sacred theology from the middle of the twelfth century. It was in use throughout the university world until the end of the sixteenth century. Thus, during the period when the most distinguished theologians of the Catholic Church lived and worked, the *Four Books of Sentences* were in use. The strongly traditional nature of the *Sentences* brought the terminology and the mentality of subsequent works into a more direct line with the thought and the expression of the Fathers. Where the school of Chartres and even the Victorines were prone to employ their own distinctive methods and disparate approaches to theological problems, the literature after the Lombard was fused as one organic expression of Catholic thought. While the Lombard and his commentators were by no means in agreement on every point in the science of sacred theology, the terminology and the process of sacred theology were so unified that it was able to progress more perfectly after the *Sentences* had been written.

The first of the *Books of Sentences* deals with the Trinity and Unity of God. The second treats of creation, the angels, the work of the six days, and man. The treatise on man includes the teaching on original sin and grace. The third book deals with the Incarnation, the virtues, sins, and commandments. The fourth book treats of the sacraments, the sacramentals, and the last things. This perfection of the order according to which St. John Damascene had disposed his books *On the Orthodox Faith* was thus secured for Latin theology as a whole. The great St. Thomas Aquinas improved this order in the *Summa Theologica*, but it was definitely an improvement of an already existing and scientifically correct disposition.

The time of Peter the Lombard abounded in these ordered expositions of all sacred theology. Between 1141 and 1148 a follower of Gilbert of Poitiers wrote a volume called *Sententia Divinitatis*. A *Summa Sententiarum* appeared in the middle of the twelfth century. Gaudulph of Bologna (1155?), Peter of Poitiers (1205) also wrote works which utilized the resources of Peter the Lombard. Peter of Poitiers was the first important commentator of the Lombard. The controversial theological literature of the time came from Alan of Lille (1202), Peter of Blois (1200), and Praepositinus (1210). Petrus Comestor (1178) and Petrus Cantor (1197) worked in scriptural theology. Roland Bandinelli, afterward Pope Alexander III (1181), carried on the work of Gratian in canon law and thus indirectly in the field of sacred theology.

G. The Early Thirteenth-Century Theologians of Paris. The most spectacular advance in sacred theology was that accomplished during the thirteenth century. The men who brought about that advance were teachers at the great universities, and in particular at the University of Paris. During the first years of the thirteenth century, that is up until the scholastic year 1229–1230, the faculty of sacred theology in the University of Paris was composed entirely of secular priests. In that year Roland of Cremona, a Dominican (1259), took one of the chairs and from that time until the end of the medieval period the religious, and particularly the Friars Minor and the Friars Preachers, played the most important part in the literary productions of the faculty, even while the membership of that body remained predominantly secular. William of Auvergne (1249), Robert Courcon (1218), Stephen Langton (1228), later Archbishop of Canterbury in England, and Philip de Greve (1236) were among the most prominent masters during the early years. These men were excellent technical theologians, well informed in Greek and Arab philosophy, and yet in no way tempted to subordinate Catholic doctrine to the dicta of the philosophers. The brilliant Simon of Tournai (c. 1219) was one of their number. The later university legends charged him with an impious arrogance which certainly does not appear in his authentic writings. William of Auxerre (1231) and Robert of Sorbonne (1274) who founded the famed theological school named after him were potent factors in the advance of the science in those times. William of St. Amour (1272) and Gerard of Abbeville (1271) were remarkable more for their attacks on the religious than for any theological excellence.

The secular masters as a whole were, however, competent and even brilliant individual scholars. As a group they had made the University of Paris the capital of the intellectual world, and had constituted the theological faculty of that university as the most influential group of scholars in history. They wrote well, and added to their commentaries on the *Four Books of Sentences* their own magnificent syntheses of Catholic theology. Still, because of their very position as individual masters, they did not form schools nor establish definite theological traditions. That function was reserved for the religious, particularly the Franciscans and Dominicans who were to take their places in the already renowned faculty.

H. Alexander of Hales and the Franciscan Writers. The first, in order of time, among the great religious doctors of the university was the English Franciscan, Alexander of Hales (1245). He wrote a *Summa Theologica* embodying all the advances in sacred theology up to his time. It was divided into four books. The first of these treated of God, the second of the creatures God has made, the third dealt with Christ and with the virtues, and the fourth with the sacraments and the last things. He followed the tradition of St. Augustine as it had come down particularly through St. Anselm and Hugh of St. Victor, and thus he stands as the founder of the Franciscan theological tradition. That tradition was carried on and developed by John of La Rochelle (1245), Odo Rigaldus (1275), and William of Meliton (1260) who was charged with the work of completing the text of the *Summa Theologica* actually left unfinished by Alexander himself. The Franciscan theological tradition, however, reached its epitome in the works of St. Bonaventure (1274) and John Duns Scotus (1308).

I. St. Bonaventure. St. Bonaventure, the Seraphic Doctor of the Catholic Church, gave definitive form to the Franciscan theological tradition during the last years of the thirteenth century.[†] His tremendous influence on spiritual theology, the scientific statement of Franciscan spirituality was expressed in his masterpiece the *Itinerarium Mentis ad Deum*, as well as in his writings on the life of St. Francis. The highly traditional and Augustinian dogmatic and moral theology of St. Bonaventure is found in his commentary on the *Four Books of Sentences*, his *Disputed Questions*, and the *Breviloquium*. This latter book is divided into seven parts. In the first the Seraphic Doctor deals with the revealed teaching on the Triune God. The second part treats of creatures, the third of the corruption of sin, the fourth of the Incarnation, the fifth of the grace of the Holy Spirit, the sixth of the sacraments, and the last of the state of the final judgment. His treatise *De Reductione Artium ad Theologiam* is one of the outstanding contributions to theological methodology.

J. St. Albert the Great. The outstanding Dominican leaders on the Faculty of Sacred Theology in the university were St. Albert the Great (1280) and his pupil St. Thomas Aquinas (1274). St. Albert inaugurated a tradition in Parisian theology by using the works and the definitions of Arab philosophers like Averroes to further his task of explaining sacred doctrine. The older secular writers for the most part, and the Franciscans after them, had shown a marked aversion for the writings of these Mohammedans. St. Albert was anxious to use these writings, to strip them of the errors that covered them, and to make the scientific and philosophical resources of the Arabs available to Catholic students. He is best known for his marvelous philosophical and scientific learning, and for the use to which he put this learning in sacred theology.

K. St. Thomas Aquinas. St. Albert's pupil and successor, St. Thomas Aquinas, is the most important figure in the history of sacred theology. Historically he may be said to have accomplished for the Dominican tradition of St. Albert the Great what John Duns

---

†   **Editor's Note:** For a contemporary consideration of the Franciscan tradition and school, see Bert Roest, *Franciscan, Preaching, and Mission c. 1220–1650* (Leiden: Brill, 2015).

Scotus was to do some years later for the Franciscan school of Alexander and St. Bonaventure, But this historical parallel would give only a very inadequate notion of the real function of St. Thomas. Today the study of these other masters is important from the standpoint of the history of sacred theology. But the theologians of the world use the writings of St. Thomas as texts. The central stream of theological tradition which came down from St. Augustine passed through Peter the Lombard to St. Thomas. The didactic literature of sacred theology today uses the works of St. Thomas as classical sources both for their terminology and their basic conclusions. His writings occupy a place apart in the literature of scholastic theology.

L. Followers of St. Bonaventure. St. Bonaventure is said to have been an intimate personal friend of his great Dominican confrere. But the men who had studied under St. Bonaventure were among the most bitter opponents of St. Thomas' theology. John Peckham (1292), the Archbishop of Canterbury, William de La Mare (1298), author of the first anti-Thomistic theological treatise, the *Correctorium Fratris Thomae*, and Cardinal Matthew of Aquasparta (1302) were all students of St. Bonaventure, as was Richard of Middletown (1307?) who taught at Oxford. This latter University had developed a strong Franciscan teaching of its own under Bishop Robert Greathead (1253), Thomas of York (1260), and William of Ware (c. 1270). Peter of John Olivi (1298), the Blessed Raymond Lull (1315), Roger Bacon (1294), and Roger Marston (1298) were Franciscan theologians who operated outside their traditional school. Some of Olivi's theses were condemned by the Council of Vienne.

M. John Duns Scotus. However, the man in whose writings the Franciscan theological tradition crystallized and found its best expression was John Duns Scotus.† St. Bonaventure had been the great scholastic rival of St. Thomas in the Faculty of Sacred

---

†   **Editor's Note:** For an overview of Bl. John Duns Scotus' thought, see Thomas Williams, ed., *The Cambridge Companion to Duns Scotus* (Cambridge: Cambridge University Press, 2003).

Theology at Paris. His immediate disciples were outstanding in their reaction against the distinctive systematic theses of the Angelic Doctor. But when the time came for the theologians of the Order to form a school, that school bore the name of Scotus, and propounded his system.

Scotus' principal literary work is the formidable *Commentaria Oxoniensis*, an explanation of the *Four Books of Sentences* written during his professorship at Oxford. There is another commentary, the *Reportata Parisiensia* which consists in the class notes of his students at the foremost medieval university. In these, and in the brilliant *De Primo Principio* he drew up a system which retains its scientific vigor and value even today. He differs from St. Thomas in practically every part of sacred theology. However, a good many of these differences arise from the variant definitions used by the two men. An instance in point is, of course, their teaching on the practical character of sacred theology. Using two distinct concepts of practicality, Scotus reasoned that sacred theology is preeminently a practical science while the Angelic Doctor held it to be more speculative than practical.

The outstanding thesis of the Subtle Doctor was his doctrine on the Immaculate Conception. In virtue of his proofs and explanations, universities which had previously been at least neutral on the matter came to require from candidates to their chairs of sacred theology a profession of acceptance for this teaching.

N. Successors of St. Thomas. The Dominican masters contemporary with St. Albert and St. Thomas were, as a whole, not identified with their tradition. Thus Roland of Cremona (1271), John of St. Giles (1258), and Hugh of Saint-Cher (1263) as teachers at Paris all taught the so-called Augustinian system, used by the greater number of the secular and Franciscan masters. This Augustinian system consisted in the use of St. Augustine's philosophy and philosophical terminology in expressing theological conclusions. At Oxford the Dominicans Robert Bacon (1248), Richard Fishacre (1248) and Robert Kilwardby (1279) followed the same trend. The last, a Cardinal and Archbishop of Canterbury, was a bitter opponent of Thomism. St. Raymond of Pennafort (1275), who contributed to the progress of moral theology, is not connected with the Thomistic school.

However, the influence of the Thomistic doctrine was not long in making itself felt, Peter of Tarentasia (1276), later Pope Innocent V, used some of St. Thomas' teachings in his own writings. Ulric of Argentina (1275) also approached the Thomistic tradition, as did the brilliant Augustinians Aegidius Colonna or Giles of Rome (1316) and James of Viterbo (1307), the author of one of the earliest treatises on the Catholic Church. The Cistercian, Humbert of Prully (1298), and the Carmelite, Gerard of Bologna (1317), also manifested strong Thomistic tendencies.[†]

John of Paris (1306) made one of the earliest explicit apologies for St. Thomas, his fellow Dominican, when he replied to William de la Mare's *Correctorium*. Ptolemy of Lucca (1327) completed the text of the Angelic Doctor's *De Regimine Principum*, while Hugh of Billon (1298) and William of Hozun (1297) wrote in defense of Thomism.

O. The Secular Masters. Henry of Ghent (1293), Peter of Auvergne (1304), and Godfrey of Fontaines (1306) were the last representatives of the great independent secular tradition at Paris.[††] They were frequently used and cited by the sixteenth and seventeenth-century theologians.

P. The Nominalists. With the fourteenth century a group of writers who are grouped as *nominalists* had an unfortunate effect upon the development of sacred theology. The precursor of this group was the Franciscan, Peter Aureolus (1322). Its most influential figures were another Franciscan, William Ockham (c. 1349), and the Dominican Durandus of St. Pourçain (1334).[†††] Francis

---

† **Editor's Note:** For more on this period and the early Thomists, see Frederick J. Roensch, *Early Thomistic School* (Dubuque, IA: The Priory Press, 1964).

†† **Editor's Note:** For recent studies on Henry of Ghent, see Gordon A. Wilson, *A Companion to Henry of Ghent* (Leiden: Brill, 2011).

††† **Editor's Note:** For more on William of Ockham, see Paul Vincent Spade, ed., *The Cambridge Companion to Ockham* (Cambridge: Cambridge University

Mayron (1327), a Scotist, favored the development of nominalism, while Gregory of Rimini (1358), an author much cited by the theologians of later centuries, manifested strong nominalistic tendencies.

Nominalism was a sort of "modernism" in the fourteenth century, put forward as a "modern way" by the masters of Paris themselves. The men who taught it had lost the fundamental spirit of sacred theology, and had grown to consider the hairline distinctions of the great theologians as mere words, devoid of any objective meaning. Naturally, the men who multiplied distinctions for the sake of manifesting their own intellectual acumen rather than to explain accurately the content of divine public revelation were primarily responsible for the appearance of this school. The school itself, in its reaction against the great works of the past, represented a definite lowering of theological standards. Those who reacted against meaningless distinctions came unfortunately to reject even those which were requisite for the proper elucidation of Catholic dogma. In so doing they presented the world with an inferior expression of Christian doctrine and prepared the way for heretics like Luther whose misconstruction of this doctrine degenerated into heresy.

John Buridan (c. 1358) was largely responsible for implanting nominalism in the University of Paris. His disciple, Marsilius of Inghem (c. 1396), brought the movement with him to the University of Heidelberg.

Peter of Ailly (1420) and John Gerson (1429) were by all means the most important of those affected by nominalism at the University of Paris. Both of these writers miscalculated the nature of that authority which Jesus Christ gave to his Church. They taught that a general council is actually superior to the Roman Pontiff in authority and hoped by this solution to resolve the

Press, 1999); William J. Courtenay, *Ockham and Ockhamism* (Leiden: Brill, 2008); Christian Rode, ed., *A Companion to Responses to Ockham* (Leiden: Brill, 2016). For more on Durandus of St. Pourçain, see Isabel Iribarren, *Durandus of St Pourçain: A Dominican Theologian in the Shadow of Aquinas* (Oxford: Oxford University Press, 2005).

problems which faced the Church in their day. However, Gerson, a voluminous writer, contributed toward the advance of moral and spiritual theology.

Q. Late Pre-Tridentine Writers. During the fourteenth century the great traditional schools of theology continued to advance. Hervé de Nedellec (1323), John of Naples (c. 1336), and Peter of Palude (1342), all Dominicans, did much to advance Thomistic doctrine. John de Bassolis (1347), a Franciscan, was studied assiduously at Louvain and Douai during the seventeenth century as an authentic exponent of Scotus' teaching. Peter of Aquila (1370) was another outstanding fourteenth-century Scotist. Peter Tartaretus (c. 1495) contributed to the advancement of Scotism during the fifteenth century, as did Nicholas de Orbellis (1455) and Stephen Brulefer (1483). The pre-Tridentine Scotistic writing may be said to have reached its highest point of perfection in the works of Trombeta (1518) and Lychetus (1520). The greatest figures among the pre-Tridentine Thomists were Capreolus (1444) and Torquemada (1468). Thomas de Vio of Gaeta, who has gone down in history under the name of Cajetan (1534), and Sylvester Ferrariensis (1528) bring us to the dawn of modern theology. Their commentaries give us answers to the difficulties raised by the first Protestants. Cajetan's commentary on the *Summa Theologica* was the first of its kind, while Ferrariensis' explanations of the *Summa Contra Gentiles* is still printed with the standard critical edition.

Outside the Thomistic and Scotistic schools, there were many influential theologians. Among these were the Carmelites Robert Walsingham (c.1310), Gerard of Bologna (1317), John Baconthorp (1348), Francis Bacon (1372), and Thomas Netter Waldensis (1430). The latter was often used by post-Tridentine writers. Thomas Bradwardine (1349) included so many inaccuracies in his teaching that he has been considered a forerunner of Protestantism. His contemporary, Richard Fitzralph, Archbishop of Armagh (1360), was hardly more successful.

In Spain Raymond of Sabunde (1437) and Alfonsus Tostatus (1455), the latter a Bishop of Avila, were outstanding for their erudition in sacred theology. In Germany, Gabriel Biel (1495), the Cardinal Nicholas of Cusa (1464), and Denys the Carthusian (1471) were important figures. The latter was by all means the most influential independent theologian of the fifteenth century.

Chapter XIII

The Development of Sacred Theology: The Post-Tridentine Theologians

The reaction against the Protestant heresy, manifest in the condemnation of Luther's teaching by Leo X in the Bull *Exsurge Domine* of June 15, 1520, and in the ecumenical council of Trent (1543–1565), produced tremendous effects in the development of sacred theology. First of all it destroyed the influence of that nominalism which had done such harm to this study during the preceding century and a half. After the revolt of Luther this unscientific and unsatisfactory treatment of sacred doctrine was discontinued. Second, it produced the gradual departmentalization of sacred theology. There had been treatises on moral theology, on fundamental dogma, and on ascetics before the time of the reformation. But, after the council of Trent, the organization of sacred theology began to take the didactic form which it possesses today.

A. The Controversialists. The immediate reaction against the errors of Luther and Calvin naturally developed where the heresy was strongest. Among those who wrote as shock troops for Catholic truth in Germany were John Eck (1543), Albert Pighius (1542), Frederick Gnau (1552), John Cochlaeus (1552), Jerome Emser (1527), Frederick Staphylus (1564), John Gropper (1559), the Dominican, von Hoogstraeten (1527), and St. Peter Canisius, S.J.

(1597). Louvain was represented by Adrian of Utrecht (Pope Adrian VI, 1523), John Driedo (1535), James Latomus (1546), Ruard Tapper (1559), Judocus Ravesteyn, often cited as Tiletanus (1570), John Hessels (1566), John Molanus (1585), John Lens (1593), and William Lindanus (1588).

The newly organized University of Douai played a considerable part in this first assault on the Protestant heresies. Richard Smith (1563), of Worcester, England, was an excellent theological controversialist, as were his fellow members of the Douai faculty, Matthew Galenus (1573) and Matthias Bossemius (1599). The traditions of Catholic Oxford and Cambridge appear in the controversial works of Cardinal William Allen (1594), St. John Fisher (1535), Cardinal Reginald Pole (1558), Gregory Martin (1582), who did the principal work on the Douai version of Holy Scripture, Stephen Gardiner (1553), and Nicholas Sanders, S.J. (1581). Thomas Stapleton (1598) was the most influential theologian of this group. His work was carried on by Matthew Kellison (1641) and by another Richard Smith (1655) who became Bishop of Chalcedon and Vicar Apostolic for England.

In France the outstanding controversialists were Claudius d'Espence (1571), Claudius de Sainctes, O.S.A. (1591), Francis Feuardentius, O.F.M. (1610), Nicholas Coeffeteau, O.P. (1623), and Davy du Perron (1618). Their work was continued by Cardinal Richelieu (1642), Francis Veronius (1649), and by Bossuet (1704). In Spain the Catholic cause was upheld by Alphonsus Ruiz de Virues, O.S.B. (1545), Peter Soto, O.P. (1563), Alphonsus de Castro (1558), Andrew de Vega, O.F.M. (1560), Didacus de Paiva de Andrada (1578), and Martin Perez de Ayvla (1566), Dominic Soto, O.P. (1560), and Melchior Cano, O.P. (1560). Cardinal Hosius (1579) wrote in defense of the faith in Poland. In Italy the opposition to Protestantism was carried on by St. Robert Bellarmine (1621), Ambrose Catharinus (1533), Thomas Bozius, the Oratorian (1610), as well as by Cajetan.[†] St. Robert's

---

†   **Editor's Note:** For a recent study of Ambrose Catharinus, see Giorgio Caravale,

Controversies constitute the outstanding individual defense of the Church in those days. His works dealt with every point of Catholic doctrine which had been attacked by Reformers.

This formidable controversial literature naturally tended to advance sacred theology as a science. Since the Protestants had set forth a body of teaching centering around the notions of grace and the supernatural, it was to be expected that there should be some diversity of opinion on these points among the Catholic authors themselves. The scientific elaboration of the Catholic position as set forth in the works of the great controversialists actually resulted in disputes.

B. Baianism and Jansenism. The first of these originated at Louvain with the writing of Michael Baius (1589). Baius despised the scholastic theologians and attempted to base his teaching almost entirely upon the writings of St. Augustine. Much as he read St. Augustine, however, Baius' own literary productions showed that he understood very little of St. Augustine's message. Baius' own teaching was heretical, and it was condemned four times by the Holy See. His own faculty of sacred theology in Louvain took the lead in opposing the teaching of Baius. Ruard Tapper, the most influential of the sixteenth-century Louvain Doctors, Driedo, Tiletanus, and Lens were bitter opponents of Baianism. Some sympathizers with Baius remained, however, on the Louvain faculty for generations. One of these, Cornelius Jansen (1638), the Bishop of Ypres, wrote a book of spurious Augustinian doctrine. The teaching of that book was condemned as heretical. Those who continued to accept the doctrine of Jansenius constituted a heretical sect which was important until the early nineteenth century. All of the important theologians since the early part of the seventeenth century exposed the fallacies of Jansenism.

C. Thomist–Molinist Controversy. The second dispute of importance was that between the Thomists and the Molinists, the controversy which reached its climax in the famous *Congregationes*

Beyond the Inquisition: Ambrogio Catarino Politi and the Origins of the Counter-Reformation, trans. Donald Weinstein (Notre Dame, IN: University of Notre Dame Press, 2017).

de Auxiliis (1598–1605).[†] Almost every one of the important post-Tridentine theologians made some contribution toward the solution of this problem. The discussion began in the north when the Faculty of Sacred Theology at the University of Louvain censured certain propositions taught by Leonard Lessius, S.J. (1623), in 1586. Two years later the same statements were censured much more severely by the theological faculty at Douai. In Spain the teachings of Molina (1600) were denounced by Dominic Bañez (1604). This debate was eventually carried to Rome where, in 1607, Pope Paul V forbade the condemnation of either the Molinistic or the Thomistic position until such time as the Apostolic See would see fit to terminate the discussion.

D. Early Jesuit Theologians. In general the great theologians of the Society of Jesus taught either the system of Molina or some modification of it. Apart from Molina himself, the most prominent Jesuit theologians of this golden age were Francis Suarez (1617), Gabriel Vasquez (1604), Gregory of Valentia (1603), Cardinal John De Lugo (1660), and, of course, St. Robert Bellarmine. Suarez was one of the most influential theologians in all the history of the Catholic Church. He is one of the few men to have been cited universally, that is by theologians of all schools and in every department of sacred doctrine. Most of his extensive writing is in the form of commentaries on the *Summa Theologica* of St. Thomas Aquinas. However, his acceptance of the basic Molinistic position brought him to differ with the Angelic Doctor in many of his theses. Modern research has made the influence of Suarez in the history of sacred theology still clearer.[††] Vasquez and Valentia

---

†   **Editor's Note:** See the editorial note above on p. 139.

††   **Editor's Note:** For more on the life and thought of Francisco Suárez, see José Pereira, *Suárez: Between Scholasticism and Modernity* (Milwaukee, WI: Marquette University Press, 2006); Emmanuel J. Bauer, "Francisco Suárez (1548–1617): Scholasticism after Humanism," in *Philosophers of the Renaissance*, ed. Paul Richard Blum (Washington, DC: The Catholic University of America Press, 2010), pp. 236–55; Daniel Schwartz, ed., *Interpreting Suárez: Critical Essays* (Cambridge: Cambridge University Press, 2012); Victor M. Salas and Robert L. Fastiggi, ed., *A Companion to Francisco Suárez* (Leiden: Brill, 2015).

were brilliant commentators of St. Thomas. The former disputed many points with Suarez. De Lugo's greatest contributions were his monograph on faith and his teaching on the Mass.

Others, equally brilliant in this first group of Jesuit theologians, and equally Molinistic in their views were Didacus Ruiz de Montoya (1632), Harrubal (1608), Herice (1626), Granado (1632), Hurtado (1646), Ripalda (1648), Turrianus (1635), Becanus (1625), Tanner (1632), Coninch (1633), Platel (1681), and Arriaga (1667). The earlier Jesuit theologians like Cardinal Toletus (1596) and Henriquez (1608) taught a doctrine more in accord with the Thomistic position.

E. Post-Tridentine Dominican Writers. The literature of modern Thomistic theology begins with Cajetan and Ferrariensis. But the school which was destined to play the most striking part in the development of post-Tridentine Thomism was the University of Salamanca in Spain. The Dominican, Francis of Vitoria (1546) wrote brilliantly himself, and taught a line of scholars who were destined to leave their mark in the history of sacred theology. Vitoria is considered as the founder of the science of international law.

His outstanding pupil was the Dominican Melchior Cano, the controversialist who wrote the first treatise on the theological places. Dominic Soto was another influential figure in this Spanish Dominican school which included Cardinal Carranza (1576) and Dominic Bañez, the great opponent of Molina. Other great Dominican theologians of the golden age were Bartholomew Medina (1581), Alvarez (1635), Massoulié (1706), John of St. Thomas (1644), Ledesma (1616), Lemos (1629), Antoine Reginald (1676), Porrecta (1614), De Medices (1622), Gonet (1681), Goudin (1695), Araujo (1664), Nazarius (1646), Nuno (1614), Labat (1670), Nicolai (1673), Contenson (1674), and Godoy (1677).

F. University Theologians. The debate on the matter of Molinism and Thomism was by no means confined to the Jesuit and Dominican theologians. The great university faculties took an active part. At Louvain the outstanding commentators of St.

Thomas, John Wiggers (1629) and John Malderus (1633), inclined toward the Molinistic position, although both rejected the system of Molina as such. At the Sorbonne of Paris, Gammache (1625), Duval (1637), and Ysambert (1642) wrote commentaries on the *Summa* and rejected the Thomistic explanation of efficacious grace. The most important secular faculty at the time, that of Douai, was strongly Thomistic. The characteristic Douai tradition of the great faculty was established by William Estius (1613). His disciple and successor, Francis Sylvius (1649), wrote one of the most valuable commentaries on the *Summa Theologica*. The Douai Thomists relied greatly on the works of St. Augustine and made a brilliantly successful use of the same scientific equipment which had been perverted by the Baianists and the Jansenists. Sylvius with his confreres, George Colvenerius (1649), Theodore Van Coverden (1658), and Valentine Randour (1653), fought brilliantly against the Jansenists. The Spanish Bishop Ferdinand Martinez Mascarhenas (1628) was a strong defender of Molinism.

Among the religious of orders other than that of St. Dominic, the Augustinians, Puteanus (1623), Basilius Pontius de Leon (1629), and the Irishman, Augustine Gibbon (1676), were Thomists, as were the Benedictines, Curiel (1609) and Reding (1692), the Cistercians Cabreyro (c. 1600) and de Lorea (1606), and the great Mercedarian Francis Zumel (1607). The Carmelite school produced some of the most brilliant Thomistic writers in the history of sacred theology with Paul of the Conception (1617), Leo of St. John (1671), Raymond Lumbier (1684), Philip of the Blessed Trinity (1671), and the authors of the most imposing work in all the history of Thomism, the *Cursus Salmanticensis in Summam Sancti Thomae*, the professors in the college of St. Elias in the University of Salamanca from 1631 to 1700. The Salmanticenses took account of every important scholastic theologian who had preceded them.

The Franciscan school continued the Scotistic tradition for the most part. Prominent among the post-Tridentine Franciscans were Luke Wadding (1657) and his fellow Irishmen Cavellus (1626),

Hickey (1641), and Ponce (1660). The Scotistic school was also ably represented by De Mazzara (1588), Macedo (1608), and Smising (1626).

G. Positive Theologians. The seventeenth century also saw the beginnings of a specifically positive theology with the writings of Petavius, S.J. (1652) and the Oratorian Thomassinus

H. Eighteenth-Century Writers. In the eighteenth century the theologians took advantage of the tremendous advances made by their predecessors. The previous writers had manifested an almost encyclopedic erudition in the development of their theological conclusions. Men like Suarez, Vasquez, and the Salmanticenses had brought out every solution advanced by their predecessors on the various problems with which they were concerned. Suarez, Bañez, Molina, John of St. Thomas, and others like them had subjected every conclusion and opinion to a most rigorous logical investigation. Estius and Sylvius had manifested a mastery of patristic thought, and particularly of the teachings of St. Augustine. The eighteenth-century writers devoted themselves particularly to the work of stating the conclusions of their predecessors in a more compendious and practical form. Outstanding among the eighteenth-century Dominicans were Billuart (1757), Gotti (1742), De Rossi or De Rubeis (1775), Concina (1756), Gazzaniga (1799), and Natalis Alexander (1724).

In the Scotistic school Frassen (1711) and Montefortino (c. 1728) were the most prominent and influential figures. The Capuchin theologian Thomas ex Charmes (1765) wrote an excellent textbook. The Jesuits Noel (1729) and Antoine (1743) wrote well, but by all means the most powerful exponent of Molinism was the Sorbonne Doctor, Honoratus Tournely (1729). Billuart's famous work was intended as an answer to Tournely's writings. The Vincentian Collet (1770) continued Tournely's works. Other important theologians of the period were St. Alphonsus Liguori (1787), the founder of the Redemptorists and the most modern theologian to be named as a Doctor of the Church, Duhamel (1705), Amort (1775), and Gerdil (1802). A distinctively

Augustinian system for the solution of the problem on efficacious grace was proposed by Noris (1704), Berti (1766), and Klupfel (1811). The Sulpician Fathers, who were entrusted with the education of many secular priests in France, exercised a great influence through the textbooks of De La Fosse (1745), Montaigne (1767), Legrand (1780), and Regnier (1790).

I. Nontraditional Currents in Nineteenth-Century Writing. The theological literature of the early nineteenth century suffers badly in comparison with that of earlier times. The students of that time were prone to prefer the theories of Descartes and Kant to the perennial philosophy which St. Thomas and the other giants of the theological tradition had expounded and employed. As a result, their interpretation of Catholic dogma was colored by a false philosophy. Some of them like Hermes (1831) and Gunther (1863) taught a kind of rationalism in the name of sacred theology and attempted to prove the very mysteries of divine revelation by the ordinary processes of human reason. Others manifested no confidence whatever in the power of man's mind and lapsed into fideism as did De Bonald (1840), Bautain (1867), Bonnetty (1879), de Lamenais (1879), and Ventura (1861). Gioberti (1852), Maret (1884), and Ubaghs (1875) taught a kind of ontologism which was, orthodox. The ontologism of Rosmini-Serbati (1855), however, was condemned by the Church.

J. The Traditional Schools in Modern Times. Good work was done in the statement of Catholic teachings at the German universities and seminaries by Moehler (1838), Lieberman (1844), Klee (1839), Heinrich (1891), and the great Matthias Joseph Scheeben (1888). The Jesuits Kleutgen (1883), Perrone (1876), Franzelin (1885), Palmieri (1909), Camillus Mazella (1900), and Emilio de Augustinis (1899) did outstanding work in the development of sacred theology. The Dominicans were represented by Lepidi (1922), Zigliara (1893), and Buonpensiere (1924). The Thomistic tradition was aided by the school of Satolli (1910), Janssens (1925), and Monsignor Paquet of Laval University in Quebec. These men were sometimes referred to as Cajetano-Thomists. Actually their teaching was another one of the numerous attempts at a compromise between the Molinistic and the Thomistic positions. In spite of a certain weakness inherent in their characteristic position, these three writers did a great deal in bringing the text of St. Thomas to the attention of the great number of Catholic universities and seminaries.

In positive theology the nineteenth century was quite rich. John Paul Migne (1875) published a tremendously extensive *Encyclopedia* of ecclesiastical sciences, a course in sacred theology and editions of the Latin and Greek Fathers. Many of the volumes in these latter collections are still the best texts available for certain patristic and early scholastic authors. Hefele (1893) and Hergenroether (1891) continued the work of conciliar theology which had been so well done by Mansi (1729) and Hardouin (1729). Vacant (1901) wrote brilliantly on the first dogmatic constitution of the [First] Vatican Council, the history of which was recounted by Granderath-Kirsch, Butler, and Mourret. Murray of Maynooth in Ireland (1877) produced the outstanding work on the Church in the nineteenth century. Cardinals Wiseman, Manning, and Newman contributed ably to English theological literature.

After the [First] Vatican Council, and particularly after the condemnation of Modernism, the quality of Catholic theological literature improved visibly. Besides the great post-Vatican writers to whom we have already alluded, Catholic theology has been enriched by the writings of the Thomistic school, so much encouraged by the sovereign pontiffs. To this school we must assign the European Dominicans, Hugon, Garrigou-Lagrange, Freithoff, Cordovani, Mingoja, Marín-Sola, Schultes, Gardeil, Berthier, Congar, Charlier, Paris, and Simonin. Gardeil was the greatest master of theological methodology. His *Crédibilité et l'Apologétique* has been of great importance in fixing the object of apologetics. His writings on theology as such, and on mystical theology have also exercised great importance. Marín-Sola and Schultes took a leading part in a controversy on the nature of sacred theology. Freithoff and Merkelbach have written on Mariology, and the latter is, of course, one of the acknowledged modern masters of moral theology. By all means the most important of the European Dominicans was Reginald Garrigou-Lagrange, the great master of the Angelico [Angelicum]. With all the richness of his published works, it is evident that his influence has been most strongly felt in Apologetics, Spiritual Theology, and *De Deo Uno.*

The contemporary Molinistic school has been defended mostly by the Fathers of the Society of Jesus. Typical of the thoroughgoing Molinists were Hugo Hurter, also the editor of many patristic opuscula and the author of the invaluable *Nomenclator,* Christian Pesch, Lercher, Lennerz, Tepe, and Beraza. The great Cardinal Billot and his successor Charles Boyer the patrologist and dogmatic theologian incline very much toward the Thomistic position. Among the non-Jesuit Molinists we may list Petroccia, Egger, Van der Meersch, Bartmann, and MacGuinness. The Thomistic cause has been upheld outside the Order of Friar Preachers by Diekamp, Van Noort, Hervé, Cardinal Lepicier, Lahitton, and the Carmelite Archbishop Zubizarreta.

Recent dogmatic theology has been rich in monographs. Lepin and the Jesuit Father Maurice de la Taille wrote explanations of the essence of the Eucharistic Sacrifice, which were disputed by the English writers Father Joseph Brodie Brosnan, and the Dominicans Swaby and McNabb among others. The controversy on the nature of apologetics has brought out the writings of the immanentist Blondel and his followers, and the rich treatises of the more traditional writers, Bainvel, Garrigou-Lagrange, Dieckmann, Dorsch, Van Laak, Felder, and Nicolás Marín Neguerela.

The great number of competent reviews which flourished before the war in Europe, and the rapidly expanding theological literature of our own land have made the early twentieth century one of the truly golden eras of theological inquiry. The results of modern theological labor have been expressed, not only in reviews, textbooks, and monographs, but also in the imposing theological encyclopedias. The *Catholic Encyclopedia* of our own country contains many articles of scientific excellence, as do the German *Lexikon für*

Theologie und Kirche and the still incomplete French *Dictionnaire de Théologie Catholique* and the *Dictionnaire Apologétique de la Foi Catholique*, edited by Father D'Ales, S.J.

In the field of positive theology a tremendous amount of work has been done by men like Duchesne, Battifol, Rouet de Journel, S.J., Kirsch, Landgraf, and Grabmann. Father Denzinger, S.J. (1883) performed an invaluable work in the publication of his *Enchiridion Symbolorum* a collection of the authentic declarations of the Church's solemn magisterium. The French theologian Cavallera wrote a similar work, the *Thesaurus Doctrinae Catholicae*. The great Jesuit *Cursus Scripturae Sacrae* continued the exegetical tradition of the Society which had been manifest in the works of St. Robert Bellarmine, Maldonatus (1553), Cornelius à Lapide (1637), and Cardinal Toletus, with the works of such great writers as Hummelaur, Cornely, and Bea. The Dominican scripture scholars under the leadership of Lagrange, Voste, Ceuppens, and Abel, the great Sulpician Fillion, and Father Vigoroux have helped to bring about the excellent status of modern scripture studies.

In the field of *moral* theology, the post-Tridentine development has been tremendous. The writers until the end of the sixteenth century generally treated moral and dogmatic theology together. But since the end of the sixteenth century the literature of sacred theology has been enriched by a section devoted to a casuistic and scholastic treatment of moral problems as such. This development may be said to have begun with the Spanish writers Martín de Azpilcueta (1586) who is usually cited in theological texts as "Navarrus," the Jesuit Cardinals Toletus, Azorius (1603), Sanchez (1610), and Mendoza (1669). Many modern manuals are based upon the works of Busenbaum (1668), Lacroix (1714), and Gury (1866). St. Alphonsus Liguori is the great figure in the development of moral theology. Among the manuals of moral theology most influential today are those of the Dominicans Prümmer and Merkelbach, the Jesuits Capello, Vermeersch, Noldin, Ferreres, and Sabetti, the Redemptorists Aertnys and Damen, Marc and Konings, and the Catholic University professor, Thomas Bouquillon (1902).

$$* * *$$

Chapter XIV

Theology in America: Retrospect and Prospect

A. The Defense of the Faith. In spite of its youth, the Catholic Church in the United States is rich in theological tradition. During the past century Archbishop Francis Patrick Kenrick (1863) wrote valuable textbooks on dogmatic and moral theology and took a leading part in the polemic theological writing made necessary by the powerful and bitter opposition to Catholicism during the nineteenth century. Archbishop Martin John Spalding (1872), Archbishop John Hughes (1864), the illustrious convert Orestes Augustine Brownson (1876), Bishop John Lancaster Spalding (1916), and the founders of the Paulist congregation, Fathers Isaac Thomas Hecker (1888) and Augustus Francis Hewit (1897), were leading figures in the glorious Catholic controversy of the nineteenth century.

The success of that controversial effort was based upon the theological excellence of the writers. In order to cope with the ever pressing objections against Catholic doctrine and practice, the early American priests used the resources of theological tradition. The pages of these writers manifest a familiarity with the works of the sixteenth-century controversialists, particularly St. Robert Bellarmine and Francis Suarez, and the best critical works of positive theology.

The founders of American theology were good Scripture scholars and good students of the Fathers. Indeed, Archbishop Kenrick's revision of the Douai version is one of the best to have appeared in the nineteenth century, and so well known was his ability in matters scriptural that so formidable a scholar as Cardinal John Henry Newman left off work on his own revision when he learned that Kenrick's revision was in process of preparation.

These sturdy defenders of the faith gave the tone and motivation to American theology as such. Occupied, as they were, almost exclusively in defeating attacks against the Church (and even the dogmatic theology of Kenrick is constructed along polemic lines), they left their successors a tradition of intense loyalty to the Church and to its visible head on earth. With their intense and personal loyalty to the Sovereign Pontiff, and the solidity and conservatism which they drew from their favorite sources, they left their students who were to follow them and continue their work in a position of unique advantage.

Those who have contributed to American theological literature have come from almost every racial stock in Europe. As a matter of fact, many of the prominent nineteenth-century writers were born abroad. Furthermore, the theological schools of the United States have been staffed for a great part with men who received at least part of their training in the various universities, institutes, and seminaries of Europe. In this way the current of American theological tradition has carried all that is best in the tendencies and accomplishments of older countries. But all of these tendencies and resources have been formed and dominated, in American theological literature, by that solidity and loyalty which is inherent in our tradition.

B. Latin Theological Literature. American theological literature is by no means as extensive as that of France, Italy, Germany, Spain, or even Belgium. Thus far it has been an affair mostly of articles or small monographs. In the line of Latin texts the United States has produced, apart from the work of Archbishop Kenrick, comparatively few works. The *Apologetica* of John Langan, S.J., the

Theologia Fundamentalis of Cotter, S.J., the treatise *De Sacramentis* by Francis Connell, C.Ss.R., the *Alpha et Omega* by John Moran, S.J., a brilliant statement of theses on the one God and on the Trinity are among the few texts in dogmatic theology written by Americans. Mazzella, De Augustinis, and Tanquerey all wrote their Latin texts while in this country, but all subsequently returned to Europe. In moral the outstanding Latin work produced by an American author was the moral theology of Thomas Bouquillon, one of the world authorities on moral, and one of the original faculty of sacred theology in the Catholic University of America.

C. Moral Theology. In the field of moral theology, particularly in its social implications, Monsignor John A. Ryan has been an outstanding writer of books and articles. His work on distributive justice has exercised a world-wide influence. The Dominican writers, Callan, McHugh, and Farrell have made valuable contributions to theology. The first two have collaborated in Scripture studies and on a moral theology in English. Walter Farrell has published two of the four volumes which will ultimately comprise his *Companion to the Summa*, the first commentary on St. Thomas' masterpiece to have been offered in the English language. The *Companion* ranks as one of the outstanding Thomistic works of modern times. Well-written articles by Monsignor James O'Brien of Cincinnati, and Doctors William Allen, and Joseph P. Donovan, C.M., have enriched the literature of moral theology.

D. Dogmatic and Positive Studies. Dr. Joseph Baierl, Monsignor Fulton Sheen, and Dr. Paul Glenn are among the outstanding American writers in fundamental dogmatic theology. Bishop Strang wrote an excellent textbook for pastoral theology. The late Monsignor William Kerby and Doctor Parente are outstanding in spiritual theology. Fathers Gruden and Berry are authorities in ecclesiology.

Among the outstanding writers on Holy Scripture in the United States we must number Doctor Rudolph Bandas, Fathers McGarry, S.J., McClellan, S.J., John Collins, S.J., Callan, O.P., McHugh, O.P., and Spencer, O.P. Doctor John Quasten's work on

Christian antiquity, continuing the research of Kirsch and Dölger has attracted world-wide attention. The studies of Monsignor Peter Guilday have been invaluable to students of modern theology. Father Bernard Otten, S.J., has written well on the history of dogma.

E. Direction of American Theology. With their resources of tradition and learning, the American theologians are well equipped for the tasks which confront them. The improved English version of Holy Scripture must bring in its wake a complete and scientific commentary upon the sacred books, and a good vernacular treatment of the various subjects covered in the introduction to Holy Scripture. In the field of moral theology the work done by Dr. Bouquillon and Monsignor Ryan must be continued. The former was outstanding for his work on fundamental morals and education, while the latter has done magnificent work in bringing out the Catholic teaching on social justice. The full measure of that Catholic teaching about human conduct is absolutely necessary in order that our republic may operate successfully and preserve its resources and advantages. It is the function of Catholic theologians to manifest the basis of morality and point out the practical and detailed application of moral principles in order that our people may continue to constitute the great democratic state. Such work has been accomplished in the recent books of Doctors James Magner and John K. Ryan.

We must have more texts and monographs on dogmatic theology, utilizing the wealth of resource at our disposal. Despite the general excellence of European theological works at the present time, the American respect for tradition and inherent love of accuracy should be able to make great advances. The new American works in dogma will utilize the documents of the existing theological literature in the only manner in which they can be employed to best advantage. The students of the future will have a far better presentation of the historical background of individual theses than that given in even the best European manuals. In these latter works there has been frequently an unfortunate tendency to stress the theses of one or another theological school at the cost of scientific exactness.

Thus the inquiry into the history of post-Tridentine theology now being conducted at the Catholic University of America will undoubtedly be helpful. The literature of those theologians who wrote during the century and a half after the Council of Trent constitutes an invaluable resource for the accurate and unequivocal teaching of divine revelation. Lately several priests of the Jesuit theological school of Granada in Spain have also taken up this same field of theological research with spectacular success. The publications of Fathers Lamadrid and Abellan, among others, are worthy of note. The American theologians must take cognizance of these endeavors and use the results obtained for the enlightenment of their own people. In the field of spiritual theology a great deal has been done, and much more is necessary. The strong adherence to God which alone can save our people demands the full force of revealed teaching on our life in God. The weak and emotional pietism which is expressed by some non-theological books of devotion is not enough. Only in the clear and unequivocal statement of sacred doctrine, as it has been stated in the works of St. John Damascene, St. Thomas Aquinas, St. John of the Cross, St. Teresa, and the great scholastic masters of spirituality such as Vallgornera, Joseph of the Holy Spirit, and Le Gaudier will the people of God find the enlightenment of which they stand in need.

The Sovereign Pontiffs have urged and commanded the teachers of sacred theology to utilize the principles and the theses of St. Thomas Aquinas. The heartfelt loyalty of the American schools to the Holy See will result in dominantly Thomistic trend in our theology. The Thomism of American writers like Connell, Farrell, and James O'Brien will certainly not possess the contentious and antagonistic character which has lessened the usefulness of some older works. The American Thomism, like that of Ferland in Canada, is eminently irenic and exact. The need of our people for an adequate and accurate statement of revealed doctrine is far too pressing to allow us to ignore or condemn the real theological acquisitions of

writers outside the Thomistic school. And at the same time that
need is too great to permit us a desultory choice among systems.
The teaching and tradition of St. Thomas, with their incalculable
force for the exact statement of Christ's teaching are at our disposal.
The theologians of our time will use them.

Because of the intensely practical background of our theological tradition, there is little likelihood that American Theologians
will be misled into thinking of sacred theology as a mere intellectual exercise, drawing from the body of revealed doctrine certain
conclusions highly interesting yet not intimately connected with
the fabric of Christian life. That tendency resulted long ago in the
blighting reign of nominalism in the schools. It brought about
the aberrations of Cartesian and eclectic theology in the late eighteenth and early nineteenth centuries. In more recent times it has
been manifest in a kind of "liberal" Catholic writing which tended to overlook or misstate the necessity of the Catholic Church
and build up bizarre interpretations of the axiom "*Extra Ecclesiam
Nulla Salus.*" Books of this sort have abounded in descriptions of
shortcomings in the membership of the Catholic Church, and have
spoken disdainfully of Catholic devotional practices.

Fortunately such literature has shown little likelihood of in-
terfering with the development of American theology. The virile
tradition of our Catholic schools makes it quite improbable that
American scholars will turn for enlightenment to the amateurish
and unscholarly works of "groups" and "movements" dedicated to
the reform of the Catholic body politic rather than to the great
scholastic tradition of sacred theology.

It is very easy to write and to speak about matters which pertain
to the field of this science, but it is extremely difficult to require it.
In order to write and teach as a theologian a man must utilize the
various resources at his disposal for the proper statement of that
doctrine which God revealed to the world through Jesus Christ
our Lord. The theologian must see how the doctrine with which
he is concerned is proposed in the authentic magisterium of the
Catholic Church. He must see how it is expressed in the divinely

revealed books which constitute Holy Scripture, and then ascertain how it was taught and developed by the Fathers. The theologian must have cognizance of the literature of his own science, and know how his teaching appears in theological tradition.

The science of sacred theology demands erudition as well as intelligence. The Church in the United States of America, strong in its faith and in loyalty to our Lord and His vicar on earth, and endowed with that ability which our country has used to attain its pre-eminence among the nations of the world, can be expected to supply the necessary industry and to advance the science of sacred theology as it was developed during its golden age. The statement of divine revelation, a statement perfected by theological research and adapted to the men of our age, is what God expects of America.

* * *

Bibliography

Aquinas, Thomas. *Selected Writings*. Edited and translated by Ralph McInerny. New York: Penguin Books, 1998.

Bauer, Emmanuel J. "Francisco Suárez (1548–1617): Scholasticism after Humanism." In *Philosophers of the Renaissance*, edited by Paul Richard Blum, pp. 236–55. Washington, DC: The Catholic University of America Press, 2010.

Bellamah, Timothy, O.P. "*Tunc scimus cum causas cognoscimus*: Some Medieval Endeavors to Know Scripture in Its Causes." In *Theology Needs Philosophy: Acting against Reason is Contrary to the Nature of God*, edited by Matthew L. Lamb, pp. 154–72. Washington, DC: The Catholic University of America Press, 2016.

Besong, Brian. "Reappraising the Manual Tradition." *American Catholic Philosophical Quarterly*, Vol. 89, No. 4 (2015): pp. 557–84.

Bolin, David P. "On the Inerrancy of Scripture." *The Aquinas Review*, Vol. 8, No. 1 (2001): pp. 23–178.

Bonino, Serge-Thomas, O.P. *Angels and Demons: A Catholic Introduction.* Translated by Michael J. Miller. Washington, DC: The Catholic University of America Press, 2016.

_____. *Dieu, « Celui qui est » (De Deo ut uno).* Paris: Parole et Silence, 2016.

Bourke, Vernon J. "The Role of Habitus in the Thomistic Metaphysics of Potency and Act." In *Essays in Thomism*, edited by Robert E. Brennan, O.P., pp. 103–109. New York: Sheed and Ward, 1942.

Boyle, John F. "Authorial Intention and the *Divisio textus.*" In *Reading John with St. Thomas Aquinas*, edited by Michael Dauphinais and Matthew Levering, pp. 3–8. Washington, DC: The Catholic University of America Press, 2005.

Brennan, Robert Edward, O.P. *Thomistic Psychology: A Philosophic Analysis of the Nature of Man.* Edited by Cajetan Cuddy, O.P. Tacoma, WA: Cluny Media, 2016.

Budziszewski, J. *Commentary on Thomas Aquinas's Treatise on Law.* Cambridge: Cambridge University Press, 2014.

Burke, Eugene M., C.S.P. "The Scientific Teaching of Theology in the Seminary." *Proceedings of the Fourth Annual Convention* of The Catholic Theological Society of America (1949): pp. 129–73.

Cajetan, Thomas de Vio. *Cajetan Responds: A Reader in Reformation Controversy.* Edited and translated by Jared Wicks, S.J. Washington, DC: The Catholic University of America Press, 1978.

Caravale, Giorgio. *Beyond the Inquisition: Ambrogio Catarino Politi and the Origins of the Counter-Reformation*. Translated by Donald Weinstein. Notre Dame, IN: University of Notre Dame Press, 2017.

Carey, Patrick. "Fenton Returns." *First Things*, No. 282 (April 2018): pp. 54–58.

Cessario, Romanus, O.P. "Casuistry and Revisionism: Structural Similarities in Method and Content." In *"Humanae Vitae": 20 Anni Dopo. Atti del II Congresso Internazionale di Theologia Morale*, Vol. III, pp. 385–409. Milano: Edizioni Ares, 1990.

_____. *Christian Faith and the Theological Life*. Washington, DC: The Catholic University of America Press, 1996.

_____. *"Duplex Ordo Cognitionis."* In *Reason and the Reasons of Faith*, edited by Paul J. Griffiths and Reinhard Hütter, pp. 327–38. New York: T&T Clark, 2005.

_____. *The Godly Image: Christ and Salvation in Catholic Thought from Anselm to Aquinas*. Petersham, MA: St. Bede's Publications, 1990.

_____. "The Importance of Steven A. Long's *Analogia Entis* within Contemporary Catholic Thought." *Nova et Vetera*, Vol. 12, No. 3 (2014): pp. 971–74.

_____. *Introduction to Moral Theology*. Revised edition. Washington, DC: The Catholic University of America Press, 2014.

_____. "Mary in the Thomist Commentatorial Tradition." In *Sapienza e libertá: Studi in Onore del Prof. Lluís Clavell*, edited by Miguel Pérez de Laborda, pp. 81–88. Rome: EDUSC, 2012).

_____. "Molina and Aquinas." In *A Companion to Luis de Molina*, edited by Matthias Kaufmann and Alexander Aichele, pp. 291–323. Leiden: Brill, 2014.

_____. *The Moral Virtues and Theological Ethics*. 2nd edition. Notre Dame, IN: University of Notre Dame Press, 2008.

_____. "The Sacraments of the Church." In *Vatican II: Renewal within Tradition*, edited by Matthew L. Lamb and Matthew Levering, pp. 129–46. Oxford: Oxford University Press, 2008.

Cessario, Romanus, O.P., and Cajetan Cuddy, O.P. "Mercy in Aquinas: Help from the Commentatorial Tradition." *The Thomist*, Vol. 80, No. 3 (2016): pp. 329–39.

_____. *Thomas and the Thomists: The Achievement of Thomas Aquinas and His Interpreters*. Minneapolis, MN: Fortress Press, 2017.

Conley, Kieran, O.S.B. *A Theology of Wisdom: A Study in St. Thomas*. Dubuque, IA: The Priory Press, 1963.

Courtenay, William J. *Ockham and Ockhamism*. Leiden: Brill, 2008.

Cuddy, Cajetan, O.P. "Thomas Aquinas on the Bible and Morality: The Sacred Scriptures, the Natural Law, and the Hermeneutic of Continuity." In *Towards a Biblical Thomism: Thomas Aquinas and the Renewal of Biblical Theology*, edited by Jörgen Vijgen and Piotr Roszak, pp. 173–97. Pamplona: EUNSA, 2018.

Dolan, Timothy Michael. *Some Seed Fell on Good Ground: The Life of Edwin V. O'Hara*. Washington, DC: The Catholic University of America Press, 1992.

Donneaud, Henry, O.P. *Théologie et intelligence de la foi au XIIIème siècle*. Paris: Parole et Silence, 2006.

Dougherty, M.V. "On the Alleged Subalternate Character of *Sacra Doctrina* in Aquinas." *Proceedings of the American Catholic Philosophical Association*, Vol. 77 (2004): pp. 101–10.

Dulles, Avery Cardinal, S.J. *A History of Apologetics*. San Francisco: Ignatius Press, 2005.

Emery, Gilles, O.P. "Biblical Exegesis and the Speculative Doctrine of the Trinity in St. Thomas Aquinas's *Commentary on John*." In *Reading John with St. Thomas Aquinas*, ed. Michael Dauphinais and Matthew Levering, pp. 23–61. Washington, DC: The Catholic University of America Press, 2005.

_____. *Présence de Dieu et union à Dieu: Création, inhabitation par grâce, incarnation et vision bienheureuse selon saint Thomas d'Aquin*. Paris: Parole et Silence, 2017.

_____. *The Trinitarian Theology of Saint Thomas Aquinas*. Translated by Francesca Aran Murphy. Oxford: Oxford University Press, 2007.

_____. *La Trinité créatrice: Trinité et création dans les commentaires aux Sentences de Thomas d'Aquin et de ses précurseurs Albert le Grand et Bonaventure*. Paris: Vrin, 1995.

Feingold, Lawrence. *The Eucharist: Mystery of Presence, Sacrifice, and Communion*. Steubenville, OH: Emmaus Academic, 2018.

_____. *The Natural Desire to See God According to St. Thomas Aquinas and His Interpreters*. 2nd ed. Ave Maria, FL: Sapientia Press, 2010.

Fenton, Joseph Clifford. *The Calling of a Diocesan Priest.* Westminster, MD: The Newman Bookshop, 1944.

_____. *The Catholic Church and Salvation in the Light of Recent Pronouncements by the Holy See.* Westminster, MD: The Newman Press, 1958.

_____. "The Centenary of Cajetan," *The Commonweal*, Vol. 21, No. 13 (1935): pp. 369–70.

_____. *The Church of Christ: A Collection of Essays by Monsignor Joseph C. Fenton.* Edited by Christian D. Washburn. Tacoma, WA: Cluny Media, 2016.

_____. *The Diocesan Priest in the Church of Christ.* Providence: Cluny Media, 2018

_____. *Laying the Foundation: A Handbook of Catholic Apologetics and Fundamental Theology.* Steubenville, OH: Emmaus Road Publishing, 2016.

_____. "Metaphysics Should Treat All the Categories." *Proceedings of the Eleventh Meeting* of The American Catholic Philosophical Association (1935): pp. 108–13.

_____. "Modern Thomists." *The Commonweal*, Vol. 20, No. 11 (1934): pp. 279–80.

_____. "Popular Thomism." *The Commonweal*, Vol. 24, No. 24 (1936): pp. 554–55.

Feser, Edward. *Aquinas.* Oxford: Oneworld, 2009.

_____. *Five Proofs of the Existence of God.* San Francisco: Ignatius Press, 2017.

De Franceschi, Sylvio Hermann. *Entre saint Augustin et saint Thomas: Les jansénistes et le refuge thomiste (1653–1663): à propos des 1ʳᵉ, 2ᵉ et 18ᵉ Provinciales.* Paris: Classiques Garnier, 2017.

_____. *Thomisme et théologie modern: L'école de saint Thomas à l'épreuve de la querelle de la grâce (XVIIᵉ–XVIIIᵉ siècles).* Paris: Artège Lethielleux, 2018.

Garrigou-Lagrange, Reginald, O.P. *Christ the Savior: A Commentary on the Third Part of St. Thomas' Theological Summa.* Translated by Dom Bede Rose, O.S.B. St. Louis, MO: B. Herder Book Co., 1950.

_____. *God, His Existence and His Nature: A Thomistic Solution of Certain Agnostic Antinomies.* Translated by Dom Bede Rose, O.S.B. 2 vols. St. Louis, MO: B. Herder Book Co., 1949.

_____. *Grace: Commentary on the* Summa theologica *of St. Thomas, Ia IIae, q. 109–14.* Translated by the Dominican Nuns of Corpus Christi Monastery, Menlo Park, California. St. Louis, MO: B. Herder Book Co., 1952.

_____. *The One God: A Commentary on the First Part of St. Thomas' Theological Summa.* Translated by Dom Bede Rose, O.S.B. St. Louis, MO: B. Herder Book Co., 1943.

_____. *The Sense of Mystery.* Translated by Matthew K. Minerd. Steubenville, OH: Emmaus Academic, 2017.

_____. *The Trinity and God the Creator: A Commentary on St. Thomas' Theological Summa, Ia, q. 27–119.* Translated by Frederic C. Eckhoff. St. Louis, MO: B. Herder Book Co., 1952.

Gleason, Philip. *Contending With Modernity: Catholic Higher Education in the Twentieth Century.* Oxford: Oxford University Press, 1995.

Hochschild, Joshua P. *The Semantics of Analogy: Rereading Cajetan's De Nominum Analogia.* Notre Dame, IN: University of Notre Dame Press, 2010.

Horst, Ulrich, O.P. *The Dominicans and the Pope: Papal Teaching Authority in the Medieval and Early Modern Thomist Tradition.* Translated by James D. Mixson. Notre Dame, IN: University of Notre Dame Press, 2006.

Hudock, Barry. *Struggle, Condemnation, Vindication: John Courtney Murray's Journey Toward Vatican II.* Collegeville, MN: Liturgical Press, 2015.

Iribarren, Isabel. *Durandus of St Pourçain: A Dominican Theologian in the Shadow of Aquinas.* Oxford: Oxford University Press, 2005.

Izbicki, Thomas M. "The Immaculate Conception and Ecclesiastical Politics from the Council of Basel to the Council of Trent: The Dominicans and their Foes." *Archiv für Reformationsgeschichte*, Vol. 96, No. 1 (2005): pp. 145–70.

John of St. Thomas. *The Gifts of the Holy Spirit.* Translated by Dominic Hughes, O.P. Tacoma, WA: Cluny Media, 2016.

_____. *Introduction to the* Summa Theologiae *of Thomas Aquinas.* Translated by Ralph McInerny. South Bend, IN: St. Augustine's Press, 2003.

_____. *The Material Logic of John of St. Thomas.* Translated by Yves Simon, John Glanville, and G. Donald Hollenhorst. Chicago: University of Chicago Press, 1955.

Kerr, Gavin, O.P. *Aquinas's Way to God: The Proof in* De Ente et Essentia. Oxford: Oxford University Press, 2015.

Ku, John Baptist, O.P. *God the Father in the Theology of St. Thomas Aquinas.* New York: Peter Lang, 2012.

Labourdette, Michel, O.P. *La charité: « Grand cours » de théologie morale.* Vol. 10. Paris: Parole et Silence, 2016.

_____. *Cours de théologie morale: Tome 1, Morale fondamentale.* Paris: Parole et Silence, 2010.

_____. *Cours de théologie morale: Tome 2, Moral spéciale.* Paris: Parole et Silence, 2012.

_____. *L'espérance: « Grand cours » de théologie morale.* Vol. 9. Paris: Parole et Silence, 2012.

_____. *La foi: « Grand cours » de théologie morale.* Vol. 8. Paris: Parole et Silence, 2015.

_____. *La justice: « Grand cours » de théologie morale.* Vol. 12. Paris: Parole et Silence, 2018.

_____. *La prudence: « Grand cours » de théologie morale.* Vol. 11. Paris: Parole et Silence, 2016.

Legge, Dominic, O.P. *The Trinitarian Christology of Thomas Aquinas.* Oxford: Oxford University Press, 2017.

Leinsle, Ulrich G. *Introduction to Scholastic Theology.* Translated by Michael J. Miller. Washington, DC: The Catholic University of America Press, 2010.

Lombard, Peter. *The Sentences, Book 4: On the Doctrine of Signs.* Translated by Giulio Silano. Toronto: Pontifical Institute of Mediaeval Studies, 2010.

Long, Steven A. *Analogia Entis: On the Analogy of Being, Metaphysics, and the Act of Faith.* Notre Dame, IN: University of Notre Dame Press, 2011.

_____. "On Natural Knowledge of God: Aquinas's Debt to Aristotle." In *Theology Needs Philosophy: Acting Against Reason Is Contrary to the Nature of God*, edited by Matthew L. Lamb, pp. 74–87. Washington, DC: The Catholic University of America Press, 2016.

_____. "On the Possibility of a Purely Natural End for Man." *The Thomist*, Vol. 64, No. 2 (2000): pp. 211–37.

_____. "The Perfect Storm: On the Loss of Nature as a Normative Theonomic Principle in Moral Philosophy." In *What Happened in and to Moral Philosophy in the Twentieth Century: Philosophical Essays in Honor of Alasdair MacIntyre*, edited by Fran O'Rourke, pp. 271–303. Notre Dame, IN: University of Notre Dame Press, 2013.

_____. "Providence, Freedom, and Natural Law." *Nova et Vetera*, Vol. 4, No. 3 (2006): pp. 557–606.

_____. "Speculative Foundations of Moral Theology and the Causality of Grace." *Studies in Christian Ethics*, Vol. 23, No. 4 (2010): pp. 397–414.

_____. *The Teleological Grammar of the Moral Act.* 2nd edition. Ave Maria, FL: Sapientia Press, 2015.

_____. "St. Thomas Aquinas, Divine Causality, and the Mystery of Predestination." In *Thomism and Predestination: Principles and Disputations*, edited by Steven A. Long, Roger W. Nutt, and Thomas Joseph White, O.P., pp. 51–76. Ave Maria, FL: Sapientia Press, 2016.

_____. "Yves Simon's Approach to Natural Law." *The Thomist*, Vol. 59, No. 1 (1995): pp. 125–35.

Lynch, Reginald M., O.P. *The Cleansing of the Heart: The Sacraments as Instrumental Causes in the Thomistic Tradition*. Washington, DC: The Catholic University of America Press, 2017.

Mansini, Guy, O.S.B. "Are the Principles of *sacra doctrina per se nota*?" *The Thomist*, Vol. 74, No. 3 (2010): pp. 407–35.

Matava, R.J. *Divine Causality and Human Free Choice: Domingo Báñez, Physical Premotion and the Controversy* de Auxiliis *Revisited*. Leiden: Brill, 2016.

de Mattei, Roberto. *The Second Vatican Council: An Unwritten Story*. Translated by Patrick T. Brannan, S.J., Michael J. Miller, and Kenneth D. Whitehead. Edited by Michael J. Miller. Fitzwilliam, NH: Loreto, 2013.

McInerny, D. Q. *Natural Theology*. Elmhurst, PA: The Priestly Fraternity of St. Peter, 2005.

_____. *Philosophical Psychology*. Elmhurst, PA: The Priestly Fraternity of St. Peter, 2016.

McInerny, Ralph. *Characters in Search of Their Author: The Gifford Lectures 1999–2000*. Notre Dame, IN: University of Notre Dame Press, 2001.

_____. *Praeambula Fidei: Thomism and the God of the Philosophers.* Washington, DC: The Catholic University of America Press, 2006.

Miner, Robert. *Thomas Aquinas on the Passions: A Study of* Summa Theologiae, *1a2ae 22–48.* Cambridge: Cambridge University Press, 2009.

Mullahy, Bernard, C.S.C. "Subalternation and Mathematical Physics." *Laval théologique et philosophique*, Vol. 2, No. 2 (1946): pp. 89–107.

Mullaney, Thomas U., O.P. "Created Personality: The Unity of Thomistic Tradition." *The New Scholasticism*, Vol. 29, No. 4 (1955): pp. 369–402.

_____. "Mary Immaculate in the Writings of St. Thomas." *The Thomist*, Vol. 17, No. 4 (1954): pp. 433–468.

Nichols, Aidan, O.P. *The Shape of Catholic Theology: An Introduction to Its Sources, Principles, and History.* Collegeville, MN: The Liturgical Press, 1991.

Nieuwenhove, Rik Van. "'Bearing the Marks of Christ's Passion': Aquinas's Soteriology." In *The Theology of Thomas Aquinas*, edited by Rik Van Nieuwenhove and Joseph Wawrykow, pp. 277–302. Notre Dame, IN: University of Notre Dame Press, 2005.

_____. "St. Anselm and St. Thomas Aquinas on 'Satisfaction': Or how Catholic and Protestant Understandings of the Cross Differ." *Angelicum*, Vol. 80, No. 1 (2003): pp. 159–76.

Nutt, Roger W. *General Principles of Sacramental Theology.* Washington, DC: The Catholic University of America Press, 2017.

O'Brien, Thomas C., O.P. *Metaphysics and the Existence of God.* Edited by Cajetan Cuddy, O.P. Tacoma, WA: Cluny Media, 2017.

____. "Premotion, Physical." In *New Catholic Encyclopedia*, Vol. 11: pp. 741–43. New York: McGraw-Hill, 1967.

O'Connor, James T. *The Hidden Manna: A Theology of the Eucharist.* 2nd edition. San Francisco: Ignatius Press, 2005.

O'Malley, John W. *What Happened At Vatican II.* Cambridge, MA: The Belknap Press of Harvard University Press, 2008.

O'Neill, Colman, O.P. "The Rule Theory of Doctrine and Propositional Truth." *The Thomist*, Vol. 49, No. 3 (1985): pp. 417–42.

Osborne, Thomas M., Jr. "Thomist Premotion and Contemporary Philosophy of Religion." *Nova et Vetera*, Vol. 4, No. 3 (2006): pp. 607–32

____. "How Sin Escapes Premotion: The Development of Thomas Aquinas's Thought by Spanish Thomists." In *Thomism and Predestination: Principles and Disputations*, edited by Steven A. Long, Roger W. Nutt, and Thomas Joseph White, O.P., pp. 192–213. Ave Maria, FL: Sapientia Press, 2016.

Pelotte, Donald E., S.S.S. *John Courtney Murray: Theologian in Conflict.* New York: Paulist Press, 1976.

Pereira, José. *Suárez: Between Scholasticism and Modernity.* Milwaukee, WI: Marquette University Press, 2006.

Perrier, Emmanuel, O.P. "L'enjeu Christologique de la Satisfaction (I)." *Revue Thomiste*, Vol. 103, No. 1 (2003): pp. 105–36.

_____. "L'enjeu Christologique de la Satisfaction (II)." *Revue Thomiste*, Vol. 103, No. 2 (2003): pp. 203–47.

Pinckaers, Servais, O.P. *The Sources of Christian Ethics.* Translated by Sr. Mary Thomas Noble, O.P. Washington, DC: The Catholic University of America Press, 1995.

Porro, Pasquale. *Thomas Aquinas: A Historical and Philosophical Profile.* Translated by Joseph G. Trabbic and Roger W. Nutt. Washington, DC: The Catholic University Press of America, 2016.

Portier, William L. *Divided Friends: Portraits of the Roman Catholic Modernist Crisis in the United States.* Washington, DC: The Catholic University of America Press, 2013.

Ramírez, Santiago, O.P. "The Authority of St. Thomas Aquinas." *The Thomist*, Vol. 15, No. 1 (1952): pp. 1–109.

Reese, Philip Neri, O.P. "Theology, Faith, Universities: From Specialization to Specification in Theology." *New Blackfriars*, Vol. 92, No. 1042 (2011): pp. 691–704.

Rode, Christian, ed. *A Companion to Responses to Ockham.* Leiden: Brill, 2016.

Roensch, Frederick J. *Early Thomistic School.* Dubuque, IA: The Priory Press, 1964.

Roest, Bert. *Franciscan, Preaching, and Mission c. 1220–1650.* Leiden: Brill, 2015.

Salas, Victor M., and Robert L. Fastiggi, ed. *A Companion to Francisco Suárez.* Leiden: Brill, 2015.

Schelkens, Karim. *Catholic Theology of Revelation on the Eve of Vatican II: A Redaction History of the Schema* De fontibus revelationis *(1960–1962)*. Leiden: Brill, 2010.

Schwartz, Daniel, ed. *Interpreting Suárez: Critical Essays.* Cambridge: Cambridge University Press, 2012.

Serry, Jacques-Hyacinthe, O.P. ("Augustinus Leblanc"). *Historia congregationum de auxiliis divinae gratiae, sub summis pontificibus Clemente VIII et Paulo V.* Antwerp: 1709.

Simon, Yves R. *The Tradition of Natural Law: A Philosopher's Reflection.* New York: Fordham University Press, 1999.

Sirilla, Michael G. *The Ideal Bishop: Aquinas's Commentaries on the Pastoral Epistles.* Washington, DC: The Catholic University of America Press, 2017.

de La Soujeole, Benoît-Dominique, O.P. *Introduction to the Mystery of the Church.* Translated by Michael J. Miller. Washington, DC: The Catholic University of America Press, 2014.

Spade, Paul Vincent, ed. *The Cambridge Companion to Ockham.* Cambridge: Cambridge University Press, 1999.

Titus, Craig Steven. *Resilience and the Virtue of Fortitude: Aquinas in Dialogue with the Psychosocial Sciences.* Washington, DC: The Catholic University of America Press, 2006.

Torrell, Jean-Pierre, O.P. *Aquinas's Summa: Background, Structure, and Reception.* Translated by Benedict M. Guevin, O.S.B. Washington, DC: The Catholic University of America Press, 2005.

_____. *Saint Thomas Aquinas*. Vol. 1, *The Person and His Work.* Translated by Robert Royal. Rev. ed. Washington, DC: The Catholic University of America Press, 2005.

Wallace, William A., O.P. *The Role of Demonstration in Moral Theology*. Washington, DC: The Thomist Press, 1962.

Weisheipl, James A., O.P. *Aristotelian Methodology: A Commentary on the* Posterior Analytics *of Aristotle*. River Forest, IL: Pontifical Institute of Philosophy/Dominican House of Studies, 1958 .

_____. "The Meaning of *Sacra Doctrina* in *Summa Theologiae* I, q. 1." *The Thomist*, Vol. 38, No. 1 (1974): pp. 49–80.

White, Joseph M. "Theological Studies at the Catholic University of America: Organization and Leadership before Vatican Council II." *U.S. Catholic Historian*, Vol. 7, No. 4 (1988): pp. 453–66.

White, Thomas Joseph, O.P. *Wisdom in the Face of Modernity*. 2nd edition. Ave Maria, FL: Sapientia Press, 2016.

Williams, Thomas, ed. *The Cambridge Companion to Duns Scotus*. Cambridge: Cambridge University Press, 2003.

Wilson, Gordon A., ed. *A Companion to Henry of Ghent*. Leiden: Brill, 2011.

* * *

Index

CLUNY MEDIA

Designed by Fiona Cecile Clarke, the CLUNY MEDIA *logo*
depicts a monk at work in the scriptorium,
with a cat sitting at his feet.

The monk represents our mission to emulate
the invaluable contributions of the monks
of Cluny in preserving the libraries of the West,
our strivings to know and love the truth.

The cat at the monk's feet is Pangur Bán, from the
eponymous Irish poem of the 9th century.
The anonymous poet compares his scholarly
pursuit of truth with the cat's happy hunting of mice.
The depiction of Pangur Bán is an homage to the work
of the monks of Irish monasteries and a sign
of the joy we at Cluny take in our trade.

"Messe ocus Pangur Bán,
cechtar nathar fria saindan:
bíth a menmasam fri seilgg,
mu memna céin im saincheirdd."

Made in United States
North Haven, CT
28 March 2025

67295485R00202